Diplomats and Terrorists

Or: How I Survived a 61-day Cocktail Party

Diego and Nancy Asencio

Produced by MAP

From a left-wing comic book, not intended as a flattering image, but Diego likes it.

PREFACE

In reviewing *Our Man Is Inside* today, we can truthfully say that we would not change one line of what we wrote in 1980. However, thirty-one years have passed and the passage of time does lend a different perspective to the interpretation of the past. Nancy was right in saying back then that we would probably stay married forever. Also, the mellowness and introspection which overtook me after my captivity slowly dissipated over time. Nancy was quick to reassure me that I was as big a bastard as I ever was. As I got into the workaday world of immigration policy, I began once more to exhibit the driven nature of my personality.

One fascinating aspect of my return to civil society was that the public information sector of the Department of State was anxious to put me before the Media. Most memorable was a luncheon meeting at The Council for Foreign Relations in New York where I was introduced to journalist Tom Brokaw, who invited me to appear on the TODAY Show. We got to meet Jane Pauley and even Willard Scott. This was followed in short order by an interview with Gail Sheehy of *Passages* fame. She was intent on determining why I had managed to survive my captivity in reasonably good psychological shape. Her conclusion was that I had become so accustomed to personifying the United States as a Foreign Service Officer and as an Ambassador that I had developed a continental-sized ego impervious to external assault. No post-traumatic stress disorder for me! On the other hand, calling my ego 'continental-sized' ruffled my feathers a bit, since I have always considered myself humble and modest. I realize that in some quarters this assertion will be met with snickers, if not outright belly-laughs.

The saddest moment in the aftermath of my adventure was the untimely death of my friend Victor Sasson, the intrepid intermediary for the Jewish community in Colombia, who was probably as responsible as anybody for getting me out of captivity safely. He was shot during an attempted kidnapping in Bogota. Irony of all ironies, someone who had helped so many kidnap victims became a victim himself.

One incident during my PR tour is vividly etched in my mind. During a speech in Chicago, some smartass asked me how I would feel about my almost thirty year career being overshadowed by what I did during those 61 days. Interesting thought, that! Had the hostage event been instrumental in furthering my career? Would I have been promoted to Assistant Secretary of State under normal circumstances? Would I have had the opportunity to shine in a high-profile position, eventually rewarded by being made Ambassador to Brazil, considered the top post in Latin America? Being a great believer in serendipity, I hold firm to the thought that my career has been a series of (relatively) happy accidents.

We managed to maintain the personal links we developed in Colombia, some of whom are now deceased: Ignacio Umana, who had offered to pay my ransom; Enrique Santos, my friend and great publisher of *El Tiempo* and his son Juan Manuel Santos, now the President of Colombia. We have also been in touch with David Manzur, the master Colombian artist, and of course, our relatives-in-law, including our grandson's grandmother, Norma Fehrmann, also an artist of international stature. We treasure the collage given to us by the late Alejandro Obregon, whose works can be found at the OAS as well as the UN. Although we never met the great artist Botero, we did manage to acquire a signed lithograph in, of all places, a consignment shop in Palm Beach Gardens, Florida. While we were in Mexico we learned that he had abandoned his workshop without destroying his molds and were able to acquire three small sculptures that his former workmen are still producing.

I have received various requests for interviews with Commander One. These have been easy to turn down, regardless of money offers. There is no way that I am going to honor this terrorist, who had threatened my life. Ironically, a Colombian movie was made about the hostage incident, but of course it tilted heavily towards the terrorists' point of view, since rebels and bandits are often admired and tolerated in Colombia. The M-19 became a legitimate but third-rate political party, and Commander One became the Mayor of Yumbo, a middle-sized town near Medellin. He was also a delegate to the most recent constituent assembly which produced Colombia's current constitution. Colombian journalist Yamid Amat told me that after consecutively interviewing President Turbay Ayala, Commander One and me, he was struck by the fact that we each felt we had been singularly instrumental in resolving the crisis. He has a point.

One of the unforeseen effects of the celebrity status caused by my captivity is that I have become a speaker in some demand for lectures on cruises, at conferences on terrorism, university assemblies and other organizations. An additional unexpected gig was being hired by Horacio Serpa as his advisor on US-Colombian relations during his presidential campaign in Colombia. I must not have done a very good job; he lost. The height of my contribution was an all-day discussion with his campaign staff that he should soften his strong nationalist image - which I felt was frightening the entrepreneurial class - by making a pre-election visit to Washington and New York. I was voted down on the grounds that this would disturb his nationalist base. I really did not enjoy pointing out to him afterwards that if he had listened to me at the time, he might have won.

I have always felt that President Ernesto Samper received a bum rap when accused of accepting narcotics money for his campaign. It kept him from realizing his potential as a great president, since he was forced to divert much of his energy towards defending himself. I proposed that he permit me to set up a foundation in the US that would hire lobbyists, defend him against these assertions, and in the process defend Colombia. I was associated with the Florida law firm of Becker and Poliakoff at the time. I discussed this with my friend Alvaro Gomez, the great leader of the Conservative Party, who encouraged me with the thought that defending Ernesto was incidental to defending Colombia. Unfortunately, the Colombian Ambassador to the U.S. at the time felt threatened by my proposal, making it impossible to raise funds or implement an appropriate policy. Curiously, he tried to set up a similar foundation of his own, which collapsed under its own weight.

There is an object lesson there that I also encountered during my early days as a civilian consultant. American businessmen would often see me solely as a door-opener. After introducing them to worthwhile contacts, I was often dismissed with a "Thank you, we will take it from here." A few weeks later, they would be back with "That didn't work." Before long, I began explaining to new potential clients that it was not just my title or celebrity or contacts that were of value, but also my experience and my knowledge of Latin American history, mores and customs. Needless to say, innate ability might occasionally play a part.

The point is that some of the same approaches you will read about in this book are still operating in my post-government life. More specifically, they made all the difference in this hostage drama, converting the likelihood of inconceivable tragedy into a process which was imaginative, creative and ultimately enlightening. The expected 'by the book' approach expounded by many of my colleagues at the Department of State was, in my view, doomed to failure and would most likely have ended in a bloodbath. Seeing my fellow hostages file out of the Dominican Embassy into awaiting buses at the end of our ordeal was a surreal and almost out-of-body experience. The feeling of elation and sense of impending freedom was nearly unbearable. Violence had been faced down by painstaking negotiation. Common sense prevailed over atavistic impulses to strike back. Diplomacy, administered in a situation for which it had never been designed, succeeded in delivering a satisfactory conclusion for all parties concerned. It worked. I think it is a hell of a great story, now judge for yourselves.

Diego C. Asencio

West Palm Beach, Florida

June 23rd, 2011

FOREWORD

February 1980 was an unsettling month for the United States. The Abscam scandal was breaking nationwide as the FBI pressed charges of bribery and influence-peddling against several congressmen and other high officials in this first of many "sting" operations. February marked the first hundred days of captivity for the American hostages in Teheran. February was also the month President Carter warned the Soviets to either withdraw their occupying forces from Afghanistan or face "the final and irrevocable decision" of a major world boycott of the 1980 Summer Olympic Games scheduled to be held in Moscow. The price of gold, an indicator that often reflects the level of world stability, fluctuated dramatically. The impasses in Iran and Afghanistan and the charges of corruption at home made for rather gloomy forecasts. The world at large was edgy.

America's self-esteem waned as we became painfully aware of our inability to act definitively in Iran. We felt tarnished and vulnerable. It was a difficult time for us, and we rather naively yearned for dramatic, heroic solutions in an unyieldingly complex world.

Fortunately, we were to have a taste of victory and glory in the swell of nationalistic pride that same February when the American Olympic hockey team overcame long odds to beat Finland and the Soviet Union and win the gold medal at the Winter Games in Lake Placid, New York. The country went wild with joy as we crowned a team of heroes. Our triumph over the Russians was as metaphoric as it was literal. We were in a dangerous frame of mind: our over-aggrandizement of heroes, some of whom were no more than serendipitous, betrayed our urgent need for them. Even Eric Heiden, who won a spectacular and unprecedented five gold medals in speed-skating competition - a truly remarkable, perhaps even heroic, feat - did not receive anywhere near the spontaneous enthusiasm and adulation accorded the members of the U.S. hockey team.

Perhaps part of the reason for this reaction was our subconscious need to overcome the odds with a coordinated team effort combining singular dedication with effective action. In the United States, where individual achievement is traditionally lauded over group achievement, we became intent on team effort. The U.S. hockey team, in effect, became a paradigm for the White House. The success of the athletes served as a galling reminder to the Carter Administration of its own inefficacy abroad.

In addition to its pressing international concerns, the Carter Administration was being relentlessly beleaguered by the traditional devils of inflation, unemployment, and the yet-to-be-balanced federal deficit. Pressure on the President to take action had begun to snowball, and with the national elections looming uncomfortably close on the horizon, the President knew he had to do something - anything. Sooner or later he would have to show some muscle if he was going to survive the elections. No one - not our allies abroad nor the American people at home - would tolerate his dodging of the political spotlight any longer.

This tension spread overseas. Even in Latin America, where political unrest is a way of life, the caution flag was up. American envoys abroad were waiting for word from Washington about changes in policy.

In February 1980, I entered my thirtieth month as the Ambassador from the United States to Colombia. My assignment to this South American nation in the upper northwest corner of the continent was my first as ambassador. I'd spent many years in Latin America holding various positions within the American embassies in Mexico, Panama, Brazil, and Venezuela, so I felt fairly confident of my ability to interpret the heart and brain of Latin politics. I had also learned to be wary: many a doctor has reviewed an EKG only hours before the patient suffers a massive coronary without seeing anything remarkable on the readout tape. A diagnosis of health in politics, as in medicine, is often no more than an educated guess - a probability - and there are enough exceptions in modern Latin history to keep anyone from calling the chain of cause and effect predictable.

Certainly we professional diplomats knew that Latin politics was notoriously volatile, but I would not have believed in February of 1980, for instance, that I would end up the prisoner of professional terrorists for two months. As a diplomat used to the low lighting of comfortable offices, I would have never believed that I'd get caught in the middle of a full-scale gun battle and have to crawl on my stomach across the floor to hide under furniture while people around me were getting shot. Worse, I wasn't prepared for the moment when I'd be confronted with the possibility of shooting down a woman. Even as a veteran negotiator, I'd never thought the time would come when I would have to marshal all my skills to bargain for my own life. No one told me about these things at the Georgetown Foreign Service School; in fact, no one even suggested they might happen one day. Yet happen they did; and I survived, but not without scars, and not without a greater sensitivity to the plight of the hostage - increasingly commonplace figures in the arena of international politics.

I also learned a lot. Not just about myself and my family, but also about myself and my government. No experience I had had in twenty-three years in the Foreign Service had ever put my relationship with the United States government to the acid test. After sixty-one days as a hostage, I had firsthand experience of the true nature of U.S. policy regarding kidnapped nationals and what it really means to someone to be in the unenviable position of hostage.

The incident brutally defined the psychic depth and breadth of each of the hostages. Many of the men and women who were captured were career representatives of their governments and as such were used to the aegis of custom, protocol, and political privilege under which international diplomacy normally proceeds. Suddenly we found ourselves cruelly severed from the lifelines of our families and governments. Denied the structure that defines diplomacy, we were held in seemingly endless uncertainty, isolation, and alienation. Men and women accustomed to act were stripped of their capability but not their desire to do so, and this in turn led to severe frustration. Most diplomats are by nature active, not passive people, and the role of submissive prisoner is difficult for them to accept. During those moments when the opportunity to act arose, I often found myself unpredictably stymied - not only by our captors, which was predictable, but also by the conventional wisdom of U.S. hostage negotiation policy. Neither a mere spectator nor a minor character in the drama, but one of the central characters - the victim - I was the fulcrum over which U.S. policy was levered into action. I found that I was victimized in more ways than one.

Ours was not an experiment in a test tube. It was every bit as real as the seizure of the American Embassy in Teheran. The invasion of the Dominican Embassy and taking of hostages cost the lives of some, and was resolved at the expense of the mental stability of others. Despair and hope, fear and courage, trust and suspicion and paranoia, love and hate, drove hostage and captor alike. And never in equal doses. Captivity itself was often unbearable, and more so was the frequent boredom, the endless monotony of waiting. We were never certain there would be an acceptable end to our journey. I was forced to suffer an ironic loneliness: even though I was always surrounded by people - captors and fellow hostages - I spent too many long hours and days profoundly alone, cast off in an inexplicable void. Worst of all was the uncertainty. Unlike the criminal prisoner who at least knows how long his sentence is and when he will be eligible for parole, a hostage doesn't have the comfort of knowing anything for sure, not even if he will be alive by the end of the day. All he has is time and his imagination, which works either for or against him.

It is difficult to convey the sense of helplessness that moved like a disease among us, breeding a crippling, existential fear. It is difficult to describe the thousand hours of fruitless waiting and the hundreds of dashed hopes. I learned to read pain and disappointment in the faces of my fellow hostages. I learned how to confront fear - my own and others' - and how to deal with it. Most of all, I learned the true relationship between myself and my peers, both in Bogota and in Washington, the not always pretty skeleton that supports the muscle and blood and smooth skin of international relations.

There were countless ironies and twists of fate that harassed us endlessly. Some of those whom we thought we could count on turned out not to be the allies we had thought them to be. Those whom we considered strong turned out to be weak; others we had dismissed earlier as ineffectual or uninformed turned out to be incisive and savvy. No conclusion and inference we made went unquestioned. Our governments proved to be as much a risk as our captors.

Looking back, I understand that some of the worst dangers came not from the people who held us at gunpoint, but from those who were ostensibly committed to rescue us.

Being kidnapped is an unforgiving experience in many ways. Memories are engraved with the steel points of fear and pain; they are unlikely to be entirely erased, although time will surely soften them. This experience has been shared with hundreds of others, yet no other person has had the same experience. I do not intend this account of the seizure of the Dominican Embassy in Bogota by terrorists to be a litany of bizarre incidents designed to entertain the casual reader with the underside of terrorism; instead, I want to tell you what happened and what I learned, to bear witness to a remarkable political and social process.

I do not believe, as Hegel did, that peoples and governments have never learned anything from history, or acted on the principles deduced from it. It's true, perhaps, that we haven't learned as much as we should have from the past, but progress, scientific and human, has always been predicated on our ability to build on the foundations of the past. We are an imperfect people. Believing in man's intent to understand and improve his lot, I offer this testament.

ONE

An ambassador's life is a curious one. It is adventure balanced with routine. As Ambassador to Colombia, I might spend the morning discussing policy with the President at his palace or with the Minister of Defense working out a major narcotics interdiction program designed to deter the heavy flow of cocaine and marijuana to the United States. In the afternoon, I might attend any of the hundred perfunctory cocktail parties to which an ambassador's liver is subject. Attending such functions is part of the job of diplomacy, and despite the myriad boors and incompetents who somehow always manage to insinuate their way into these gatherings, they are important. Mountains of hors d'oeuvres and rivers of alcohol set a scene in which businessmen, government officials, and diplomats try out ideas before presenting them formally in the offices of government. The cocktail party is also the rumor market typical of capital cities in which speculation, innuendo, and blatant accusation are traded daily. If you know how to listen properly, the chain of receptions that ring the city can act like the Distant Early Warning line and alert the wary to what is in the air.

One such event an ambassador is obliged to attend as a gesture of courtesy is the national day celebrations of other embassies. Protocol is rigorous in capitals, so an ambassador and other high-ranking embassy personnel will make at least a brief showing at a national day party before returning to business.

On February 27, the Embassy of the Dominican Republic celebrates the independence it won from neighboring Haiti in 1844. Its newly appointed Ambassador in Bogotá, Dr. Diogenes Mallol, sent notes to the diplomatic community inviting it to participate in the celebration. I made plans to attend at midday, greet the new Ambassador, say hello to a few friends, and then get back to work. My wife, Nancy, usually comes along with me to these things, but the morning of the reception she complained she wasn't feeling well, so I didn't press her to go.

My retinue of bodyguards and I arrived at the Dominican Embassy as the reception was getting off the ground. About sixty people, representing many Latin and European countries, had gathered. In addition to the ambassadors from Egypt, Israel, Austria, Switzerland, the Soviet Union, and some of its allies, the Pope's own representative was milling around making small talk and eating canapés. The atmosphere was typical of such functions: informal but slightly restrained. Ambassador Mallol welcomed me. As I started making my rounds, I ran into Virgilio Lovera, the Ambassador from Venezuela and an old friend from my days as Deputy Chief of Mission in Caracas. He snagged me by the cuff and took me aside because he wanted to talk about my proposal to allow his country rather than the Soviets to buy up surplus Colombian beef. Ambassador Lovera told me his country was hesitant to make such a deal with Colombia because Venezuela needed to protect its own cattle industry. As we talked, I noticed the Soviet bloc envoys start to leave en masse. They offered their apologies to our host, explaining they were invited to a reception at the East German Embassy following the presentation of the new East German Ambassador's credentials to the President of Colombia, Dr. Julio César Turbay Ayala.

Taking their cue, I started to inch toward the front door because I was anxious to get to a luncheon engagement. I started to say my goodbyes when two well-dressed couples walked past my four bodyguards outside the front door and came into the Embassy. They were young and self-assured, so they didn't create any immediate suspicion. Because there was virtually no security provided at the reception except for an aged guard who was more of a doorman and car-watcher, no one bothered to check their credentials, and they walked into the Embassy unannounced. That wasn't unusual in itself because gate-crashers are common at diplomatic receptions in Colombia. Many of them are professional crashers and have colorful reputations as regular fixtures on the embassy and government circuit. They are derogatorily known as *lagartos*, or "lizards," and are tolerated with some amusement. The solemnity of the two couples at the front door was disturbing, but before anyone could question them, they opened their jackets, pulled pistols from their belts, and started firing at the ceiling.

For a fraction of a second there was nothing but stunned silence. Then all hell broke loose. The restrained and stately civility of one second disintegrated into the raw panic of the next. Women screamed. Men shouted. I dove to the floor and crawled for the nearest cover, a sofa against the front wall. Others whose reflexes were not as quick stood stone-still in either shock or disbelief. I doubt any of us were fully able to comprehend what was happening. It was all too fast, too dramatic. Nevertheless, I've always believed that when someone starts shooting at you, you don't ask questions, so I tried to be as inconspicuous as possible as I wedged myself between the sofa and the wall. When I looked up, I saw the horrified Dominican Ambassador, who had a moment ago been so gracious, run from the room screaming. Offstage, his wife shouted the piercing command, "Mallol, act like a man!" which brought him back to his senses, and back to the room.

As soon as the shooting began, another twelve terrorists who had been kicking a soccer ball around in a playing field across the street stormed the Embassy. Still dressed in green warm-up suits, they pulled shotguns, carbines, and pistols from their gym bags and fired at the security men who had been lounging near the front of the Embassy. The terrorists broke through their weak cordon and scrambled through the front door. As the lead terrorist burst into the Embassy, he glimpsed a man with a carbine to the left of the door near him. Reflexively, he opened fire on the other man and threw himself onto the floor as the other man fired at him simultaneously. As the terrorist looked up, he realized the man he had tried to kill was only his own reflection in a large mirror behind the door.

My bodyguards and some of the other security men, caught off guard, started to return fire. Pablo Oliveros, my chief bodyguard, was hit four times as he bravely tried to get into the Embassy to rescue me. He was seriously wounded, but fortunately survived. Police patrolling the National University across the street heard the gunfire and rushed over to join the small, ineffective force of security men who were no match for the heavy firepower of the terrorists.

By then, sixteen terrorists had forced their way into the Embassy and barricaded themselves inside the building. People rushed around, it seemed, without sense or order. The noise was deafening. Above the shooting I could hear people swearing, shouting, and pleading. Time and space became entirely disjointed. Bullets crashed through the tall, large windows only inches above my head and showered me with broken glass. I could hear the bullets thudding into the wall behind my head with sickening insistence. At first I was terrified, and my mouth was sour with fear. I sensed death at my shoulder. But then something curious happened to me. My fear turned into rage, and with it the action around me, which had seemed speeded up at first, now turned into slow motion.

The scene was like a confused, nightmarish hallucination, a grotesque charade. Everything I saw seemed distorted; everyone, everything, was out of character. In the midst of that heavy barrage of gunfire, I was still convinced my death was at hand, and I performed what was probably the most perfect and sincere act of contrition in my life. I repented a lifetime of sin and asked God to receive me in His embrace.

While I was concentrating on the prospect of death, the heavy arms fire escalated into a pitched battle. One of the terrorists, a young boy, was fatally shot in the head near the front door and collapsed like a puppet with cut strings. He died instantly. Another terrorist, a young woman, was wounded by a bullet that grazed her scalp. With blood streaming down her face, she continued undaunted to fire her carbine out the door where passersby were still scrambling for cover. A bus driver, unaware of the siege, drove through the line of fire, and an unsuspecting student passenger was mortally wounded and died en route to the hospital.

Inside the Embassy, the Paraguayan Honorary Consul General was seriously wounded in the shoulder. He clutched his shoulder and winced with the pain while others around him were still scurrying for cover. In those initial moments when one had to react without thinking and rely on reflexes and not intellect, some people were still too shocked to move. The Ambassador from Costa Rica, a young woman attending her first diplomatic function, stood motionless on the staircase until one of the terrorist women, seeing her recklessly exposed to danger, shouted, "Get down! You'll get shot!" Ambassador Chassoul had arrived in Bogotá only three weeks before. We'd chatted for a few minutes before the invasion, and I felt sorry for the rude way she was being introduced to the Colombian political scene. When the terrorists rushed the Embassy, she first thought they were thieves and tried to hide her jewelry. A burst of weapon-fire from the outside showered her with glass, and yet she remained hunched over the banister without moving. She told me later that she was remembering what some friends had said about being shot — that "you feel something warm come out" — so she had closed her eyes and was trying to see if she could feel anything warm! The dead terrorist was only a few feet away from her, and, when she finally opened her eyes after the guerrilla had shouted to her, she must have been terrified by the sight of the corpse covered with blood. The terrorist woman, sensing the Ambassador's distress and her inability to protect herself, shouted over and over, "Get down!" The Ambassador then began to realize the real danger and ducked down on the staircase. Ambassador Chassoul wasn't the only one incapable of responding to the crisis quickly: the Costa Rican Consul General, with his drink still in his hand, was walking around the room in a daze until another of the terrorists pulled him down to the floor.

Bizarre thoughts went through my mind. I remembered that in Norman Mailer's war novel *The Naked and the Dead* some of the protagonists had trouble controlling their bowels under fire. So much for literary convention. I wasn't having that problem. My worry was staying alive. In the middle of my detached thoughts, the Ambassador from Uruguay interrupted me as he started squirming and swearing. "Sonofabitch," he started repeating in English, "sonofabitch!"

"Keep quiet!" hissed the Ambassador from Mexico, who was also on the floor near us. "And keep still!"

The Brazilian and Mexican ambassadors were then both hit by ricocheting pellets from a shotgun blast. I saw a petite terrorist woman crouched on the floor near me get shot squarely in the chest. The force of the bullet nearly knocked her over. Incredibly, she continued to fire her carbine. She wasn't fazed by a shot that should have killed most men. When I realized she wasn't even bleeding, I knew she must have had a bullet-resistant vest hidden under her clothing. These terrorists were well armed and well prepared.

The swarm of bullets continued to pock the walls and break all the windows in the heavily glassed building. Later, I counted seventeen bullet holes in one window alone. After the first few minutes, nearly everyone had taken cover, so there was little movement except for the skidding of splinters of wood and glass across the floor. A Peruvian hired to work the reception foolishly tried to stop the guerrilla onslaught and was shot for his trouble. He started crying pathetically for mercy when one of the terrorist women told him to shut up.

"I'm a mestizo and a poor man," he insisted. "Please don't shoot me!"

In response, the woman pointed her rifle at the Peruvian. "If you don't shut up, you sonofabitch," she threatened, "I will shoot you."

Meanwhile, the Ambassador from Peru took advantage of the melee and, with the help of the wife of one of the hostages, slipped out the back with only some minor bruises. Even more fortunate was the Ambassador from Argentina, who pulled up to the Dominican Embassy just after the terrorists rushed the front door. When he saw what was happening, the Ambassador exercised good judgment and drove off, hoping no one would miss him. A story also circulated that the Ambassador from Spain, also arriving late, insisted on trying to get into the besieged Embassy by pounding on the front door and shouting, "Open up! I'm the Spanish Ambassador! Let me in!" But the terrorists, already happy with their catch, refused to let him in.

Government troops began arriving on the scene in force with armored cars. Besides my bodyguard Pablo, four other soldiers were wounded in the shoot-out and taken to local hospitals. The army quickly consolidated its position, barricaded the streets, and began a systematic evacuation of nearby residents. After fifteen minutes the shooting began to taper off as officers exercised greater control over their troops. Even so, I couldn't breathe any easier. Around me men were bleeding and groaning in pain. Others were crying or praying. The room was in ruins: furniture torn up and overturned, windows and mirrors shattered, and people huddled motionless in every corner. I was still convinced I was going to die and decided that if my time was up, I would go with a measure of dignity. Strangely, this thought, in addition to my having made peace with my Creator, gave me considerable strength.

I later reflected on whether it had been my Hispanic heritage with its popularly ascribed concepts of fatalism and machismo which gave me the strength I needed to stand up to this moment. Octavio Paz, the Mexican author of *The Labyrinth of Solitude*, talks about this mystique in Hispanics when he writes: "To die and to kill are ideas that rarely leave us. We are seduced by death."

My childhood had been replete with lessons illustrating the proper conduct of an honorable man. From a Spanish primer, I remember a story about a group of courtiers in the service of a medieval Spanish king who were marveling at a caged wild lion when one of the ladies capriciously dropped her glove into the lion's cage in order to test the chivalry of the gentlemen present. One of the courtiers promptly entered the cage at the risk of his life and gallantly retrieved the glove. With a sweeping bow, he returned the glove to the damsel. Before she could acknowledge his chivalry, the courtier slapped the startled lady across the face for presuming to test the intrepidity of Castilian gentlemen. The courtier then turned to the rest of the astonished crowd and challenged any man to a duel in the field of honor if he believed he'd acted unjustly or dishonorably. No one challenged him.

It occurred to me later that, in the case of our captivity, both the heroes and the waverers among the hostages were for the most part Hispanic. So much for tradition. There was, however, an old Spanish adage we used among ourselves to stiffen our spines at moments of stress and danger: *"Nadie muere en la víspera"* (No one dies on the eve of his death). I wasn't dead yet, and there was no reason to sulk about death's inevitability. If there was anything that put me in good stead from my heritage, it was a sense of pride. I knew there was no way I could return to my wife and children, to my friends and colleagues in the Foreign Service after collapsing in a heap and saying, "I can't cut it." While I was gathering strength, a terrorist ran over to me in a crouch, and motioned with his rifle for me to follow him toward the front door. I could tell by his grim face he was determined to make me go. Reluctantly, I crawled out of my hiding place to where the dead guerrilla was sprawled on the floor. I felt a remarkable detachment as I studied the face of the corpse. The boy couldn't have been much older than seventeen or eighteen, dead for a cause he probably didn't even understand. What a waste!

I surveyed the eerie sight around me. What I saw gave me little comfort: anxiety and fear were written broadly across the faces of hostages and terrorists alike. Everyone was waiting, although I doubt anyone knew what he was waiting for. Faces were taut, strained with worry. A few people were shivering uncontrollably. The shooting had almost died out completely, and the intervening silences were as macabre as the sound of gunfire.

The terrorist gestured toward the door. "Tell them to cease fire," he said anxiously as he forced me to stand in full view of the front door. I wasn't about to argue with the man.

With all the voice I could muster, I shouted in Spanish, "Don't shoot! Hold your fire!" I still shudder to think what a target I must have made to the troops outside. Only the police's restraint kept me from being shot full of holes. I remember being surprised I could stand there — in the face of such danger — with relative equanimity and even a certain amount of disdain while occasional bullets continued to whiz past my ear. Like the Spanish courtier who retrieved the lady's glove, I would like to have slapped the terrorist for his rash use of me.

The terrorist, satisfied with my performance, then shuttled me upstairs to a window at the back of the building where he made me call again to the troops for a cease-fire. Other terrorists followed suit and herded different hostages, even Ambassador Chassoul, to the windows to shout, "Don't shoot! We are diplomats!" The refrain turned into a litany that lasted about ten minutes, and ultimately it worked. The shooting stopped. Many of the hostages, fearing for their own safety, pleaded with the soldiers not to try anything foolish.

The situation first looked as if it were starting to come under control when one of the terrorists cried out in a panicky voice, "Tear gas!" It turned out a canister of tear gas had been lobbed through an upstairs bedroom window.

The guerrilla leader shouted, "Throw it back out!" but no one volunteered to go into the bedroom, so the canister spent itself harmlessly, doing no damage other than badly scorching the floor. It was a reminder, however, of what the police and army could do. I was as terrified of their rescue attempts as I was of the terrorists. If the army decided to gas us, the confusion could be fatal.

We then realized it was in our own best interest if the soldiers didn't try anything, so the chorus began again, this time voluntarily. The Ambassador from Mexico, already slightly wounded, called out for a cease-fire with the conviction of his strong voice, and the Papal Nuncio, a thin, frail man, tried to explain to the troops that the terrorists had hand grenades and would blow everyone up if the troops tried to overrun the Embassy. We urgently appealed for calm and order, worried that the soldiers might be trigger-happy and prone to heroics at our expense.

The firefight lasted about thirty minutes, and for someone under fire, that's a long, long time. Sporadic shooting went on for another hour and a half. Once we convinced the troops to hold their fire, I breathed somewhat more easily, but I dreaded what was ahead of me. I had no idea who these terrorists were or what they wanted. I suspected they were trying to pull off some kind of spectacular kidnap plot at our expense — and it was becoming increasingly obvious that that was their intent — but I couldn't make myself face the possibility that this might be another Teheran in the making. What it turned out to be, in fact, was the longest and largest barricaded hostage crisis in modern political terrorism.

The terrorist who had forced me to call for the cease-fire was impatient and nervous, and held me at gunpoint on the second-story landing near the staircase. I could hear people moving around haphazardly as the terrorists tried to round up everyone. Soon some of my colleagues joined me. We listened to the guerrillas as they ranged the house, trying to figure out the army's deployment and how best to secure their position. One man, apparently the leader, barked orders to his comrades and assigned them to sentry posts while others stood over us with rifles. Those were anxious, solemn minutes.

Everyone was to some degree reluctant to move, as if a larger script had been written for the event, and we were blindly awaiting our directions. Even the terrorists seemed hesitant about exactly what they should do next as if they were waiting for their director to prompt them. The atmosphere was both tense and tentative, on the verge of going out of control. We waited. The terrorists waited. Everyone waited, as if in the eye of a massive storm, each second, it seemed, a century.

The terrorists, it turned out, despite their outward display of what they considered military precision and dedication to principle, were a ragtag bunch of self-styled freedom fighters motivated by a blind and awkward idealism and a massive dose of adrenaline. At first they were as lost as we, but once the situation became more stable, they tried to act military — orderly and disciplined. The leader, a slight but intense man with glasses, shouted orders while his soldiers ran about attempting to establish some sort of positive control over a large group of shaking wrecks. Some of the women were weeping; others were totally out of it with shock. The terrorists, as frightened as we, were jumpy and intolerant. When someone tried to speak, a guard would gesture threateningly with his rifle and tell him to shut up. No one dared open his mouth while we listened to the terrorists scramble about the building as they took up new positions.

The leader divided us into groups according to our value to him. Ambassadors were segregated along with other high-ranking officers, while the wives and employees and middle-rank diplomats were moved at gun point to other rooms. Some of the terrorist men, still afraid the army might try to overrun the Embassy, took hostages to strategically vulnerable points around the building and held them as shields. They made it painfully clear that if the army tried anything, we would be the first to die.

Finally, I was forced into the library on the second floor with several other ambassadors where we sat on the floor awaiting the terrorists' next move. We were dirty, disheveled, and disoriented. The scent of fear in the air was sharp.

Of the sixteen guerrillas that stormed the Embassy, one was dead — the young boy I had to step over near the front door — and a couple of others were slightly wounded. Of the fifteen remaining, six were women. The woman with the head wound was alert, but her hair was matted with dried blood. They called each other by revolutionary names or by numbers, a tactic common to Latin revolutionaries. In order to confuse outside intelligence, they assigned only odd numbers to themselves, thereby creating the illusion that there were twice as many terrorists as there actually were, a ploy that succeeded in confounding army intelligence for several weeks once it took the "bait" that the guerrilla known as Number Twenty-nine was one of twenty-nine terrorists. The leader was a young man in his early thirties known simply as *Commandante Uno*, a man of some leadership capability who ran a tight ship from beginning to end. When Commander One gave an order to jump, his people jumped.

Once he felt the Embassy was secure, Commander One brought all the hostages together. There were more than fifty of us, including the ambassadors of fifteen nations. We were an impressive catch by any standard, and to my knowledge we represented the largest group of high-ranking diplomats ever captured. Besides the ambassadors, the terrorists had several chargés and consuls general. Even more unfortunate were the wives of all levels of personnel. As soon as I saw them, I thought of Nancy and how fortune had been standing by her that morning. The thought of Nancy among the hostages infuriated me, and my heart went out to the women whose only crime was to be married to diplomats.

The Commander was a former school teacher from the southern Colombian city of Cali. He was dark-skinned and had straight, almost Oriental-looking, hair which reminded me of the Goan refugees I had seen while stationed in Portugal. His black-framed glasses and his decisive but decidedly pedantic manner enhanced his air of a school teacher. His real name, we later found out, is Rosenberg Pabón Pabón, and he claimed to have been named after Ethel and Julius Rosenberg, the American couple who were executed in 1953 for passing sensitive atomic secrets to the Soviets. Pabón announced in his grandiose manner that we were the hostages of a special Column of the Movement of April 19, named after Jorge Zambrano, a young M-19 member who had been arrested two weeks earlier by the national police as a suspected terrorist. Two days after his arrest, Zambrano's savagely beaten body had been found lying on a city street: thus he became one of the cause's martyrs.

Commander One was blunt in telling how he intended to use us. He was going to demand the exchange of 311 political prisoners, including several of the M-19's High Command, many of whom were being held in La Picota, the national penitentiary. In addition, he wanted a ransom of $50 million in cash and the worldwide publication of the M-19's charges of brutality against the Colombian government.

The first order of business, he declared, was to get the police to withdraw from their close perimeter. The police were breathing down our necks waiting for the word to storm the Embassy, and their presence made everyone nervous. If the police didn't withdraw, Commander One said he would blow up the building and everyone in it. He told us his soldiers had wired the building with high explosives, and we already knew from the M-19's past reputation that they were capable of carrying out the threat. Their tactics were notoriously bloody and heartless. In its relatively short history, the M-19 had earned a reputation for violence, brutality, and cunning. They had used explosives before with devastating effect, and I wasn't willing to call their bluff. Commander One insisted he would be willing to begin negotiations with the Colombians only if and when the police pulled back.

Commander One also suggested we elect a group of ambassadors to represent the hostages both to the terrorists and to the Colombians once negotiations got under way. I understood this was no idle request on Commander One's part; in fact, he insisted we choose from among ourselves carefully because he anticipated this committee would play an important role in his plans. He then made the initial nominations of Ricardo Galán Mendez, the Ambassador from Mexico; His Excellency Angelo Acerbi, the Papal Nuncio; Virgilio Lovera, my friend from Venezuela; and me. Taking him at his word, we quickly went into brief session and ratified his nominations. We wanted to move as quickly as possible, and I suppose somewhere in the backs of our minds we hoped we might be home for dinner.

TWO

The favorite choice for a position on the ambassadorial hostage committee was the Ambassador from Mexico. Ricardo Galán Mendez, a forty-one-year-old career diplomat, already had an unsettling reputation for dealing with terrorists. It seemed no matter where Mr. Galán went, trouble was waiting for him. While appointed to an office in Haiti, he had dealt with Haitians seeking refuge from the repressive "Papa Doc" Duvalier regime. In Honduras he had sheltered a group of terrorists who sought refuge in the Mexican Embassy after trying to blow up the central power plant in the capital city of Tegucigalpa. When Ambassador Galán was assigned to a post in Paris, he ended up a hostage in his own Embassy by a disgruntled and slightly insane Spanish Civil War veteran who came into his office with bombs strapped to his chest and waving a pistol. He demanded a million-dollar ransom to release Mr. Galán alive, and held a gun on him for twenty-four hours before police dressed as waiters overpowered him.

Not long after his unfortunate incident in Paris, Ambassador Galán was appointed to the head post in Nicaragua, where he had the uneasy responsibility of protecting political refugees who were desperate to escape the Somoza regime. When one such guerrilla tried to seek asylum in the Mexican Embassy, a Somozan general barged into the building with a machine gun and demanded that the guerrilla be turned over to him. Ambassador Galán, in true heroic fashion, faced down the furious general and "escorted" him out of the Embassy. The general was so incensed that he threatened Galán and told him he would never leave Nicaragua alive.

The Mexican government took the threat seriously enough to recall Galán from his post and bring him back to Mexico City for reassignment. They decided to give him a post that would be free of apparent danger.

As luck would have it, he was given the ambassadorship to Colombia. Ambassador Galán was a natural as a spokesman for the hostages, and he accepted the nomination, but not without trepidation.

The same was true for Angelo Acerbi, the Papal Nuncio, Dean of Bogota's diplomatic corps. We elected him to the ambassadorial committee because of the religious influence we hoped he would have with the guerrillas, if they wouldn't listen to the voice of government, then we hoped they would listen to the surrogate voice of God. The word of the Church and the Pope should carry some weight in a Spanish-speaking country.

We also elected Virgilio Lovera, the Ambassador from Venezuela, for his senior political status and polish, as well as for the importance of his country in the Colombian context; and lastly, I was elected to the group of four because of the supposed clout of the United States.

Our work was cut out for us from the beginning. Our first act was to call the Foreign Minister, Diego Uribe Vargas, on the Embassy telephone and convey the demands of the terrorists. Ambassador Galán made the call while the terrorists listened in on another phone. The Mexican patiently reiterated the terms of our release. He spoke cautiously and slowly. He also passed along Commander One's request that former Foreign Minister Alfredo Vásquez Carnzosa come to the Embassy to meet with Commander One and his command staff. Commander One's specific request for Vásquez Carrizosa didn't surprise anyone. As a leader of the Conservative party, Vásquez Carrizosa had made a name for himself in Colombia as a progressive advocate of human rights. He had founded a group of activists known as the Human Rights Association, which had taken every opportunity during the last year to point out blatant human rights infractions by the Colombian government. Commander One believed there was an ideological kinship between his and Vásquez Carrizosa's goals. Uribe Vargas listened to Galán but stayed noncommittal. He would see, he told the Mexican, what he could do.

As soon as Ambassador Galán got off the telephone, it started to ring as reporters began their own untiring assault on us. Commander One, in a recorded interview with the Todelar Radio Network, was blunt about his intentions. After repeating his demands, he revealed part of his task force's motive: "We are informing world public opinion that political prisoners do exist in Colombia," he pronounced in his overblown oratory, "and it is not just one but more than one thousand political prisoners." When a reporter asked him about the fate of his hostages, Commander One said he would guarantee their safety only if the riot police and government troops withdrew immediately from the outside of the Embassy. If they weren't pulled back, Commander One threatened in his best dramatic voice, he would start executing us. "Pay attention to what I'm going to tell you," he said as he gave his stern, chilling warning. "If the troops continue attacking us, we shall be forced to the painful task of executing hostages as a security measure."

I didn't want my life reduced to nothing more than "a security measure."

Telephone calls continued to pour in. At first the terrorists were beside themselves with joy for the opportunity to broadcast their grievances to the world, but the flood of calls so tied up the guerrillas that they had to turn the telephones over to the hostages in order to concentrate on their defense. We didn't hesitate to accept their offer to talk to reporters.

Ambassador Galán pleaded for the police to exercise caution and good judgment. He was worried that if the troops decided on some daring course of action "a slaughter would occur inside the Embassy." He knew we were sitting ducks if anything went wrong. Galán also urged that Uribe Vargas open channels with the M-19 as quickly as possible.

I found out that a rumor was circulating that I had been seriously wounded, a confusion that arose when the press saw a bleeding man being helped into my car during the shoot-out. The first journalist I spoke to asked me in a shaken voice, "How are you?"

"Fine," I answered in a way that must have sounded terribly glib. "How are you?" He asked me if I'd been shot, and I told him no, at least not that I was aware of.

For the next few hours we handled calls from the United States, Mexico, Brazil, and a number of other Latin countries. Commander Zero, the noted leader of the Sandinistas of Nicaragua, called from Managua to congratulate Commander One on his coup. Leonard Greenwood of the *Los Angeles Times* called and asked me if I had panicked during the shooting.

"I'm about to panic right now," I told him. "I'm down to my last pinch of pipe tobacco and I don't know where I'm going to get any more." I asked Greenwood if he'd be kind enough to call my staff at the Embassy in Bogota and ask them to send me a can. I still wonder if Greenwood didn't think I'd come unhinged. In truth, my pipe-smoking was a constant source of comfort in captivity. Think on that, you psychologists!

We spent anxious hours waiting for Vásquez Carrizosa to arrive, never certain that he would. I tried to think through our predicament. The silence in the wake of the gunfire was haunting, and it only highlighted the threat. I was thankful for the opportunity to speak to someone, anyone, on the outside because it kept my mind from more despairing thoughts. Outside, I knew wary troops were massing around the perimeter and barricading the immediate area, which was jammed with civilian and military vehicles. The few glimpses I could get of the street were chilling. I was in a war zone. Men with their weapons at the ready were crouched behind cars awaiting orders. It was a strained, tense truce. Everyone — the soldiers and the police, the hostages and the terrorists — was waiting.

Nancy was at home trying to sort through the conflicting bits of information that were cascading through. Frank Crigler, the Deputy Chief of Mission and second in command in the American Embassy in Bogotá, called the house to tell Nancy that a group of terrorists had attacked the Dominican Embassy, but that he had no information about my status. The news went through her like a shot. As Frank told her the sketchy details, Nancy, who'd been standing with her back against a wall in the office, slid down onto the floor in momentary shock. Her first words were, "I should have been there with him…" She sat on the floor trying to surface from the flood of feelings that engulfed her with the force of a tidal wave. Her concern for me was mixed with guilt and anxiety for not having gone to the reception with me.

My capture didn't come as a total surprise to Nancy. We'd often discussed the possibility of a terrorist attack on the Embassy among ourselves and with other friends who were diplomats. There were enough precedents — too many, in fact: Nicaragua, Guatemala, Mexico, the seizure of the American Embassy in Kuala Lumpur in 1974, and, of course, the seizure of the American Embassy in Teheran. In Latin America alone there had been a dozen embassies that had been seized during the last two months. There were another dozen major incidents in the rest of the world, not including the assassination of Adolph Dubs, the American Ambassador to Afghanistan, in 1979 by extremist Moslem terrorists, and the assassination of the British Ambassador in the Hague that same year. Embassies were rapidly becoming prime targets for any radical group of armed men with a cause. Despite heavy security, no embassy was any longer immune to the violent radicalism of the population that surrounded it.

Nancy and I were both aware that the age-old doctrine of diplomatic immunity was crumbling throughout the world. Even our five children, who are tuned into the state of extremist politics in Latin America, expressed their concern for us on occasion. The problem was, however, that we had prepared for such an event only in a vague, intellectual way. Now we had to confront the reality of the problem emotionally, something we were completely ill-prepared for. The distance between the indefinite and indistinct intellectual acceptance of such a contingency and the definite, pressing emotional crush of the event itself when it happens is so awesome that the one has no relationship to the other. Inwardly, I suppose, Nancy and I believed it would never happen to us. Naively, we believed, like all our colleagues, that it always happens to other people. We felt reasonably safe in Colombia because the government was friendly, and outwardly there was no reason to be concerned.

The truth is, no post is safe. As Foreign Service officers we are aware of an element of risk involved with the job, but few people safeguard themselves against that risk with anything but superficial considerations unless they are stationed in a country in the throes of revolution or social upheaval. Americans are notoriously slow to react to danger, and we can be characterized as anything but overcautious. The Department of State has a two-day course for overseas personnel exposed to the threat of terrorism. It needs such a program to help victims such as myself and the families of victims such as Nancy and our children to deal with the effects of terroristic crimes.

Although Nancy considers herself a realist, when she heard the uncertain news from Crigler, she felt as though a part of her had been severed. Every ounce of will drained away with the uncertainty about my fate. She quickly got up off the floor and turned on the radio and then turned up the volume on the Embassy's emergency radio network. She waited anxiously for some word of what was happening. Things were jumping. First a local announcer claimed that the Ambassador from the United States had escaped but had been badly wounded and was being rushed to the Military Hospital.

Nancy's first reaction was one of sheer relief. I was out of the Embassy, and that was something definite, something she could deal with. She didn't believe I'd been "mortally wounded," as one announcer claimed. I was alive and out of danger. She grabbed her purse and started for the door when she heard loud and clear on the Embassy radio: "The terrorists have taken the Dominican Embassy! Our man is inside!"

Within moments, the telephone rang. The caller was a good friend of ours and a prominent neurosurgeon in Bogotá, Dr. Solomon Hakim, who was at the Military Hospital and told Nancy not to listen to the news reports. I wasn't on the way to the hospital, and I hadn't been shot. (I later learned that the overzealous press mistook me for Pablo Oliveros, who had been taken to the Military Hospital in my limousine.)

Nancy vividly remembers the crushing feeling after hearing the truth: I was taken hostage by terrorists. She was overwhelmed. It was easier for her to accept that I was hurt and out of the Embassy than unhurt and being held captive by a largely unknown enemy. She felt absolutely powerless. There was nothing she could do but sit tight and wait for more news, relay it to the rest of the family, and pray, something she did a lot of during the next sixty-one days.

Uncertainty is a difficult emotion to handle because it has no apparent beginning, middle, or end. Uncertainty can be devastating because it stealthily robs you of hope. It is an endless continuum of darkness fraught with doubts. The ordeal was every bit as trying for Nancy as it was for me. Families of hostages undergo equal trauma even though only one life may be in danger. With death, a family can grieve for its lost one. It is part of a reconciliation process. But with uncertainty there can be no grief, only constant waiting and insidious frustration.

It hurt most, Nancy later told me, the first morning after my capture. At that floating moment before she actually awoke, Nancy felt my presence next to her strongly. When she turned to my side of the bed and saw the emptiness she remembered what had happened to me. My absence was profoundly real at that moment, and the feeling was shattering.

Nancy held up well under pressure. Before long, many of the other wives of hostages looked to her for comfort, strength, and direction. Nancy is a remarkable woman, and our family's calm and strength undoubtedly flowed from her behavior.

THREE

M-19, until its grandstand play of seizing the Dominican Embassy, was pretty much unknown outside Colombia. The M-19 is the most sensationalist of the half-dozen terrorist organizations in Colombia, and its blatant publicity-seeking has put it on the international terrorist map.

In almost any reference to the modern-day political situation in Colombia, it is necessary to begin by mentioning the name of Jorge Eliecer Gaitán. His presence seems to seep into contemporary events much as Banquo's ghost did at Macbeth's feast. This charismatic leader of the Liberal party was gunned down at the height of his popularity in 1948 at high noon in downtown Bogotá. Some say he was killed by a jealous husband, more are convinced that his death was sought by the radical right who feared his immense popularity was leading him to the presidency. His death was marked by a popular surge of violence that led to the torching of a considerable portion of Bogota, indiscriminate looting, attacks on the presidential palace, and 2,000 people killed. The *Bogotazo*, as it is referred to by observers of Latin America, coincided with a meeting of foreign ministers of the Organization of American States in Bogotá. The U.S. delegation, headed by General George C. Marshall, and the foreign diplomats had to scurry for cover, holing up in their embassies and hotel suites. Among the ravening mobs was said to be a young Cuban student by the name of Fidel Castro.

Beyond the drama of the moment, the *Bogotazo* intensified the chronic internecine fighting in the Colombian countryside between adherents of the Liberal and Conservative parties that became a part of Colombian life. Entire rural districts were wiped out as people fled to the cities to escape the wholesale slaughter of thousands. This intermittent warfare lasted for ten years and claimed well over 100,000 lives — some say as many as 300,000. It came to be known in Colombia simply as *La Violencia*, not unlike "the trouble" in Ireland. Armed bands of various ideological persuasions roamed the countryside, enforcing their philosophies with violence. Others were less ideologically inclined and their acts bordered on simple banditry. Still others transcended the Liberal-Conservative polarization and were much more radically inclined. In all cases, their actions were devastating.

A number of the guerrilla movements and subversive groups currently in existence trace their roots back to *La Violencia* and those that do not can be said to have been created by the conditions of the period. With the inability of the traditional leadership to contain the situation, General Gustavo Rojas Pinilla took power in 1953, the only member of the military to have done so in this century. He was to rule for four years, but when his populist tactics were perceived as threatening to the traditional parties, he was deposed.

In 1957 a remarkable political instrument was forged that came to be known as the National Front. The Liberal and Conservative parties were to rotate the presidential office and to apportion between them the executive branch, the Parliament, and the governorships of the states. Succeeding presidents then governed with the support of both parties and with the assistance of an almost continuous state of siege decreed intermittently by the executive to defend against the remaining, radicalized guerrilla groups. While *La Violencia* waned, distinct vestiges remained. In 1965, I first went to Bogotá while working with the Alliance for Progress, the economic development program proposed by President Kennedy to address the social and economic inequities of societies like Colombia. While I was there, a leaflet bomb was detonated inside the American Embassy to protest U.S. involvement in the country.

In 1970, General Rojas Pinilla reemerged on the national scene, this time as a candidate for president under the banner of the National Popular Alliance. He proposed a "third way" in response to the National Front and, with his considerable gifts as an organizer and his populist leanings, put together a powerful coalition of the disaffected. While there is no question that the alliance of the two major parties had brought a virtual end to *La Violencia*, political critics observed that it had frozen Colombian politics at the year 1948. They denounced its basically elitist orientation as static and unfit to address the problems of an industrializing and urbanizing Colombia. Nevertheless, in the elections of 1970, large segments of the population that had been apathetic since 1948 seemed to be swept up in the excitement generated by the General's campaign. He offered hope to the nation's urban poor and downtrodden with his mix of populism and demagoguery. The poor understood his language and his promises, and they believed, despite his former dictatorial methods, that he was their man. Rojas Pinilla started out the front-runner in the contest, but he ultimately lost the election to the Liberal-Conservative establishment. It was a close election and President Misael Pastrana Borrero won with a plurality of a mere 65,000 votes.

Carlos Toledo Plata, one of the current leaders of the M-19, claimed that candidate Rojas Pinilla, whose platform was based on an intense, almost jingoistic nationalism that provided for sweeping reforms, was the victim of what he described as "the oligarchy, the Liberals and the Conservatives" who perpetuated a "fraud and stopped the people from choosing." Toledo Plata later said, "I think that was the moment when I decided I had to look for a political movement and military organization, to create a clandestine group and start fighting using these methods." Thus a new guerrilla faction was born.

The people seemed to revert to their former apathy. In 1974, a schism in the semi moribund political organization developed after the General's death and a "socialist" splinter group emerged that was soon disowned by the parent organization. It was from this group that the M-19, as a clandestine armed group, seeking by subversion what they claimed had been denied to them through the ballot box, came forth. The name is taken from the date of the 1970 election: it is known formally as the Movement of April 19, thus M-19. Over the years the M-19 developed a distinctly leftist cast and incorporated the disillusioned and the politically disenfranchised. Current intelligence characterizes the ranks of the M-19 as a combination of Maoist, Castroite, Trotskyite, and Guevarist revolutionaries, but although their ideology might most kindly be described as heterodox, the primary thrust of the M-19 is Marxist.

Toledo Plata also became enamored with Peronism while he was a medical student in Buenos Aires. He has openly advocated the institution of a socialist republic through armed insurrection, and he has linked himself with the Tupamaros of Uruguay and with Fidel Castro.

The M-19 surfaced from time to time during the seventies with actions that can only be described as guerrilla theater. Keenly aware of the value of publicity in a revolutionary cause, the M-19 developed a marked penchant for the highly dramatic. They took their lead from the Tupamaros and from the Montoneros of Argentina, and heeded the guidelines from the basic text of urban guerrilla warfare by Carlos Marighella, The Mini Manual of the Urban Guerrilla. The M-19 made national headlines for the first time in January 1974, when a select group of its members broke into a national museum in Bogotá and made off with a national treasure: the sword of the great South American liberator, Simón Bolívar. The M-19 claimed the sword in the name of "the people who struggle for freedom" and resolved never to return the sword until democracy was fully restored to Colombia. "His [Simón Bolívar's] sword now begins new combats," a note left behind read. "Now it confronts the Yanqui, the exploiter, those who deliver our country to sorrow, the landowner, the capitalist, the oligarch."

The M-19's first sortie into the consciousness of the Colombian people was not without careful preparation. In the weeks before the theft of the sword, the M-19, then virtually unknown even inside Colombia, bought advertising space in the national newspapers and ran ads that said cryptically, "Wait for the M-19." Vásquez Carrizosa later remarked, "Nobody knew if it was something to clean your floors with, or cigarettes, or what."

As far as anyone knows, the M-19 still has possession of the Liberator's sword.

Naturally, the theft of Bolívar's sword created a great deal of national press, and it wasn't long before the M-19 was at it again, creating incidents designed to enhance its popular image. In most cases, the M-19 was careful to inform the press beforehand to ensure adequate coverage. In several theatrical, almost melodramatic gestures, guerrillas hijacked milk trucks and drove them into the slums where they distributed the milk free to the children. Another favorite M-19 publicity stunt is to commandeer buses loaded with passengers and then lecture them about the abuses of the government and the goals of the M-19. On other occasions they have kidnapped prominent businessmen and taken them to secret "people's prisons" — usually no more than a pit dug beneath the floor of a house — and forced promises from them to give raises and other concessions to their workers in return for their lives and freedom. In a few cases, this coercion actually worked, and the "exploited workers of capitalists" were given wage increases.

By 1976, the M-19 accelerated their terrorism with the assassination of anti-Communist labor leader José Mercado Martínez, whom they had charged with betraying the working class. They believed his union was responsible for making sweetheart deals with management and that Mercado himself was an agent of imperialism who had not fully supported a general strike instigated in 1976, which had been severely repressed by the government at the cost of several lives. Originally the M-19 asked for an exchange of Mercado for one of their own members who had been captured, but when the government flatly refused to cooperate, Mercado was executed "in the name of the people." One of the women terrorists in the Embassy told me that Mercado had been lured to his kidnapping by a beautiful woman. In her opinion, Mercado was a "pig" who deserved to be killed because of his eye for pretty women.

On New Year's Day, 1979, the M-19 committed one of their most daring exploits by tunneling 250 feet into a national armory north of Bogotá and making off with about 5,000 weapons of all kinds.

The reaction of the government was swift and severe. By invoking a national security statute, the President of Colombia empowered the Minister of Defense, Luis Carlos Camacho Leyva, to make mass arrests and conduct house-to-house searches for terrorists. The military enforced a sweeping dragnet which left virtually no stone unturned during eighteen months of searches. Nearly 2,000 people were seized by the national police during the roundups. Of those, more than 400 men and women were arrested and held in prisons as suspected members of the M-19. Nine other people were killed resisting arrest. The majority of arms that had been stolen from the arsenal were recovered (the government claimed to have repossessed 95 percent of the stolen armaments). Some of those arrested were innocent of any connection with the M-19 and were subsequently released, but at the time of the Embassy seizure, 219 M-19 suspects were still being held prisoner at La Picota Prison pending their courts-martial, a very slow process in Colombia. The right to a speedy trial is not guaranteed by the Colombian constitution.

Under the provisions of the national security statute and because Colombia has been in an official state of siege for most of the last thirty years, the suspected terrorists were subject to military and not civilian jurisdiction. The army claimed to have obtained confessions from 109 of the prisoners.

Camacho Leyva, who became a focal figure during the massive anti-guerrilla campaign, was convinced that the military action had been so thorough as nearly to wipe out any remnants of organized urban guerrilla dissidents in Colombia. He made a public announcement to that effect only days before the last of the M-19 showed their remarkable resiliency by capturing the Dominican Embassy.

Cartoon implying that the Colombian Minister of Defense, General Carlos Camacho Leyva, is Ambassador Asencio's Agent, an accusation that did not make the General particularly happy.

Ambassador Diego Asencio with President of Colombia, Julio Cesar Turbay Ayala, who was instrumental in effective resolution of the hostage crisis.

The seizure of the Dominican Embassy was an act of desperation. Mindful of its public image, although incapable of perceiving that image correctly, the M-19 had lost major ground during the anti-guerrilla campaign and therefore had to do something spectacular to recoup lost prestige and power. The taking of the Dominican Embassy and its hostages was, if anything, intended to be a magic, grandiloquent gesture. With a minimal investment of personnel and matériel, the M-19 intended to create a major international incident that would reestablish the group as a powerful threat to what the M-19 considered to be its detractors and the enemies of democracy.

Until February 1980 it had seemed that the back of the M-19 had been broken. But rumors would surface that the M-19 was going to start rural campaigns. M-19 spokesmen related the results of secret "people's courts" in which exploiters were tried and condemned in absentia. Meanwhile, the Colombian government attributed ninety-five criminal acts, including twelve murders, during 1979 to the M-19. The M-19, furthermore, began to form alliances with extra-national terrorists in the hopes of consolidating its power and resources.

The connections the M-19 has with other organizations are still unclear. Toledo Plata, forty-eight, a doctor and an ex-member of Parliament, and Jaime Bateman Cayon, thirty-six, a former law student once involved in the youth movement of the Communist party, supply the leadership to the M-19. Currently Toledo Plata is in prison awaiting trial, though Jaime Bateman Cayon is still at large.

The membership of the M-19 has traditionally been comprised of professional white-collar workers and intellectuals: doctors, lawyers, university students, professors, artists and the like; but the current membership is probably less sophisticated because many of the leading members have been captured. The young guerrilla who was killed in the initial shoot-out at the Dominican Embassy was a seventeen-year-old high school student who had been involved in radical politics for less than a year. His family described him as poor and naive.

The M-19 has been repudiated by the last vestiges of Rojas Pinilla's populist party and by other leftist organizations such as the legal Communist party in Colombia. It has, despite its attempts to curry favor, little popular support. The majority of the M-19's funding has come from an active and lucrative kidnapping program. Among the more infamous kidnappings was that of Nicolas Escobar, a general manager of Texaco in Colombia. Escobar was being held for ransom when Colombian government troops conducting an anti-guerrilla raid accidentally stumbled into the M-19's "people's prison." The troops and the guerrillas battled it out, but when the tide turned toward the army, the terrorists dynamited their hiding place with themselves and Escobar in it rather than be taken prisoner.

Even more infamous was the kidnapping and murder of Chester Bitterman III, who was kidnapped after the taking of the Dominican Embassy. Bitterman, charged by the M-19 as a CIA front man, was, in fact, a field worker for the Summer Institute of Linguistics in Texas, part of a concern that has hundreds of representatives working worldwide to study the native languages of countries' indigenous peoples, such as many of the Indian tribes in Colombia. After a harrowing series of negotiations, which ultimately failed, the M-19, or a group claiming association with the M-19, executed Bitterman and left his body in an abandoned bus on the streets of Bogotá.

The M-19 has extorted many millions of dollars of working capital by its illegal acts, much as Joseph Stalin once supported himself by robbing banks in the early days of his career. The M-19's connections with Moscow, if there are any, are tenuous at best, and up until the seizure of the Dominican Embassy, the M-19 was a self-supporting group of mavericks. When Commander One was asked in the first hours of the assault why he had taken over the Embassy, he gave the classic Marxist response of "praxis": "We believe," he said stuffily, "that theory is constructed by doing something, not in making theoretical polemics." We never did find out what the theory he was "constructing" was.

FOUR

The city of Bogotá is at the northernmost end of the Andean mountain chain and sits at an elevation of 8,600 feet. Evenings in February can be chilly, even downright cold. With most of the windows of the Embassy shot out, the frosty air invaded the building. There was no heat, and we were still dressed in our party clothes, so we concentrated on trying to stay warm.

We waited to hear whether the government was going to send Vásquez Carrizosa, the former Foreign Minister, according to Commander One's request. It was possible Uribe Vargas would refuse to send anyone. The government's aversion to any kind of dealing with terrorists was well known. It might decide, for instance, to turn the siege around and deny us food and water until the guerrillas submitted to the government's terms. There would be casualties with that approach, but the message would be irrefutably clear: the Colombian Government would have no truck with terrorists, whatever the consequences.

If Vásquez Carrizosa showed up, then his presence would be a good sign: it meant the President and the Foreign Minister at least were willing to test the water. I had dealt with the two officials before; they were sensitive and intelligent men, so there was little reason to believe they would adamantly refuse to talk to Commander One. But terrorism was an emotionally charged issue in Colombia. There was no safe way to predict what anyone might or might not do.

The late afternoon light faded toward dusk. We still had no word about Vásquez Carrizosa. The guerrillas were impatient, and we tried to calm them down by explaining the complicated procedure involved in asking Vásquez Carrizosa, to act on behalf of an administration he was no longer part of, and then convincing him to endanger his life by coming to the Dominican Embassy to make first contact with a bunch of trigger-happy terrorists. First, President Turbay would have to agree to the proposal, I explained to Commander One in an attempt to calm him. Then the president would contact former President Misael Pastrana Borrero, under whom Vásquez Carrizosa had been Foreign Minister. This procedure was a peculiar twist in Colombian political protocol: the President would not try to contact the former Foreign Minister himself, but only through the original chain of command. Pastrana would then petition Vásquez Carrizosa to come to the Embassy. A time-consuming process. And a sensitive one. Once Commander One understood the complexity involved in his request, he stopped threatening to start executions to demonstrate the seriousness of his intent.

The terrorists continued to move us around at gunpoint, trying to decide how best to split us up and where to keep us. Staying alive was my top priority, and I was careful not to do or say anything to antagonize Commander One or any of his henchmen. They were fidgety and impatient, just as ready to shoot as to talk. I could hear them arguing among themselves about what strategy to pursue. I was later advised that one terrorist, a mean-tempered and pathologically angry man, argued violently for my execution. Fortunately, I was spared from hearing that particular argument.

Vásquez Carrizosa finally arrived after what had seemed like a century. I was ushered downstairs with the other ambassadors in the committee-elect. We sat in the darkening room and waited patiently, not sure of what to expect. Commander One, wary of a trick, doubled the guard. He pulled a bandanna over his face to protect his identity, a practice that became de rigueur for the duration. I prayed everyone would remain calm and act politic, if this first meeting failed or went wrong, our chance for another meeting would be reduced dramatically. My colleagues and I were all eyes and ears. Although we had discussed among ourselves how to make the best out of an encounter with Vásquez Carrizosa, we were uncharacteristically quiet while we waited for the government's emissary.

When Vásquez Carrizosa entered the room, he had a physician in tow to treat the wounded. Vásquez Carrizosa was his usual urbane, imperturbable self, but the doctor was obviously terrified. They made a striking contrast: Vásquez Carrizosa, elegant and calm, and the unnerved physician, who obviously wished he were elsewhere. Commander One greeted them nervously, and then ordered sentries posted at the front doors and windows in case Vásquez Carrizosa was a ploy for the army to attack.

We pretended, against impulse, to be civil, but the meeting was strained and awkward. As we sat together among the ruins of the battle-torn room, we appeared to be calm, rational statesmen discussing a proposal in a boardroom when, in fact, we were seething inside as we tried to disregard the explicit threat to our lives.

We quickly launched into the first of many talks. Under Commander One's tutelage, we outlined the predicament and the cost of our safety. Meanwhile, it was getting dark as night settled into the Embassy. When the Ambassador from Brazil started to turn on a light, Commander One brusquely stopped him. He was afraid of snipers and didn't want any lights on to silhouette a target for a sharpshooter. So we sat in the dark and talked by the feeble light that filtered through the heavily barred windows. We later resorted to lighting one small candle so we wouldn't be entirely in the dark, but the pathetic flickering flame seemed only to highlight the absurdity of the meeting.

Commander One again reiterated his demands with his typical bombastic flair. He insisted on the release of 311 political prisoners, whom he would name later, a ransom of $50 million in cash, and the publication of a list of M-19 grievances in the major presses of the hostages' countries. He also told Vásquez Carrizosa he would be honored if the former Foreign Minister would himself act as the intermediary for discussions with the Colombian government. From the tone of his voice, I could tell Commander One respected Vásquez Carrizosa and his record and dedication to correcting the state of human rights in Colombia. The terrorist leader urged the statesman to mediate the crisis; he was a man both sides trusted.

The splendid old man didn't bat an eye and discussed the terms calmly. He thanked Commander One for his vote of confidence, but apologized that his writ was strictly limited to coming to the Embassy and finding out what his people wanted. Vásquez Carrizosa, cautious as he was polite, said he'd be pleased to do anything he could to settle the crisis amicably, but it was up to President Turbay to determine what steps would be taken and how. In the meantime, he was authorized to say that the President had agreed to withdraw the army to an outlying perimeter and would not attack unless the lives of the ambassadors or any of the other hostages were in immediate danger. Here the old man was explicit: if Commander One did anything to harm his captives, then he could expect the army to come crashing through the front door. At first, the threat sounded like a godsend because it would make the guerrillas think before they did anything rash, but it later turned out to be a mixed blessing.

In response to Vásquez Carrizosa's message, the Commander got back up on his high horse and emphasized the seriousness of his mission. He told the former Foreign Minister he was prepared to stay in the Embassy as long as it took to accomplish his goals — "one or two months, if necessary," he said — and that all his demands were negotiable except the release of the prisoners. On that point he was adamant, and no amount of discussion would make him or his comrades change their minds.

After forty minutes the meeting broke up, and Vásquez Canizosa and Dr. Martinez left quietly. Commander One herded us back upstairs to the library for the night.

For the first time since I'd gone downstairs, I noticed the cold as the night air seeped into the room through the broken windows. There was no food, no light, and little solace. The mansion itself was old and poorly maintained. Ironically, the building had once been owned by General Rojas Pinilla, who later sold it to the Dominican Republic. I recalled one version of the story that said Rojas Pinilla had transferred the title of his mansion to Trujillo as part of the conditions of his asylum in the Dominican Republic when he was deposed. If that story was true, then the added irony deepened as Rojas Pinillas men returned to reclaim his property.

But now the building was decrepit, with leaky ceilings and broken parquet floors, conveying a sense of shabby gentility and faded elegance. It had few conveniences and the ones it did have worked poorly or not at all. The place was hardly equipped to house and feed more than seventy people: it had no hot water and no refrigeration. We had to get along with what we had, and that was precious little. We ended up jury-rigging things to make do, which brought out our creative spirit. I was constantly amazed at our inventiveness: necessity mercifully created a band of amateur inventors and handymen.

Inventiveness turned out to be one of the keys to our survival. In inventiveness came flexibility and alternatives to action: We met every impasse with this sense of innovation, and more often than not, it would help provide the key to unlocking the seemingly impossible dilemmas that confronted us. At first, we applied our creativity only to our living conditions, but eventually we turned the same energy to an effort to find solutions to the impasses between the terrorists and the Colombians.

I was put to the test that first evening. By the time I got back to the library, most of the other hostages were trying to sleep, though with little success. There were no beds and only a few mattresses scavenged from the bedrooms and thrown on the floor. The hostages, still dressed in party clothes, were sprawled everywhere. I could see bodies turning restlessly, trying to get comfortable. A few were sitting on the floor staring off into the darkness. I tried to get comfortable in a chair, but it was hopeless. I was far too big for the small, rickety chair, and no matter how I tried to settle in, the chair fought back. Finally, one of the terrorist women took pity on me and pulled a mattress she had been using to buttress her guard station onto the floor for me. I ended up sharing the mattress with Ambassador Galán, and we spent a restless, sleepless night.

In the hush of night I reviewed the Colombian government's policy in dealing with terrorists. In the past it had been adamant to the point of inflexibility by refusing not only to give in to demands, but by refusing even to talk with them. The government's policy was explicit and hard-line, and so far it had not deviated an inch from that stance. I had experienced it firsthand in the case of Richard Starr, a Peace Corps Volunteer kidnapped in 1976. All of my requests for flexibility had been rejected out of hand by the Colombian authorities. They had been prepared to countenance Mercado's assassination in the name of policy. They were not likely to change their position lightly. Vásquez Carrizosa's appearance was meant only to probe the terrorists and find out something more about them. I couldn't expect the meeting to count for much else.

Commander One had yet to reckon with the Minister of Defense, General Camacho Leyva, a tough-minded and shrewd man who was the rare combination of a military man and lawyer. Camacho Leyva wasn't the sort of man who would give in to the pressure of other governments whose representatives were being held hostage. He would be a tough man to beat.

Colombia's policy closely paralleled the United States' posture on dealing with terrorists as defined by Henry Kissinger during his tenure as Secretary of State. By refusing to deal with terrorists or even consider their demands, we hoped to discourage trafficking in human lives. Even if Colombia took the unprecedented step of opening negotiations with Commander One, the prospect of releasing more than 300 political prisoners, many of whom had been charged with felonies such as kidnapping, extortion, and murder, was remote if not impossible. So was the ransom demand for the outrageous sum of $50 million.

There was some talk among the hostages that a major power such as the United States might try to intervene, but even if the Colombian government allowed the U.S. Department of State to intrude in a domestic affair — which was highly improbable — they would certainly take the same hard-line stance.

As much as we wanted out, and as much as our governments wanted us out, we didn't entertain any illusions. As diplomats we were expendable, and we knew we could be sacrificed if it became necessary to safeguard policy, that is, to protect our other colleagues in the future. It was a painful realization, and at times it was difficult to deal with when the cruel reality of the issue confronted me. No longer was it just an intellectual point: it became a highly charged emotional one as well. Yet I took some comfort in knowing the Department of State does not callously abandon its people in the field. I assumed the people at State would explore every avenue carefully and conscientiously, just as I hoped the Colombian government would. I was out on a long, precarious limb along with the other ambassadors and officers. All I could do now was be patient and turn over the possibility in my mind.

In the somber stillness of night, I felt strangely apart not only from Nancy and my colleagues and friends at the American Embassy, but also from my government. They all became inexplicably distant, and the feeling was unsettling. Even though I was uncomfortably squeezed between dozens of other hostages in the same predicament as myself I felt alone in what Milton calls "the palpable obscure," as if a tremendous void had opened and swallowed me, obliterating my former life as I had known it and severing my lifelines to family and country. I was in an unknown land where logic and law had gone topsy-turvy. I realized I no longer had the same set of rules to play by, and that I didn't even know the new rules or if I could play by them. I wasn't feeling panic — fear had already blunted its edge on me — I was feeling a disconcerting sense of isolation and unbreachable distance. I was alone — although I wasn't to realize how alone I really was until weeks later — and for the first time in twenty-three years in the Foreign Service I was "without instructions" and without recourse. I didn't want to be the anvil on which U.S. policy was forged; I wanted to leave the Dominican Embassy unharmed and with honor. I wouldn't abandon my responsibilities as an ambassador, nor would I allow those responsibilities to become jeopardized; by the same token, I wouldn't allow myself to become a martyr for the sake of expediency. My fatalism was being stoked by another consideration. Even if I survived, my career was at an end. I could think of no American ambassador or Foreign Service officer whose career had thrived or prospered after such an incident.

I slept fitfully that evening as my semiconscious mind began to write the hundred scenarios of my future, ranging from superhuman heroism to ignoble defeat.

FIVE

The next morning we were back at the telephones. I was grateful for the opportunity to speak with the outside because it gave me something to do, something to say, to feel as though I were accomplishing something concrete.

That morning I spoke to Nancy for the first time. I was depressed and pessimistic about my chances of surviving, but I didn't want Nancy to know how I was feeling, so I decided to sound positive and optimistic about my chances of getting out quickly. I called Nancy at the residence; our connection was weak and she sounded far away.

"Hi," I said as though I was away on an overnight trip. "How are you?"

"Oh! Darling, it's you!" she exclaimed with a mixture of excitement and concern. "How are you?"

"I'm fine," I said trying to convey a sense of confidence. "It's uncomfortable, but I'm getting along." The fact was I was thinking this was the last time I would ever speak to Nancy; it was my valedictory to her and my children. "I love you," I said pensively. "And give my love to the kids."

"I will," she said quietly. "I love you too."

I tried not to let my voice give me away. "Listen," I said, "this shouldn't last too long. We're already starting to work things out."

"Are you hurt? Are you all right?"

"No, I'm in good shape. I didn't sleep well last night."

"Well, you'll get out soon," Nancy said.

In retrospect, it was obvious we were both pretending. Nancy later told me my voice was serious, but comforting. She took my lead and returned the confidence. In that way we boosted each other's morale for the weeks to follow.

Commander One, who was monitoring the telephones, was anxious to use his hostages as pressure points on the Colombian government. He reasoned that by allowing us to talk to our wives and embassies, pressure from the outside would be brought to bear against the Colombians. It was, as far as he was concerned, an unexcelled opportunity to force the

Colombians to deal with him. I tried to explain to Commander One the United States government's intractable position on hostage and ransom negotiations, and I tried to make him understand that he might not have the valuable merchandise he thought he had when he captured the American Ambassador. I wasn't a feather in his cap, at least not as he supposed. He watched me thoughtfully while I explained all this to him and then gave me a glib response. "It would be such a shame," he said mockingly, "to have to shoot you just as I was getting to know you."

I found the hostility directed toward me as the representative of the United States by some of the guerrillas distressingly tangible. While I was grateful for still being alive, I was anxious about my prospects of staying that way. From the beginning, a few of the terrorists made no bones about the fact they despised me as an agent of American capitalist imperialism. I was a monster from a monstrous country.

My greatest antagonist was a hostile, pugnacious man who was a former *Tupamaro* and was known to us only as Omar, Number Three. Omar was the second in command and was responsible for maintaining discipline and security. He often proved himself a nasty, surly man. Omar was the man who had forced me to the front door to call for a ceasefire during the shooting. He was also the man who was arguing in favor of my execution. Omar's gruff demeanor and martinet-like attitude put him at odds with the other hostages and with his own comrades from time to time. He was an extremist on the far left, so far in fact, that he made some of the other terrorists look like political conservatives. Omar was clearly a man to avoid.

Later in the day, when sentries spotted three people moving stealthily into a house across the street, Commander One automatically assumed they were police trying to infiltrate the terrorists' position. Because the immediate neighborhood had been completely evacuated the evening before, the assumption seemed reasonable. Omar, who considered himself a man of action, immediately sought me out and forced me at gunpoint to kneel on a table before one of the library windows facing the building where the sentries had spotted the intruders.

Omar crouched — cowered might be a better description — behind me, and using me as a shield, fired his carbine into the windows where the intruders had been seen. I felt the hot muzzle blast against my leg. At my size (I weigh over 200 pounds), I knew I made an excellent target: a sharpshooter could have hardly missed. Even though I was shaken, I found myself determined not to betray my fright to Omar, so I pretended not to be concerned by his callous treatment of me. While Omar hid behind me waiting for an answer to his volley, I asked him impatiently if he were finished. The tone of my voice and the disgust I felt for his behavior must have been obvious because Omar let me get down from the table, but not before he scowled at me.

Telephoto of Ambassador Diego Asencio taken from the Press Bivouac.

The animosity between us never let up. We were committed enemies to the end, although we eventually learned to respect each other's distance. As it turned out, the police "infiltrators" Omar had shot at were not police at all, but members of a family who had sneaked back into their apartment to rescue their pet canary. Fortunately, no one was seriously injured although two of them were lacerated by flying glass. The Ambassador from Brazil, Geraldo Eulalio Nascimento e Silva, having witnessed Omar's rash use of me, approached Commander One and pointed out that while we were all ambassadors and theoretically equal, some of us were surely more equal than others. Obviously, the Ambassador from America could be a valuable hole card in the future, reasoned the Brazilian, so if Omar felt he had to use an ambassador as a shield, then "Why don't you use one of the Central Americans?"

Humor became a critical part of our routine in the days to come. It brought the hostages closer together even if the joke was at the expense of one of us. Humor helped keep us sane, and those of the hostages who didn't have a sense of humor were among those who suffered most. Nancy particularly understood the importance of a light heart, and she made it a point always to have a joke for me during our daily telephone conversations even if she had to call friends in the States to keep up her supply. Our friend Bob Graham, the governor of Florida, went so far as to send her the list of jokes he utilizes as speech openers. In turn, I would usually pass the joke along to the other hostages. We savored those moments, and it became something of a daily ritual that we looked forward to sharing. It took the edge off the strain.

Humor also allowed us to communicate with our captors. Whenever things weren't going right, I'd resort to humor to involve those hostages who wanted to withdraw. Humor was a bond that kept us going, and there were many funny moments worth their weight in gold. Without them, the heavy aura of desperation would have crippled us. Humor made an impossible situation possible.

The group of four ambassadors elected to the negotiating group decided, in the meantime, that it was important to establish cordial relations with our captors. It was a premise derived of conventional wisdom that while Latins can be cruel, they find it difficult to be cruel or even rude to people they know. Even a momentary hesitation of the finger on the trigger would be worthwhile. If it kept them from killing us, all the better. At least it would make our condition more tolerable.

The hostage leadership group posing with Commader One, from left to right: American Ambassador Diego C Asencio; Brazilian Ambassador Geraldo Eulalio Nascimento e Silva; Commander One, Rosenberg Pabón Pabón; Mexican Ambassador Ricardo Galan. Photo by Luis Guzmán.

Fortunately, Commander One reciprocated, and when he later caught one of his own men abusing one of the hostages, he chided him for being so "politically immature" as to harass a prisoner. In fact, the terrorists were courteous to the extreme by insisting on addressing us by our full diplomatic titles. While this is a basic formality of most Colombians, it seemed rather strange coming from people who were holding guns on us and threatening to shoot us if we didn't obey their every order.

Commander One later told me that he believed if our captivity was managed properly, then tension would correspondingly ease, thereby creating less of a security problem for him. I also learned later that Commander One's insistence on treating us with respect and limited deference is a hallmark of hostage-takers. It has been suggested that this unexpected behavior is an unconscious attempt to mask the innate brutality of their acts. In a paradoxical double-twist, the terrorist, who so openly flouts law and convention, turns around and insists on courtesy and convention for his victims. I was glad to be the benefactor of such pretzel logic. As a result — whatever its cause — the terrorists' general conduct made life within the Embassy bearable.

Commander One was, on the whole, forthright and rigorous about the maintenance of order and security both in his own ranks and in ours. He listened thoughtfully to what others had to say and acted accordingly, whether his advice came from his own people or from one of us. Generally he exercised good judgment in tactical matters, but I found his sense of strategy severely lacking.

The ambassadorial negotiating committee met and decided we had an opportunity to affect the direction of the negotiations. We didn't know exactly how much pressure we could exert on our captors, but it was a reasonable assumption that our active involvement in the developing state of affairs could help determine the outcome. We decided to test the water by urging Commander One to release the wounded and the women on humanitarian grounds. We used the argument that because the world was watching, Commander One should be careful to cultivate the M-19's image. He needed to establish the M-19 as a group of idealists whose quarrel was with the Colombian government and not with the innocents who had come under their control. Furthermore, if the Paraguayan Honorary Consul General were to die because of inadequate medical care for his shoulder wound, then the guerrillas were certain to be labeled as murderers, barbarians who couldn't be reasoned with. If there was any sympathy for the M-19's cause, the unwarranted death of any of the hostages was bound to destroy it. This shift, we argued, would give the government the upper hand.

The Commander accepted our argument and agreed to release the wounded and all the women except the five women diplomats. He said he would eventually release them too, but he wanted to keep them as a bargaining point for the return of one of his own soldiers, the woman with the head wound. Commander One was concerned lest she need to be hospitalized, and he intended to ensure her return to the Dominican Embassy by trading her for the five women.

By four in the afternoon, after further discussion with the Colombian government on the phone, Commander One kept his promise and released thirteen hostages: ten women, among them the wives of the Israeli and Guatemalan ambassadors, a bewildered and frightened fifteen-year-old waiter, and two wounded men, who were quickly driven away in ambulances. In response to the Commander's action, and by previous agreement, Colombian Red Cross volunteers carried twenty crates of food and supplies into the Embassy. It was the first food we'd had in nearly thirty hours, and many of us were nearly starved even though the food was an unappetizing fare of Vienna sausage and potato chips.

The guerrillas were suspicious of the food and were afraid it was poisoned or drugged, so they abstained from joining us. Meanwhile, Dr. Jaime Gómez, a well-known Colombian neurologist, and another medical colleague were allowed into the building to examine the guerrilla Renata's head wound. He concluded that the wound was superficial and that she didn't need hospitalization. He dressed the head wound and a minor leg wound. As soon as Dr. Gómez left, we pressed Commander One to live up to his word and release the other five women. He brusquely put us off and told us to be patient.

Outside, the Colombian government was reviewing the M-19's demands. In a flurry of communiqués to the anxious press, the government announced it was carefully "examining" the facts. President Turbay also issued a communiqué stating that these demands constituted what he called "a good basis for the examination and decision of the Government." No one knew what exactly this meant, but at least it was a start. Dialogue had begun. In the streets around the Embassy, the army consolidated its position. Troops carrying riot shields and machine pistols stayed out of sight while students from the National University chanted pro-M-19 slogans and verbally harassed the troops. Others, standing out of harm's way, simply stared at the spectacle.

The Austrian Ambassador and I were ordered to carry the body of the dead guerrilla known as Camilo out of the house on one of the sofas. We turned him over to the Red Cross. Camilo's body had begun to smell, and its presence in the house was a constant reminder of how close it had been for us. The smell of death lingered on for days, always intruding into our consciousness. After Ambassador Selzer and I carried Camilo into the street, Mr. Selzer told me he'd almost made a run for it while we were carrying out our grisly task.

"What made you change your mind?" I asked.

"You!" he smiled. "You're so big you blocked the door!"

We spent the rest of the day on the telephones talking with our families and respective governments and giving them our appraisal of the situation. Our calls were constantly monitored by the wary M-19 — an inconvenience we would have to learn to get used to — and we were made to speak in Spanish so they could understand what we were saying. The American Embassy recorded all the conversations, and Nancy had the onerous task of translating all our conversations into English. The Ambassador from Israel, whose wife spoke only halting Spanish, oftentimes was allowed to lapse into Hebrew, which I perceived as a tactical error on the part of the M-19. He was allowed to speak freely and at length even though at times no one knew what he was saying.

Except for what we could learn through our staffs and what Nancy would read to me over the phone, we knew little of what was going on outside. The Foreign Minister, Diego Uribe Vargas, tried to keep us informed, but he was a busy man in the beginning as he worked to establish a common working ground between his government and the M-19.

That evening we ransacked the five-bedroom mansion for mattresses and rugs to sleep on. All of the diplomatic personnel were squeezed into the library, while the remaining hostages were boarded in the bedrooms. The entire house was in disrepair. The rooms were dingy and grimy; the bathrooms were in terrible condition. There was little water pressure and the water heater didn't work. We started to learn how to make do with what we had, which seemed precious little. We had to sleep crosswise, four to a mattress, which made for an impossibly uncomfortable fit.

One of the ambassadors took heart and joked with the only female Ambassador among us, María Elena Chassoul of Costa Rica. He jibed that her reputation would surely be ruined once the press found that she had spent the night with nineteen men. As the saying goes, politics does indeed make strange bedfellows.

Left to right, Venezuelan Consul General Francisco Pacheco, Ambassador Diego Asencio, a female rebel with knee and head wound, gatecrasher Luis Valencia, photo taken a couple-three weeks into the event.

Tongue in cheek, I asked Number Seven, whose *nom de guerre* was Alfredo, why they hadn't picked a more comfortable embassy to raid. I suggested the American Ambassador's residence would have been ideal because everything was in top working order, and it was large enough to handle all of us comfortably. Alfredo's reply was intended to reveal the degree of preplanning the general staff had done before the takeover. He said they had surveyed a number of possible sites — embassies among them — as they tried to determine the best location for their mission. Alfredo told me they had considered other locations besides the Dominican Embassy. According to him, they had spent six months carefully collecting intelligence, planning, and making

44

preparations for the takeover. Alfredo also told me the M-19's intelligence forays were accomplished by couples, often with children, to help avoid suspicion. This "family" disguise supposedly allowed them to take photographs of access points to the embassies without creating suspicion. A guerrilla woman by the name of La Negra was supposed to have surveyed the American Embassy but had found the security there too formidable. Hence the M-19 command decided on a much more vulnerable embassy whose diminished security would allow them relatively easy access. By determining the dates of the independence day celebrations on the calendar, they could plan in advance when and where the ambassadorial community would be on any given day.

I found the M-19's claims of intense surveillance improbable. Most of the provisional task force assigned to this sortie were newly recruited and from out of town. They didn't know their way around Bogotá well enough to effect such an intelligence-gathering operation. But there was another, more valid reason that I found Alfredo's story suspect: there was evidence to suggest that the Dominican Embassy takeover was an inside job and that the M-19 had a plant inside the Embassy who helped coordinate plans by providing information, securing and hoarding supplies, and spying on the hostages themselves. This suspicion was more than the result of hyperactive, slightly paranoid minds. As hostages, we quickly learned there was an informer among us, someone who dutifully reported our private conversations to Commander One. There were several instances when Commander One cautioned us about following through with some escape plans we toyed with from time to time.

This had the automatic effect of making us cautious of what we said to one another. It was a distressing feeling to know there was a traitor among us. We started to break up into little enclaves, each party suspicious of the next. Speculation about who the informer might be was rampant. We were cautious of those we didn't know well and careful what we did and said around them.

One convenient happenstance nagged at the members of the ambassadorial negotiating committee. The day of the seizure there had been virtually no security at the Dominican Embassy. Ambassador Mallol told us he had informally requested police protection by sending a houseboy to the local precinct station to ask for it. The proper, formal procedure, however, would have been for him to have addressed a diplomatic note to the Foreign Ministry, which would have ensured the presence of security personnel. But Ambassador Mallol had not done so, preferring to rely on informal and less effective methods. Or at least that's what he told us. The overworked local police, if they had received such a request, apparently hadn't assigned a particularly high priority to so ineptly handled a request from such a small — from the standpoint of Colombian interests — embassy.

Except for the chauffeurs and the bodyguards of the various ambassadors, there had been only one aged guard stationed at the entrance to the Embassy. The M-19 couldn't have asked for better circumstances. Some of the hostages smelled collusion because circumstances were too convenient for the terrorists. A few people suggested Ambassador Mallol was involved, and that he only claimed to have asked for security when, in fact, be hadn't, knowing the Embassy would be wide open to attack. Others found that interpretation too farfetched and said the traitor was more likely the houseboy who had been sent to the police station. As an M-19 collaborator, perhaps he had only pretended to have asked for police protection. Still others claimed we were all crazy, and that our imaginations had run away with us. Fortunately, however, time would tell which one of us was right.

Alfredo told us that M-19 spotters had evaluated the security and the identities of the guests before deciding to attack. Once they were satisfied that conditions would never be better, they committed themselves to action and took advantage of the rarely afforded opportunity before them.

The presence of the spotters and their role in identifying the ambassadors who were present raised some intriguing questions about the convenient exit of the Soviet bloc ambassadors minutes before the attack. One ambassador claims to have seen the Soviet bloc ambassadors passing around a slip of paper to one another before leaving en masse. Was there any connection? It doesn't seem likely the M-19 would have risked being exposed by warning the Soviets and their allies, and it's more likely the spotters waited until the Soviet bloc was gone before giving the signal to attack. At any rate, the presence of the Soviet bloc ambassadors as hostages would have created some complications and embarrassment for Commander One, and it was certainly convenient — even remarkable — that they escaped capture so cleanly. I chaffed Commander One on this point several times, but he insisted he would have been delighted to have gotten his hands on the Soviet Ambassador.

Another theory was that the M-19 had made their move the moment I'd started for the door to leave because they wanted to make sure I was included in their net. In either case, I would like to think that my Soviet bloc colleagues weren't part of the conspiracy and that the spotters were acting on their behalf without their knowledge. Still, I have to conclude that their departure so close to the raid can be characterized, at best, as an amazing coincidence.

The security of embassy personnel on foreign soil, especially those in unstable or hostile nations, has become a question of primary importance within the Department of State. There are larger questions involved that encompass much more than the bodily security of overseas personnel. They affect the method and therefore the result of our efforts to deal with the political business of nations, and they are questions that must be carefully considered at all levels of those engaged in serious diplomacy.

Last year, Congress was asked to appropriate $25.7 million for fiscal 1981 to install and/or modify the existing security apparatus in the United States embassy network. The state of the art of security technology is unquestionably sophisticated and for the most part effective against unsanctioned physical violence directed toward these installations. (The seizure of the United States Embassy in Teheran by Iranian militants who had the overt support of the revolutionary government demonstrates that no facility on foreign soil is impregnable.) This technology may protect the embassy itself, but it doesn't protect the ambassador. At least not if he's going to do his job properly.

An ambassador confronting his position in an unstable or unfriendly country has two primary options: either he can develop a bunker mentality and seclude himself in his fortress and thus feel secure, or he can face the calculated risk of capture, injury, or even death by conducting his business in his host country's forum. Then even the most comprehensive security system in the world can't protect an ambassador.

In my own case, I was accompanied everywhere by a security contingent of at least four armed men. My car, an armored Chrysler, was always followed by an escort car. The ambassador's residence is protected by a tall brick wall surrounding it, and the only entrance is through a chain-locked iron gate. Sensors scan the tops of the walls and alert security to intruders. Inside, a guard force continuously patrols the grounds. The house itself has another intruder alert system which sounds an alarm if anyone tries to come up the stairs or penetrate the doors into the private quarters. The door to the bedroom is steel-plated and can be barricaded from the inside with a sliding cross-bar. It is an elaborate safeguard system designed for most contingencies, and nothing short of an army can pierce its defenses.

At the office, anyone who tries to enter the Embassy grounds must pass through a magnetometer. The visitor must then proceed to the receptionist, seated behind a sheet of bullet-resistant glass, and wait to be escorted to the person be wishes to see after the appointment has been properly verified. Each floor has at least one armed guard on it, and, in addition, a squad of marines is on standby in case of an emergency. The door to the ambassador's office is also bullet-resistant glass, and access is possible only by opening a combination lock or by activation of a release mechanism inside the office. It is a formidable defense system. The amount of organizational planning and logistics required to mount a successful assault against either the residence or the Embassy would discourage all but the most zealous.

Even here it should be noted that any individual, automobile, building, or fortification is vulnerable no matter how strongly protected, armored, or fortified. It comes down to a matter of tactics and resources. Ask the French of the Maginot Line or the Germans of the Siegfried Line. No office building, no matter how elaborate the security precautions, is infinitely defensible. The defense of our embassies abroad is predicated on the arrival of assistance from the security authorities of the host government in the event of attack. Where such authorities are hostile or abdicate their responsibilities, it is not surprising to see embassies overrun.

Still, an ambassador who restricts his activities to his residence and the mission would be relatively safe, at least compared with the ambassador who goes out into the streets and offices of his host country. Compliance with principles of near absolute security presupposes a passive existence in which business is handled by telephone and message and personal contact is restricted to those willing to come to the embassy. Modern diplomacy requires more. An ambassador is not merely the conduit by which governments speak to each other or solely the guardian of U.S. interests in the country to which he has been assigned. To be fully effective, he must represent the United States to the citizens of his host country. He must engage in discussions and negotiations with the officials of the government to which he is accredited. He must be available to the local media in order to explain U.S. policies. He must, as his country's standard-bearer, represent the United States at the various traditional functions, ceremonies, and receptions to which he is invited, not as an individual but as an agent of his government. In short, an ambassador must function in public.

During my ambassadorship to Colombia, on any typical day I might attend meetings with government officials in their offices in the morning, have lunch with any number of business or private associations, and participate in a television interview in the afternoon. In the evening, I might drop in on two or three cocktail parties and would then wind up at a formal dinner party at an embassy or in someone's home.

This much journeying, of course, makes the ambassador susceptible to guerrilla attack. Unfortunately, it is this kind of exposure that makes diplomatic personnel so attractive a target to terrorists. No assassination attempt against a President of the United States was ever made in his office. It has always occurred when he was away from his desk, either in a crowd or en route. That is true for the majority of terrorist acts against individuals of rank or importance in any country. Certainly that's not surprising: it is an application of mere common sense. Such tactics require only a modest investment for the possibility of a major return and offer a manifold increase in the probability of success.

Yet the government of the United States — or any country — cannot allow the activities of a few to dictate the method by which we conduct international diplomacy. We cannot revert to paranoia and lock away our emissaries, making them inaccessible and difficult to communicate with. That would be dramatically counterproductive. Nor can we surround ourselves with such technological excess that we appear to those who see us from the outside as a nation of intimidated, frightened people. National self-esteem is at stake. We cannot cower or retreat from the threat; we cannot compromise our confidence in our ability to be a vigorous and forthright nation, which requires a certain amount of openness in our relations with foreign countries. Our role as a global leader depends on it. We must pursue an open policy of diplomacy despite the increased threat of terrorism.

SIX

Nancy devoted herself entirely to the crisis. Every thought and every ounce of her energy went into support for me and the family, which made an incalculable difference in our morale. Our daily telephone conversations were a critical link, and I relied heavily on merely the sound of her calm and reassuring voice.

Nancy worked hard to orchestrate fulfillment of my needs. She was selfless, and her untiring drive seemed inexhaustible. Whether working to mobilize support for me among political leaders in the United States or acting as an information clearinghouse for our family and friends, she stayed on top of every development. She is not the kind of person who sits back and lets "those in charge" take care of the situation; instead, she becomes fully involved and in this case made a major contribution to the effort to free me. She may sometimes go against the grain and ruffle a few feathers perhaps, but she cannot be a passive woman when it comes to matters of the family. Nancy is fiercely protective of us.

While I was being held captive, she patiently listened to my gripes, my concerns, and my analyses of the situation. She would read me news clippings over the phone, and occasionally she would smuggle a particularly interesting and sensitive article into the Embassy past the scrutiny of both the Colombian government and the terrorists. Receiving her little surprises was like receiving contraband, and I looked forward to it.

At the American residence, Nancy worked diligently to keep our five children carefully informed. One of her initial overwhelming fears in the first hours of the crisis was that the distorted news about the takeover would reach our children before she could talk to them and assure them that I was alive and well. In the massive confusion, many erroneous reports were circulating that I was not only badly wounded but in fact dead, and they persisted to circulate once the crisis began to stabilize. So Nancy, with the help of a close friend, tracked down each of our five children, who were spread out across half the United States, and explained the situation to them. Nancy also coordinated the early family decision not to talk to the press until I was safely released. We'd seen the way the press had invaded the lives of the Teheran hostages' families, and we didn't want that additional burden on us.

The press, sensitive to our wishes, was generally respectful. Nevertheless, one day a camera crew appeared at the front gate of the U.S. Embassy residence with their cameras and equipment and started to set up. Nancy's secretary, Marcela de Child, went outside with our trusty butler, Don Jorge Santana, who had been working for the Embassy for thirty-three years and considers himself the "responsible man" who runs the house, and politely asked the two gentlemen to leave. Nancy was upstairs and happened to glance out the window, and when she saw the camera equipment, set up and rolling, she jerked the upstairs drapes closed and called the kitchen on the intercom to tell the maid to pull the downstairs drapes quickly. Nancy's command must have been crisp and nervous because she scared the poor little girl half to death. She thought the M-19 was outside the gate trying to get in!

In more ways than one, Nancy was as much a hostage as I. She was barricaded inside the compound, which had stepped up its security arrangements. My fate was continually up in the air, and as a result, so was hers. She experienced the same amount of uncertainty as I, and she had to confront many of the same psychological pressures. Fortunately, many of our friends went out of their way to offer support, and for Nancy, that made a difference. The Embassy became a busy place. Nancy is a religious woman, and she had our chaplain at the English-speaking Catholic Church come to the residence twice a week to say Mass. Father Bean, a giant of a man at six feet seven, led Nancy and our friends, and everyone in the household staff including the servants, guards, and the gardener, in prayer. They were generous with their prayers and prayed for the hostages and their families, the terrorists, the leaders of the countries involved, everyone. Many of the people involved derived strength from these spiritually uplifting sessions. Father Bean gave general absolution at the beginning of each Mass and even the non-Catholic participants were invited to take Holy Communion. There were some recalcitrant members of the faith who had not taken Communion in fifteen or twenty years, and I think my captivity did more to regenerate faith in our community than anything in recent history.

Similarly, Nancy was concerned about my spiritual needs. I can't say I've been consistent with my faith, but being under fire does wonders for restoring one's faith in God. Bishop Acerbi, the Papal Nuncio, was the natural man to conduct Mass inside the Embassy, but as a politician he was not quick to take up the role as father confessor. The Nuncio procrastinated about celebrating Mass until he received his "kit" from his secretary, which included his vestments, the Host, and sacramental wine. In fact, since the last Vatican Council there has been some noticeable progress in Church liturgy, especially the concessions permitted in time of emergency. A priest has the option of dispensing with the usual formal confession and giving general absolution instead. Also, vestments are not necessary, and normal bread and wine can replace the Host and sacramental wine. Nonetheless, the Nuncio, sensitive about his position as a diplomat, insisted on a more formal role. Even when his kit arrived, three days into the crisis, it wasn't for a month that an outside confessor was arranged and many of us could receive Communion for the first time. When Nancy found out, she was furious. In her mind a priest was a priest, no matter what the circumstances. Finally, Father Bean explained to her that in Rome things were different. The Nuncio, a bishop of Rome, had to answer to the Curia, a most formal group of gentlemen, and that accounted for the Nuncio's radical conservatism. Still indignant, Nancy wrote a polite letter to Bishop Acerbi, but she never got a reply.

Ensconced in the fortress of the Ambassador's residence, Nancy and the security people were constantly on the lookout for anything strange. This created a hypertension that set people off easily, such as the kitchen maid's panic at the appearance of newsmen. It was conceivable that the M-19 might try a ploy against the American Embassy or the residence itself. There was increased concern among the security personnel because of the construction of a ten-story building directly across the street. The new building offered an excellent vantage point over the residence grounds and could be an attractive site for terrorists. Early on in the crisis, eight young people (wearing *ruanas* and carrying shoulder bags) were seen milling around the front of the residence. Security, nervous about their loitering, decided to investigate when the young people went into the building under construction. The caution flag went up immediately, and everyone waited to see what security would find out. My chauffeur, Jaime López, who had gone through the trauma of the Dominican Embassy seizure and had dodged bullets from innocent-looking young men and women whom he had seen playing soccer only minutes before the attack, was particularly upset. Nancy and the household staff held their breaths waiting for word. The tension mounted.

When the security men caught up with the young people, they found them in the backyard of the new building studying the low wall to the American residence garden. The security officers approached the foreman and quietly questioned him about the young people's presence.

The security men returned with smiles on their faces. The suspicious-looking characters turned out to be architecture students from National University who had been assigned to examine the building under construction. Everyone breathed a sigh of relief and went back to business. Just the same, Jaime was adamantly suspicious. Nancy later had a fantasy of blowing up the new building that so threateningly loomed above us, an ever present reminder of what might happen.

Frank Crigler, the Deputy Chief of Mission, and his wife, Bettie, went to great lengths to keep Nancy informed and help her with running the residence. Frank and Bettie spent the first night with Nancy, and then afterward made a point of coming to the residence every day throughout the entire crisis. Frank would arrive each morning before eight o'clock and tell Nancy what was brewing on his end. Bettie normally showed up a few minutes later and spent the rest of the day screening the flood of phone calls. Their help was inestimable, and we are forever grateful.

One telephone call did get through, however, that shouldn't have. A caller, announcing himself as Commander One, demanded to speak to Nancy.

"Who is this?" asked Nancy.

"Commander One. How much money did you get up for ransom?"

"If this is Commander One, let me speak to my husband," Nancy asked, starting to suspect the caller.

"I guess you're not interested in saving your husband."

"I am," insisted Nancy. "I just don't believe you are really Commander One. If you are, let me speak to my husband."

"You're making a mistake," the voice accused nervously. "You'll be sorry." Then the caller hung up.

Even though Nancy was suspicious, she wasn't one hundred percent sure, and the call unsettled her. If there was the smallest chance that she was jeopardizing my life, she was worried. When I spoke to her later, I assured her the caller was a quack and that Commander One hadn't tried to deal with her. We never found out if the call was merely a crank or if someone, trying to masquerade as Commander One, was hoping to connive ransom money for himself by victimizing a distraught wife who would do anything to see her husband free.

In fact, the guerrillas liked Nancy and found her to be one of the more colorful conversationalists. They enjoyed monitoring our calls and would sometimes interrupt us to thank Nancy for some delicious meal she had sent in. Nancy found this attitude of bonhomie and politeness toward her impossible to understand. She even went so far as to challenge their presumptuousness in considering themselves champions of human rights when they were violating the human rights of their captives, and in return they thanked her for the delicious food she had prepared for us. There was still a lot for her to learn about the bizarre way people often think and act under pressure.

I insisted that Nancy try to lead a normal life. This included the Swedish exercise class held in our basement, in which she participated with other Embassy wives. I usually called in the morning and the class was at 8:30 A.M. "If Diego calls, give me a long unbroken buzz on the intercom," Nancy told Bettie Crigler.

Nancy was on a shoulder stand doing yoga exercises when she heard the buzz. She jumped over three bodies and ran upstairs.

"Oooh, ooh," Bettie was saying as she usually did when I called. But she was adding something different. "It's Jimmy, it's Jimmy."

Nancy took the call. When she returned to the exercise class, she looked crestfallen. The other women asked if I had called.

"Oh, no," Nancy said. "It was only the President."

SEVEN

Standard operational procedure for hostage situations generally involves following one of four basic options, any one of which was almost equally possible, and at first I didn't rule out any of them. One option entailed a direct assault by heavily armed troops. There were some successful precedents — Entebbe, Uganda, and Mogadishu, Somalia — wherein specially trained commando forces raided the unsuspecting terrorists and safely secured the release of hostages. There were also some failures.

The second course of action entailed the employment of sniper sharpshooters, a tactic the Munich police resorted to in 1972 when they tried to eliminate eight Black September terrorists after they captured nine Israeli athletes in the Olympic village. The terrorists were demanding the release of 236 Arabs in Israeli prisons, a demand similar to the M-19's. Tragically, however, the attempt failed and resulted in the death of all the Israeli hostages, five of the terrorists, and one policeman.

A third option included the use of chemical agents such as tear gas, but that seemed particularly risky. No gas works so fast that it will immobilize the terrorists before they have a chance to retaliate, and the more effective "hot" burning projectiles could easily start a fire in that old mansion, as we had seen with the one canister that had scorched the floor.

The last option, negotiation, seemed the most likely. It was also the most time-consuming. The Colombian government had indicated a reluctant willingness to negotiate with the terrorists, so the first action we assumed it would take was to stabilize the crisis and then slowly begin the negotiating process, always testing the water, never moving quickly or rashly. The accepted doctrine among those experienced in dealing with kidnappers and ransom negotiations is that the longer the captor and captive stay together, the more likely the captive will survive. The greatest physical danger for the hostages is in the initial minutes; conversely, however, the psychological danger increases proportionately with the amount of time spent in captivity. Successful negotiations are more than just an attempt to meet the demands of the aggressors. They attempt to handle the elements of crisis in such a way as to minimize the anxiety and tensions of the terrorists; they are, in a general way, a form of therapy that urges calm, reason, and amicable agreement.

Terrorists are the most difficult group of captors to deal with — more so than the professional criminal or the psychotic — because they have rationalized their need to commit the act on the basis of what they perceive as correct behavior. They are often prepared to die for their beliefs, and in the beginning of dramatic episodes such as ours, they are emotionally supercharged. The adrenaline is flowing and sometimes, in the crush of those first moments, they will make snap decisions that tend to be polar — either yes or no, with nothing in between. Given time to think, to consider their position and the true nature of the options available to them, however, the resolve to die fades, and the terrorists become more amenable to discourse and flexible negotiation. This was the avenue I assumed the government would pursue, although I realized the dangers of trying to second-guess what the people on the outside intended to do.

I was also skeptical about the ability of either the United States or the Colombian government to come to our aid quickly. We were likely to be in for a long, unpleasant siege. It came down to the fact that I would have to rely on my own inner resources and the resources of my colleagues who were able to stand up to the rigors of adversity.

Few of my colleagues seemed promising in this regard. Even though many of them were old hands at the political game and claimed to be realists, it was apparent from the beginning that they believed they would be rescued in Robin Hood-like fashion. Many of them were anything but realists; they spent a great deal of time waiting for their swashbuckling rescuers while others of us worked hard at finding a workmanlike solution. It was a bitter pill to swallow, and there were many times when I wished for a dashing, heroic end to our captivity. But the risks of such an attempt were, realistically, unacceptable, and as long as there was the possibility of a peaceful solution, I was intent on accomplishing it. Rashness, for all its glory if it succeeds and for all its ignominy if it fails, is for Hollywood.

Some of the hostage-diplomats were destined to be heroes, while others were destined to be cowards, knaves, or just plain fools. There were four men whose presence I found particularly comforting. The Ambassador from Mexico, Ricardo Galán Mendez, was dark-haired and slight, possessed a wicked wit, an incisive mind, and unusual courage. A jogger whose exercise schedule had been frustrated by the Embassy takeover, he made his early morning calisthenics a fixture in our lives.

The Ambassador from Brazil, Geraldo Eulalio Nascimento e Silva, was a balding, athletic man of sixty-two with one nearly blind eye. He was an international lawyer of world reputation with considerable experience in the Inter-American System. A Cariocan — a native of Rio de Janeiro — he had the charm associated with those born near Pão de Açucar, Copacabana, and Ipanema. I had first heard of him years ago when he was sent as his country's ambassador to the Dominican Republic shortly after Lyndon Johnson had sent the 82nd Airborne Division there to quell a large-scale rebellion. When the M-19 terrorists shouted their favorite slogan, "Win or Die!" he pointed out to them that he'd had a full life and was at the pinnacle of his career. Death was something he could face without qualm. They, on the other hand, were mostly in their teens or early twenties and should consider that winning was infinitely more desirable than dying.

"The Diplomatic Club," left to right, front row: Paraguayan Chargé Oscar "La Metro" Gorostiaga; Sacconi; Guatemalan Ambassador Aquiles Pinto Flores; Haitian Ambassador; Dominican Consul. Left to right, back row: female terrorist; Sassan; Papal Nuncio Angelo Ascerbi; Venezuelan Consul General Francisco Pacheco; Venezuelan Ambassador Virgilio Lovera; Mexican Ambassador Ricardo Galan; Commandante Uno; Israeli Ambassador Eliahu Barak; Brazilian Ambassador Geraldo Eulalio Nascimento e Silva; American Ambassador Diego Asencio; Peruvian Consul General Alfredo Tejada; Guatemalan Consul General Roberto Castaneda; Dominican Ambassador Diogenes Mallol; Egyptian Ambassador Allubah; Swiss Ambassador Jean Bourgeois. Photo by Luis Guzmán.

The Ambassador from Venezuela, at sixty-three, was the oldest of the hostages. Mr. Lovera was a senator and highly regarded in the councils of his country's Christian Democratic party. His courtly manner and high-spirited singing of an incredible repertoire of tangos and boleros quickly made him a favorite of hostages and guerrillas alike. The guerrilla women in particular were infatuated with him. With his craggy features and shock of silver hair, he had the look of someone Central Casting would consider the idealized Latin-American politician.

In contrast to the Venezuelan was Eliahu Barak, the Ambassador from Israel. A former tank commander, Ambassador Barak had fought in all of Israel's wars. He was affable and genial, yet he didn't hesitate to express his convictions. His mustache and bald spot, together with his pipe, gave him a professorial air, but he was a tough, uncompromising man. The terrorists were the first to learn this. He took the first occasion to tell them that if any harm came to him, there would be no place on earth they could hide. His people would find them, hunt them down like dogs. His threat plainly frightened the guerrillas, and he was probably the most carefully watched of all the hostages. He was treated with deference and respect. Since they knew his threat was anything but idle, the terrorists were always attentive to Ambassador Barak's needs.

Because of his vigor and his military experience, we put Mr. Barak in charge of housekeeping. He took his assignment seriously and would occasionally send a recalcitrant diplomat back to redo a sloppy piece of housework. His attitude created some tension because some of the other diplomats weren't particularly concerned with the appearance of the mansion. In one episode, Ambassador Barak sent the Dominican Ambassador back to the bathroom because he hadn't scrubbed it thoroughly. "But, Eli," I told him, trying to explain the difference between the Latin state of mind and his military efficiency, "for him it's clean!"

The most heartening experience in the early days of captivity was the promise by the Red Cross that deliveries would be made on a regular basis. The volunteers brought us necessities such as brooms, warm clothing, soap, and toilet tissue. Commander One allowed us to receive individual CARE packages from our families and embassies, but not until they were thoroughly searched. Just the same, the supplies were a great comfort and morale boosters that helped buffer the feelings of alienation and isolation. We found out later the police also searched the packages for anything that might be used as weapons or for other contraband such as news clippings.

Another heartening development in the early days was that Commander One kept his promise to release the women diplomats. He let five women go on the third day, including the Ambassador from Costa Rica, the Vice Consul of Venezuela, and the wife of the Dominican Ambassador. That brought the total of released hostages to eighteen.

Meanwhile, the Foreign Ministry kept in close touch with us. Having been presented with "the necessary conditions for the establishment of a dialogue," they set the first negotiation session for the fifth day of captivity. After much discussion back and forth between the M-19 and the Foreign Minister, using the four-man ambassadorial group as the relay point, the modalities of the negotiations were laid out. After the terrorists refused to meet inside the Embassy for fear of trickery, both sides agreed to meet outside in front of the Embassy in a delivery van with its doors removed so both sides could see what was happening inside. The government and the terrorists were intensely suspicious of each other, so they made sure the van was parked halfway between both sides so that armed members could reach it in short order.

Once the Foreign Minister refused to negotiate personally, he elected two of his assistants as the primary negotiators for his side. I knew one of them, Camilo Jiménez, slightly from his position as the Assistant Secretary for International Affairs. I didn't know the other man, Ramiro Zambrano, a retired army major who was the Deputy Director for International Organizations. Both men were of ambassadorial rank, but neither had been at the Foreign Ministry for more than a year. It is standard negotiating practice in situations such as these to assign middle-rank men to the actual discussions, and when Commander One found out that Uribe Vargas wasn't going to be present in the van, he followed suit by refusing to represent the M-19. That meant that Omar would probably be assigned the task of negotiating on behalf of the guerrillas, and that worried us. With him as spokesman, the talks were sure to fail because of his highly doctrinaire, intractable, gruff attitude. We didn't waste any time telling Commander One that we hoped he had more sense than assigning Omar to the task. Fortunately, the Commander was aware of Omar's shortcomings, and he assured us he would appoint someone more suitable.

We spent some time speculating on who that might be. The next possibility after Omar was Number Seven, Alfredo, and he didn't seem aggressive enough to handle the hardships of negotiating. And so we went down the line, trying to figure out who Commander One had in mind.

He chose Number Nine, Norma. She had been resolute and brave during the shoot-out, and she was the one who had threatened to shoot the babbling Peruvian if he didn't keep quiet. She was also the woman with the bullet-resistant vest whom I had seen get shot in the chest without effect. Norma seemed an inordinately tough, uncompromising woman. Once things settled down, however, we found her engaging and pleasant. She was short, rather stocky, about five feet two, with an impish smile and slightly protuberant but expressive eyes. The press dubbed her "Chi-qui," short for "Chiquita," and made her internationally famous as the resolute female negotiator of the terrorists. Norma was also Commander One's "revolutionary spouse," which was a euphemism for his lover, and they shared a private room. A sociologist by training, Norma had been working among the Indians in Colombia's hinterland and had joined the M-19 in protest at the flagrant injustices she had witnessed. She told me about her family and her sister in particular, who apparently looked very much like her and had been arrested by the national police, who mistook the sister for Norma. As a consequence, she said her sister had been beaten, and Norma herself was tried in absentia.

She also had a light side, and she amused me with a story about her anxiety in rushing the Dominican Embassy. In the planning stages, she was told she would have to scale a low wall in order to gain entrance to the Embassy. Because she was so short, she was worried that she wouldn't be able to get over the wall. When she reached the front of the Embassy and saw that the wall was only two feet high, she felt silly worrying about a wall that was ten feet high in her mind.

We suspected, with good cause, that Norma would be tough and insistent as a negotiator. We also felt she would be careful to listen to what the other side was saying. If we were right about Norma, she would be fair-minded and compassionate, and probably the best choice the Commander could have made. Besides, Norma had the private ear of Commander One, and that could only help.

We knew from the beginning that the sticky point in the negotiations would be the M-19's "nonnegotiable" demand for the release of the prisoners from Colombian jails. President Turbay was not likely to countenance a violation of Colombian law, and neither would General Camacho Leyva, who was himself a lawyer. The military, which is a powerful presence in Colombian society and politics, would certainly not favor such a move, especially after the lengths it had taken to destroy the radical movement.

President Turbay was facing a more complicated and sophisticated problem. On assuming office in August 1978, President Turbay had begun a lengthy reconstruction of the legal apparatus based on a tough law-and-order platform. He had overhauled the judicial system and redesigned the penal code in such a way as to make sure that any guerrillas who were convicted during the state of siege would stay in prison once the siege was lifted. Past civilian courts had a record for overturning the convictions of military tribunals. If President Turbay released any or all of the guerrillas demanded by the M-19, he would, in effect, be undoing everything he had accomplished. Worse, he would come out of the crisis looking "soft" or blatantly weak in his dealings with the terrorists. If that happened, it would be certain death for his administration and loss of future electoral votes for his party. Although the President had limited power for amnesty, there was little doubt that he couldn't move without first consulting the Congress. There was certain to be a great deal of pressure from both the military and private sectors to refuse to capitulate to the demands of the terrorists. Then there was always the nagging threat of the possibility of a military coup.

The M-19 balked at submitting a list of the names of the prisoners they wanted released because they feared for the safety of the prisoners and wanted to wait until their release was imminent before specifying which of the prisoners they wanted. It was generally supposed, however, that the names would include 209 prisoners being held in La Picota Penitentiary as M-19 suspects, and at least another seventy union and peasant leaders who were also being detained for trial. The M-19 said it didn't want to prejudice the prisoners' chances of being released by normal juridical means before it had to resort to coercion.

Commander One still wanted the hostages' governments to publish a document outlining the M-19's charges of torture and political repression by the Colombian Government. Colombia had been coming under recent fire in the international press for its alleged infractions of human rights by such watchdog organizations as London-based Amnesty International. Colombia had previously enjoyed a good reputation for human rights, and President Turbay had on many occasions expressed a desire to improve the world's reproachful attitude about Colombia. The massive anti-guerrilla campaign had, however, seriously damaged his claim of concern for human rights. There had been an uproar within the country by opposition politicians, the press, and members of the Liberal and Conservative parties condemning the administration's failure to observe fundamental civilian rights such as habeas corpus, a right that had been suspended during the raids. Dario Echandia, a former President and leader of the majority Liberal party, even went so far as to accuse General Camacho Leyva of trying to establish himself as a dictator.

The political climate in Colombia was uncertain. An old saying in Colombia says that the Colombian's fatal flaw is that he wants to be president. This creates a political arena that is always brimming with political hopefuls who are constantly jockeying for position and thrusting the spear of criticism into any opponent's side. Charges are usually followed by countercharges. Politics in Colombia are Machiavellian. Trying to reconcile the terrorist crisis without alienating some group would be virtually impossible. President Turbay was acutely aware of the thin line he was walking, and he was also aware that a squadron of vultures was circling his head waiting for him to falter. It is an unenviable position for any man, and especially for a man with other serious business to tend to, but such is the accepted state of politics in Colombia.

Most of the hostages were aware of the political ramifications of President Turbay's decisions, and of course we were troubled. But as the Austrian Ambassador pointed out in characterizing how our dilemma would be perceived by the Germans and by the Austrians: the Germans would say "the situation is serious but certainly not hopeless," whereas the Austrians would say "the situation is hopeless, but certainly not serious."

EIGHT

On the morning of the fifth day of our captivity, a Sunday, Norma walked out the front door of the Embassy, escorted by Ambassador Galán, and into the cream-colored van in which the negotiations were scheduled to begin. The hostages were crammed in the windows trying to get a view of the proceedings while the two approached the two men designated by the government to conduct the opening dialogue with the M-19. Norma caused a considerable stir when she walked out in full view of the press and photographers because she was wearing a tight T-shirt over her amply endowed breasts without a brassiere. The press and the two government negotiators weren't prepared for a woman, much less an attractive, rather sensuous female who was flaunting her best features. Clearly, everyone was taken aback in those first moments, and I'll never know whether they were pleased or disappointed.

In order to protect herself from being identified, Norma wore a white woolen hood over her head so that only her expressive eyes showed. Dressed in blue jeans and an open warm-up jacket, she stood outside the van with the Mexican while her comrades made the melodramatic gestures of raising their black, red, and blue standard on the Embassy flagpole and singing the Colombian national anthem. Even the two government negotiators, who had been seated, rose for their anthem in respect to their country.

Ambassador Galán, amused at this display of theater, patiently waited for the talks to begin. Unshaven but alert, the Ambassador had agreed to witness the negotiations as an observer and as a member of the four-man hostage committee. He would report to Commander One and to the hostages in order to keep us informed of the progress or the sad lack of it.

There were few amenities in the first session as Zambrano and Jiménez took their seats across from Norma and Ambassador Galán. They were trying to size up the situation as quickly as possible, which must have been a difficult task. Not waiting for an invitation to begin, Norma immediately reiterated the M-19's demands. Zambrano didn't hesitate to engage Norma and pointed out that Colombia was a country of juridical norms in which there was a specific division of powers. The President was not omnipotent. On the question of the liberation of political prisoners, the men indicated that a formula would have to be found that would preserve the integrity of the federal institutions of law. The government negotiators refused to consider the question of ransom, but would discuss an alternative of allowing other governments to pay ransom for their representatives.

And so it went back and forth for an hour and forty-five minutes. Neither side budged from its original position. Both sides were testing each other and no one really expected much to be accomplished during the first session. But it was a beginning. And it was a big step to have the

Colombian government sitting down at the same table with its declared enemy. It was something akin to having the Israelis sitting down at the same table with the Palestine Liberation Organization. When I saw Norma exit the van, I felt a surge of relief. Despite the fact that the negotiation could be described as inconclusive at best, at least the dialogue had begun. I began to believe at that moment that a nonviolent solution was truly possible. Negotiating was something I understood, and it was something I could certainly take part in. I no longer felt helpless, a victim of circumstances over which I had no control. My two decades in the Foreign Service and my experience as a negotiator could now serve to save my life.

My first overseas assignment in the Foreign Service was in 1959 when I was stationed at the American Embassy in Mexico City as a junior officer in the Consular Corps. The advantage of being a consular officer is that it thrusts you headlong into the society around you, including its worst elements. Unlike many other officers who are protected from the country to which they have been assigned, I was given the somewhat unpleasant task of acting as a liaison between the Mexican government and American citizens in distress because I could speak fluent Spanish and function well in Mexican society. But I wasn't prepared for the traumatic situations in which I was involved with the police, the courts, murderers and bank robbers, con-men and prostitutes on a daily basis. I got more than a glimpse of the netherworld of crime, mental sickness, and foul play. The Consul General, my avuncular supervisor, told me that if I could survive this assignment, then I could survive anything the Foreign Service could throw at me. Although his remark was slightly exaggerated, I later learned there was a strong foundation of truth in what he had said. In Mexico, where even the children are born haggling, I found myself constantly negotiating with the federal criminal system on behalf of my clients who had gone afoul of the law.

I was amazed by the number of schizophrenics and psychopaths who travel in a vain attempt to escape their problems only to find them accentuated in a foreign culture. Inevitably, these people get into trouble abroad, and then it becomes the Consulate's responsibility to try to help them. I spent many hours negotiating with the authorities on their behalf to keep them from being thrown into Mexican prisons. Usually the authorities would strike up some kind of agreement to export the troublemakers to the States so they wouldn't clutter Mexican prisons, cost precious tax dollars, and use up severely limited manpower.

In the three and a half years I was assigned to the post, no American was ever indicted in my district. We reasoned that these people were not subject to ordinary justice, and the Mexicans were forthcoming on this: if I would pay the fare, then they would supply the muscle to escort the violent types back to the border.

We were so successful, in fact, that I got a telephone call from Sheriff Flores in Laredo, Texas, a border town where we had been leaving off many of our clients. "Listen," he warned, obviously fed up with our dumping all those maniacs into his jurisdiction, "if I ever catch you coming through Laredo, I'm going to take care of you." After that, I made it a point to avoid Laredo whenever possible.

I learned several lessons in Mexico that became important to my career. The Mexicans taught me the subtle art of negotiating and the art of insistence. In essence, you never pay the first price asked. That is a major cultural difference between the Latins and the Americans. In the United States a person will rarely try to bargain with a shop-owner. The price asked is usually the price the seller expects. But in Latin America, the price asked is seldom what the seller expects. It is only a starting point for negotiations. Both parties realize this, and the haggling begins and doesn't end until both parties are satisfied with the renegotiated price. It is an equitable system in many respects, but anathematic to Americans, who will often pay the first price under the mistaken assumption that it is a case of "buy it at this price or go somewhere else."

I also learned how to deal with the criminal element and how to talk social languages other than my own. I learned the importance of understanding the culture you are in and of working within that culture. It's not enough merely to understand the society in which you are embroiled, you have to enter it, become part of it, in order to be successful. Despite the glamorous connotations of being an ambassador or working in an embassy abroad, the underlying truth is that the role of an embassy is to create a means by which governments speak to one another and endeavor to work out their differences. This cooperation requires a basic, common language.

That is not just the language of diplomacy; it is broader and more comprehensive than that. It consists of a mutual understanding of the integrity of its culture. An ambassador or any officer of an embassy must realize the importance of cultural relativity, must empathize with the cultural milieu in which he has been involved. It is more than being able to speak the language of the country to which one is assigned, although that's part of it. I have seen Foreign Service officers fail at their task because they attempted to lay American values and methods over the surface of a diametrically opposed system of accomplishing goals.

A person who understands cultural relativity can go into a strange culture with an open mind and not feel threatened by it. Rather, he will be interested by what's going on around him and learn how to adapt and use the materials of that culture to integrate a picture of that society in order to be able to deal effectively with its government. As a hostage, I was therefore not only able to talk with my captors, but also to think like them. I knew their hopes and their fears. This sensitivity allowed me to communicate with them on various levels, and ultimately it was a major consideration in negotiating our release. While our long-term objective was to get out of the Embassy in one piece, I had several short-term objectives as well. Besides getting the guerrillas to know us, I wanted to create some doubts in their minds about their ideology.

At first they chastised me as a symbol of American Yankee imperialism and as one of the elite who victimized the poor. I was an enemy of the people. I was an enemy of democracy. The terrorists didn't shy away from telling me what they thought about me as a representative of an exploitative government.

I immediately took the counteroffensive, not because I fancied myself the champion of democracy and the United States, but because I was offended by the callously naive way in which they thoughtlessly attacked the United States and its interests abroad. As the son of a shipyard worker who emigrated to Newark, New Jersey, from Spain, I told them that they were the bourgeoisie, and I was the worker's son. They were amazed by my simple beginnings and the fact that I'd started out in a lower middle-class family and worked my way up to becoming an ambassador. Such an achievement in Colombia was impossible, they said. In Colombia only the favored could achieve any level of political prominence without having to resort to subversion. I think I was able to de-mythicize some of the mistaken concepts that many other peoples have about Americans at large. We are often convenient hate objects, and much of the biased political rhetoric in the texts and minds of self-styled guerrillas takes advantage of the stereotype of the ugly American. When I, as the American Ambassador, was able to reveal to them the person behind the rank, they were intelligent enough to discern a dichotomy. I apparently did not match their concept of an American ambassador, and I doubt there are many in the diplomatic corps that would.

Our ability to communicate was part of the key to achieving understanding. Through mutual understanding, we were eventually able to work out a nonviolent solution to the impasse that might have stalemated us for months. If I could not have communicated with Commander One and his people fluently, then the stereotype of the self-centered, arrogant American ambassador might still be standing.

The ability to speak Spanish well was not enough by itself; what was equally important was the ability to correlate both our cultures so I could hear what was not being said in addition to what was being said. Cultural subtleties and nuances can make all the difference. Oftentimes what is not said or what is inferred is as important as or more important than what is specifically verbalized.

Beneath the mystique of a Foreign Service officer — the treaties, diplomatic notes, programs, demarches, the cocktail parties, the representation of U.S. interests, the writing of reports — there is a simple concept. We act as the channel of communications by which societies talk to each other. Sir Henry Wotton said that a diplomat was an honest man sent to lie abroad for his country, an atrocious pun of his time since "to lie abroad" also meant to live overseas. A diplomat does, however, carry his society's message. In order to accomplish this, a certain minimum of preparation is necessary. He must know his own country reasonably well — its history, politics, economics, and culture. To the foreigners he is dealing with abroad, he is the United States. On the other hand, he has to know or at least learn very quickly the nature of his foreign constituency. In conveying his message, he has to be aware of the best way to present it and to determine the impact of that message on the recipients. This demands both sensitivity and insight.

It is often argued that with modern communications, peripatetic Secretaries of State, and the travel of special missions, modern diplomacy is superfluous. If you accept my metaphor of the Foreign Service officer as a cultural bridge or pipeline guaranteeing that in the conversation between governments, societies, or peoples, the message is not garbled or is as static-free as possible, it can easily be demonstrated that he is more valuable than ever. He, after all, is the one who knows the society to which he is assigned. The other emissaries are passing through, are transitory, and must rely on him to make certain that the message is effectively transmitted. As an old-time Ambassador once exclaimed to me, when working on a team seeking to computerize the work of the Foreign Service, "How do you quantify judgment?" It was his thesis — a bit extreme, but with a germ of truth — that most of the work at a Foreign Service post was designed to keep the upper echelons pleasantly employed and gaining experience. The value of an experienced ambassador ultimately rested in the ten- or fifteen-minute period of a crisis, which might occur every few years or so, when he was called upon to exercise his judgment and make the right decisions. Those decisions are, of course, dependent on the ability of the ambassador to relate to the society in which he has been posted.

The ability of Americans to function in other cultures has become severely jeopardized by a widespread indifference to learning languages other than English. This attitude has had a major impact on international diplomacy.

The simple ignorance of Americans can be read by other nations — to our danger — as egocentrism verging on xenophobia. As a superpower that contends it is interested in the well-being of other nations, we too often contradict ourselves. Being able to speak and read the languages of those nations with which we conduct politics would seem to be a basic requirement. Multilingualism is not merely a convenience, it is a critical necessity. Allen Kassof, the Executive Director for the National Council on Foreign Languages and International Studies, states there are fewer than ten people in the United States who can speak any of the languages of the interior Soviet Union, and of those ten, only two or three have enough breadth of experience and knowledge to aid the State Department. These are depressing statistics.

Paradoxically, the Foreign Service no longer requires fluency in a foreign language as a condition for entering its employ. This change in entry requirements was the result of a dearth of applicants who were bright, intelligent, and proficient in a foreign language. Once an applicant is accepted into the fold, he or she will learn a language at the Foreign Service Institute, our own university-level training academy, which sees to it that new officers learn a language in about sixteen to twenty weeks for a world language and longer for some of the more exotic idioms. The institute is probably one of the best language training schools in existence and is staffed by native speakers. Fluency in a second language is a necessity for eventual promotion within the State Department.

The deficiency of language ability in Americans is a reflection of the society at large. Whereas competence in two, three, or even four languages is often a necessity for survival in the multilingual cities of Europe, knowledge of a foreign language and culture in the United States is often taken as evidence of ethnicity in a country that prides itself on its homogeneity. While there has been a surge of ethnic pride in the past decade in parts of our nation, there is no evidence of reciprocal increase in language training other than English.

Language training and sensitivity to cultural relativity are not, of course, cure-alls. There is a story at the Department of State, probably apocryphal, of an ambassador who was perfectly fluent in six languages. Unfortunately, he was a fool in all six as well. But without so much as basic ability to interpret the native language well, a Foreign Service officer is not likely to understand or empathize with the cultural milieu in which he or she has been assigned. This only increases the gap between us and other peoples, a gap we should be endeavoring to close. The success of negotiations in the Dominican Embassy incident was directly related to our ability to participate in the process; if that had not been possible, the crisis might have ended in tragedy.

It was my background as a boy growing up in Newark that made me appreciate the importance of cultural relativity and taught me how to apply its principles. My father, an Andalusian from the province of Almería in southern Spain, emigrated to Argentina, where he worked several years as a gaucho with his brother. I remember a story my father told me of his exodus from Argentina. He and his brother had gone to Buenos Aires for the weekend and, after having visited a few cantinas, were wandering the streets looking at the monuments and tall buildings when they came to a square with a magnificent equestrian statue. They halted an elegant urban dandy to ask who that might be on the horse. It was, of course, the great liberator of Argentina, General José de San Martín. The sophisticate, spotting my father and his brother as country bumpkins by their clothes and Spaniards to boot by their accent, replied, "That's the fellow who made the *gallegos* [a pejorative nickname for Spaniards in parts of Latin America] soil their britches!" Incensed, my father - intent on defending his Spanish honor in the same way as the Spanish courtier who retrieved the glove from the wild lion's cage had - pulled his pistol from his belt and shot up the statue of San Martín. I understand it took the Spanish Consul several weeks to get him out of jail, and he was put on a boat going north, eventually to dock in New York.

My father made his way to New Jersey and settled in Newark, where he worked in a shipyard. When it came time for him to marry, he returned to his native Almería and took a wife. Eventually I was born, and we all returned to Newark.

Newark was a port city on the most industrialized portion of the eastern seaboard. The city was dominated by New York but remained an enclave apart. One crossed the river to see shows or first-run movies or visit friends. One returned with gratitude from those excursions, happy to be home, having left behind the frenetic pace of the big city. I lived in a working-class neighborhood until I went off to college at eighteen. Like other industrialized melting-pot cities of the nation, Newark had embraced succeeding waves of immigrants attracted by the possibility of work, from Germany, Italy, Poland, Hungary, Syria, and Spain. In fact, Newark is still accepting them. Although it is a predominately black city now, Newark has solid populations of Portuguese and Cubans.

As the immigrants grew more prosperous, they left the inner city and moved out into the suburbs, but they invariably left behind residues of their cultures. In my neighborhood — the Ironbound Section — there was a broad spectrum of nationalities. You could go down the street and have a first-class Italian dinner (something I haven't been able to duplicate since, not even in Rome), then go to a genuine Irish bar, go to a Lithuanian dance, drink German beer, date a Polish girl, and take her to a kosher delicatessen. The East Side High School yearbook read like the membership of the League of Nations. Even the football team was made up along ethnic lines: the Poles, who tended to be large, played the front line, while the smaller Italians, who were fleet of foot, tended to play the backfield. As an Andalusian, I played guard.

Although there were some ethnic conflicts, we were generally a free and easy society in which we learned to appreciate the diverse customs and foods around us. Cultural relativity was a natural part of my formative process. As a result of my peculiar melting-pot neighborhood, I am a Hispanic who has been raised as something of an Irish Catholic — the only kind of Catholicism we had there — with a penchant for Italian cuisine, kosher food, and the English language. I was used to dealing with other people. As Philip Roth, a fellow Newarker of my generation, said recently in an interview, "Rather than growing up intimidated by the monolithic majority — or in defiance of it or in awe of it — I grew up feeling a part of the majority composed of competing minorities, none of which impressed me as being in a more enviable social or cultural position than my own." As Roth did, I left for college looking for those other "so-called Americans who were also said to be living in our country," carrying with me my background of ethnic diversity, my hybrid-ness, but "with my consciousness and my language — shaped by America."

In the end, that atmosphere created a method for me to create a common ground with the M-19. As a result, we were able to institute a second major round of negotiations.

Theoretically, the dialogue was completely circular: the hostages traded information with their governments, their governments then spoke to the Colombian government, the Colombian government spoke to Commander One, who then spoke to us. The circle went both ways, because we would then advise Commander One, who then passed much of what we had suggested to the Colombians, who in turn passed it on to the representative governments, and so on. Of course the information was constantly being distorted or modified from source to source, but it did flow from one group to another. Metaphorically, the flow of information was a spinning wheel — 'round and 'round it went…

NINE

Within ninety minutes of the first negotiation, Commander One ordered the release of five additional hostages, bringing the total of freed hostages to twenty-three. The released prisoners were "nonessential personnel" in Commander One's master plan — three waiters, a physician, and a captain retired from the Colombian navy.

The Office of the President meanwhile quickly issued another communiqué: "This first contact served to make known to us the demands of the occupiers of the Embassy," it read, "and for the Government to make known to them its interest in resolving this uneasy situation within the Constitution and the laws for the prompt liberation of the hostages, all of whom are innocent of the outrage that has been committed." The mood inside the Embassy, while short of elation, was one of growing self-confidence. We were no longer stalled; something, although we weren't sure what, was being done. A second round of talks was scheduled for later in the week.

Ironically, however, there was no urgency because of the congressional by-elections known as *la mitaca*, which were slated for the following Sunday, March 9. We didn't know if the government wanted to clean up our mess before the elections, but if not, then little would be done before then. This slowdown would favor Commander One, who wanted the attention of the world press so he would have a platform from which to harp on his charges of political repression and torture in Colombia.

Life inside the Embassy, meanwhile, started to develop a routine. The Papal Nuncio gave his first Mass; we established schedules for cooking and housecleaning; and the Red Cross continued to truck in supplies to make us comfortable as possible. We even received a shipment of mattresses, which were no more than thin foam rubber pads but infinitely more comfortable than sleeping three and four to a bed. The three Embassy phones were in constant use by the hostages as we called our families and our embassies trying to keep abreast of events outside. I spoke to Nancy daily and she kept me informed about our children, all of whom were anxious to help any way they could. I also spoke to Frank Crigler, the Deputy Chief of Mission, who told me that Washington had sent Frank H. Perez, the Deputy Director of the State Department Office for Combatting Terrorism, to Bogotá at the beginning of the crisis. Not surprisingly, Perez reiterated that the United States was not taking part in the current negotiations, and that it supported the judgment of the Colombian government. The United States was taking at least an outward stance of neutrality.

About the same time, the Haitian Foreign Minister called from Port-au-Prince and spoke to Commander One. The Foreign Minister asked the terrorist to be compassionate and release the Ambassador from Haiti because he was a diabetic and the only son of a widow. A sad story, the

Commander mused, but the answer was "no." Several days later, however, Colombian Foreign Minister Uribe Vargas called and told us that Ambassador Selzer's wife was on her deathbed in Vienna. The negotiating group decided to intercede on behalf of the Ambassador and ask that he be released so he could join his wife. The Mexican Ambassador and I approached Commander One and appealed to his humanitarian interests. Engaging in a tactic often utilized by former Secretary of State Henry Kissinger, we tried to give him a reputation to uphold and told him he had to show compassion. To our surprise, he agreed to let Ambassador Selzer go. I was to miss the Austrian and his exceptional sense of humor. It wasn't until much later that I learned he had been separated from his wife for several years.

Ambassador Selzer had not shied away from the terrorists. He professed to be a dyed-in-the-wool socialist and the representative of a socialist government and had tried to convince Commander One that Austrian socialism offered an appropriate and more humane model for the M-19. He even translated a synopsis of the Austrian Socialist party program into Spanish and gave it to Commander One, who was very attentive. In fact, Commander One referred to Austrian socialism as a model for his country in one of his later communiqués.

The Red Cross continued to deliver packages of personal effects. Ambassador Galán got his antacid tablets, and Bishop Acerbi got his official kit for giving Mass. Because none of us could cook, and we couldn't convince one of the released waiters who had cooked for us to stay, even after the Venezuelan Ambassador offered to triple his salary, we were left to our own devices. Our meals were simple because there was no refrigeration: rice, beans, sausage, plantains, and the like. Nancy, who believed in the value of positive reinforcement, made a habit of sending me food often. She let me know how much she was thinking of me by including four quarts of fresh strawberries from our garden, which my son Charlie had painstakingly planted the year before. It was a sensitive, meaningful touch. As the personal packages of food and staples arrived, I made it a point to share with others. I even gave a piece of cheesecake to Omar on his birthday, though I knew that Melba Zavala, the Cuban wife of the manager of the Bogotá Hilton, would object if she knew that her lovingly made cake was gracing the stomach of a hardened terrorist. Still, I felt it was a good investment. I shared the rest of Melba's cake with other hostages. The gesture was so well received that it quickly became the standard of conduct, with one notable and some minor exceptions.

The Ambassador from Uruguay, Fernando Gómez Fyns, was particularly hard hit by his captivity. His brooding aloofness was conspicuous, even among such a generally depressed group of people as ourselves. Ambassador Gómez refused to join in the work details assigned by Ambassador Barak on the grounds that he had dislocated his arm during the shoot-out. He was atypically uncooperative, and we began to worry about his mental state. Ambassador Gómez resolutely refused to share any of his food, of which he had received a lot, and he even went to the extreme of letting his food spoil rather than share it with anyone else.

But life in the Embassy went on. Amidst the high drama there was plenty of low comedy. In the early days, the Red Cross asked Commander One for permission to complete a mission of mercy. When Commander One asked for the details, a Red Cross volunteer sheepishly explained that one of the evacuated families had accidently left behind their pet Pomeranian. The poor dog hadn't eaten in nearly a week, the volunteer explained, and the military wouldn't let anyone go back into the building to save him. Commander One, always suspicious, reluctantly agreed, and poor, hungry Pelusa was saved. Meanwhile, the Dominican Foreign Minister was on the phone listening to the plaintive tone of the Dominican Ambassador, who was complaining he hadn't been fed all day.

We endeavored to keep ourselves entertained however we could. When one of the hostages found that Omar, the wiry, dour *Tupamaro*, had pretensions of being a poet, we got Aquiles Pinto Flores, the Ambassador from Guatemala and a poet of considerable reputation, and Omar together for a poetry reading. Omar showed up with a batch of poems in hand, anxious to read his work and match lines with Ambassador Flores. The event wasn't much of a match. Omar's poetry was either sentimental or blatantly propagandistic. Because we were a captive audience, so to speak, we praised his poetry shamelessly.

I remember one of Omar's poems about the class struggle, in which he talked about "killing death" as the object of revolution. The line reminded me of the last line of John Donne's Holy Sonnet "Death be not proud," which reads: "And death shall be no more; death, thou shalt die." I was also reminded of a half-forgotten phrase from Hemingway's Death in the Afternoon, which I looked up after my release, in which he speaks of the "feeling of rebellion against death from its administering." Hemingway adds:

But when a man is still in rebellion against death he has the pleasure in taking to himself one of the Godlike attributes; that of giving it. This is one of the most profound feelings in those men who enjoy killing.

In these days of potential nuclear holocaust, it is the fanatic Omars of the world who are fully capable of pressing the button that will unleash universal destruction and thus "kill death."

Our concerns inside the Embassy were a bit more mundane. I, and others, realized early that part of the key to keeping our mental health was to stay busy. Besides the assigned chores, we engineered a very distinct and organized work day. We managed to do some exercise whenever we were removed from our rooms to speak on the telephones. While someone was on the phone, we did calisthenics, ran in place, and marched up and down. We even used these exercises as a form of psychological warfare against the terrorists by telling them, with a smile, that if it became necessary to jump out of a second-story window, we wanted to be in good physical shape.

After the first week, when we were in danger of drowning in our own garbage, we set up work details. The accumulated filth was creating a serious health hazard, so we established rigorous guidelines for hygiene. I also made up my mind to come out of the siege in better physical condition than when I went in. In addition to exercise, I watched my diet (which wasn't very difficult to do) and took daily vitamins, which Nancy sent me. The Red Cross brought us games — backgammon, chess, cards, Chinese checkers, and dominoes — and tournaments became a way of passing time pleasantly.

Our personal comfort improved once more when, on returning from kitchen detail, I found that they had moved most of the ambassadors out of the library into the master bedroom. The most notable feature of this room was that it was served by a large and quite adequate bathroom, while the one in the library was small and in bad condition. The walls and ceiling of the bedroom had been peppered with shot. Most of the windows had been broken, and we used considerable ingenuity in getting them boarded up with cardboard and plastic sheeting. The most incredible luxury of all was that the guerrillas had come across a color television set that had just been purchased by our host and was still in its original crate. It was moved into the bedroom and a smaller, black and white set was made available to our junior colleagues in the library. This caused a considerable amount of good-natured ribaldry concerning the egalitarian nature of our captors' socialism. I pointed out that in George Orwell's Animal Farm some animals were more equal than others so that we were still within the bounds of orthodoxy. Nevertheless, a sentry point had been established in a small alcove that led from the bedroom to the bathroom and overlooked the front entrance to the building — an ever-present reminder that we were still prisoners.

That first evening, we watched a dubbed-in version of Quincy. As time wore on, television became an ever more popular diversion. The rating services never called, but our top shows were all American entries. One afternoon, my colleagues and I watched with interest as The Incredible Hulk turned green in front of us. The Brazilian Ambassador turned to me. "Don't you think there is something terribly decadent," he said, "not only about our sitting here enjoying this show, but also about having looked forward to it with anticipation?" Perhaps observing someone who could knock down walls bare-handed eased our sense of frustration and impotence.

Another net gain was that we left behind the Paraguayan chargé d'affaires, who was a super-snorer. In fact, he did not snore, he roared, which earned him the nickname of "La Metro," courtesy of the Metro-Goldwyn-Mayer lion. Occasionally, he would be awakened by sentries who complained that it was impossible for them to determine whether anyone was sneaking up on the Embassy.

By observing my colleagues and our captors, I noticed how the true nature of an individual's personality rises above the various personae one adopts during a lifetime. Those who were superficially strong faded quickly because a prisoner under stress must draw on reserves of inner strength if he is fortunate enough to have them. Being held hostage revealed one's true character, and it was fascinating and enlightening to watch personalities adjust and adapt in some cases, and utterly disintegrate in others.

Each hostage's emotional tenor wavered from day to day depending on the state of negotiations, news from our families, and our own introspection. Despite the fact there were always people around, some of the hostages were terribly alone and retreated into a shell that was nearly impossible to crack. Some of the hostages felt utterly abandoned, as did most of us at one time or another. Others rose to meet the challenge, took strength from those around them, and, in turn, gave strength. There was a remarkable contrast in the variations of human behavior, and always, it seemed, the behavior was unpredictable. Men you would have thought would be strong, crumbled. Others whose capacity to sustain duress you would have seriously questioned, showed remarkable courage and tenacity.

And then there were times when I had to test the outer boundaries of my own experience. One incident early in my captivity made me confront the hard reality of killing another human being. One morning, as I went into a bathroom which some hostages shared with terrorists, I found a .45-caliber automatic pistol on the lid of the water closet. I recognized it as Commander One's because of the oversized bullet clip protruding from the base of the grip. I had seen it many times before; Commander One had the nasty habit of playing with the pistol while he spoke. Other times it was sticking out of his waistband.

My first thought was to try to escape from the Embassy. I was ready to take the risk for a chance for freedom. Immediately outside the bathroom door, in the dressing-room alcove, the terrorist we called La Doctora was at her guard post. I was reasonably sure I could surprise and disarm her. If she resisted, I was prepared to use force. She was no match for my physical size, and it would be easy to overwhelm her. But would I use the pistol? I wondered if I had the determination to shoot and perhaps kill a woman. Or anyone, for that matter. I'd never fired a shot in anger before, and now I was confronted with the prospect of shooting my way past fifteen terrorists. Then I remembered that some of the terrorists had hand grenades. Provoking a shoot-out was one thing, but the effect of a fragmentation grenade in close quarters would be devastating. Some of the hostages would be maimed or killed. Even worse was the possibility that the troops, hearing the shooting, would initiate a major assault. It was bad enough risking getting shot by the terrorists, but then I had to worry about getting shot by the soldiers.

I weighed the responsibility of the .45 and tried to decide what to do. Commander One would realize his pistol was missing before long and come looking for it. I didn't have much time, so I had to act fast. Trying to escape was an enormous calculated risk that could have had catastrophic results. And the success of my escape depended heavily on my unflinching resolve to pull the trigger on other people. I might have been able to bluff some of the guerrillas, but not the hardened ones like Omar. I didn't doubt Omar would delight in calling my bluff, and then I would be faced with the prospect of shooting the man down. I knew Omar wouldn't hesitate to kill me — he probably would have enjoyed the opportunity — but that knowledge wasn't enough for me to kill categorically.

Rational thought insinuated itself between the impulse to act heroically. If I was still convinced that a negotiated settlement was possible, then was my recklessness warranted? I might have been able to justify it if I was the only hostage, but did I have the right to jeopardize the lives of the others by trying to escape?

As I hesitated, it occurred to me that Commander One might have been setting me up to test my responses. He could have jammed the pistol's mechanism or removed either the bullets or the firing pin. All these thoughts raced through my mind in seconds. The dominant thought, however, was that I really didn't want to kill anyone. Not while there was the possibility of a peaceful solution.

I opened the bathroom door and called to La Doctora. She came over to me as I was standing in the door and asked what I wanted. I suggested to her that she get the gun the hell out of the bathroom before either I or one of my colleagues was tempted to use it. When she saw Commander One's pistol, she looked startled and quickly retrieved it. I was relieved my temptation had been removed.

I never told any of the other hostages about the incident because I wanted to avoid the scorn of the belligerent ones and the concern of the conservative ones. Several times during the future negotiations I came near to regretting not having taken advantage of the opportunity, but looking back now, I'm convinced I made the right decision. I don't think it would have been possible for me to kill another person under those circumstances.

The pace of life was agonizingly slow inside the Embassy. The second negotiating session was taking days to materialize. It was obvious the government was intending to take its time and wear down the M-19. With the by-elections at hand, the government had a good excuse to procrastinate and it apparently intended to do just that. Still, the Colombian government was under heavy fire from its critics, who were intent on forcing the issue of the administration's competency as part of their own pre-election strategies. Some of the smaller political parties complained to the commission which oversees the elections that the government was capitalizing on the crisis to suppress opposition campaigning. The Worker's Socialist party, one of the smaller leftist groups, charged that Turbay had "started a campaign of intimidation, militarization, and greater abridgement of the guarantees of democracy." It is a familiar charge in Latin politics.

The real danger was much more subtle. The constant interplay between the military and the revolutionary has often set the stage for severe repression and strict authoritarianism in Central and South America. The classic example of this was in Uruguay, where the *Tupamaros* terrorized society and the establishment during the late 1960s and early 1970s. The civilian administration was so beleaguered by the *Tupamaros* that it ceded increasingly greater powers to the military in order to crush them. Unfortunately, the military ended up seizing control of the country. Political spectators have noted that leftist action often benefits the right-wing elements within a country. This is part of the left's strategy: to provoke a coup, which in turn creates an intolerable political state, thereby effectively sowing the seeds for a broad-based popular revolution.

The actions of the M-19 were bound to favor those who were inclined to a military coup, unless President Turbay could find a legally tolerable and peaceful method of resolving the crisis. There was little question that the President was fighting for more than his political life. He was fighting for democracy itself in Colombia, and the challenge was coming not only from the left, but indirectly from the right as well.

Part of the irony was that the challenge came just as conditions were improving in Colombia. The military, convinced it had effectively liquidated guerrilla resistance, had geared down its anti-guerrilla campaign, especially after the international outcry about human rights violations.

As ambassadors we were aware of these political exigencies, and many of us were also aware of the true nature of the crisis the M-19 had created. We tried to stay informed through our embassies, but because we were always being monitored by the terrorists, the flow of information between ourselves and our staffs was inhibited. The police had also effected a partial news blackout, but we got some news from smuggled-in news clippings and from what we could glean from the radio and television.

Our concerns were more immediate. Many of the ambassadors were fiercely in favor of meeting the terrorists' demands up front. They insisted that their protection superseded any self-imposed interdiction by the Colombian government against dealing with the terrorists. About this concept, men such as the Mexican and Brazilian ambassadors and their representative governments were adamant. The United States' stance was, if anything, a fly in the ointment, and several of the diplomatic hostages resented its inflexibility regarding terrorists. The Brazilians had commerced with terrorists on several occasions, and usually with satisfactory results: the captives were freed in return for the release of political prisoners and/or a cash ransom. The Brazilians had so much experience with terrorists, in fact, that they had developed a technique for negotiating with them. This technique, however, almost always favored the demands of the terrorists.

I was acutely aware of a growing animosity toward me, both for my stance in favor of American policy and as a representative of that policy. On several occasions, an ambassador would attempt to dissuade me in the vain hope of something akin to sympathetic magic: if he could convince me, then by magic the argument would automatically be accepted in Washington and policy would instantaneously reverse itself. Needless to say, their attempts were a lost cause, although they did allow the speaker to vent some of his frustration. The Colombian government was acting autonomously, and theoretically the position of the United States government was immaterial, but it was generally felt that the Colombians would respond to pressure from the hostages' home countries. Several countries had already started to apply pressure on President Turbay, but the United States's explicit policy of neutrality and its vote of confidence in the Colombians' ability to handle the situation under their own terms was a clear affirmation of its intractable doctrine of refusing to deal with terrorists. If the United States had been more vocal and critical of the Colombians' procedure, the result might have been very different, although it is difficult to say exactly how.

Nonetheless, as the situation grew increasingly more desperate, the hostages' support of Colombian capitulation to the M-19 grew noticeably more intense. My country's policy and my support of it alienated several former friends whose only concern was expediting the crisis. A few didn't care how it was resolved and at whose expense (other than their own), so long as it was resolved and resolved as quickly as humanly possible. In the beginning, however, we were all convinced that the best path was to find or create a loophole or a legal formula that would allow the release of political prisoners without compromising Colombian constitutional law. If we could work within the legal context and find some method of mediating the demands of both parties, then we could leave with honor. I and several other colleagues, however, were not willing to compromise our political or personal integrity simply to save our own skins.

We felt that as long as we were searching for a solution we could overcome the violent objections of those hostages who wanted solidarity among the nations represented to coerce the Colombians into acceding to the terrorists' demands. Most of the time it worked, but there were times, especially when a particularly promising gambit failed, that their vehemence resurfaced and put us at odds with one another.

On March 5, the eighth day of captivity, the second negotiating session took place around the table inside the van. Again, Norma acted as the guerrilla spokeswoman, and she was again accompanied by the Ambassador from Mexico, Ricardo Galán. The meeting lasted two and a half hours, which we thought was a good sign, but in reality progress was limited. The negotiators changed protocol somewhat after being accused by the Colombian press of paying homage to the terrorists during the first negotiating session. The press had photographed Jiménez and Zambrano standing while the M-19 was raising its standard on top of the Embassy, and they interpreted the gesture as one of undue respect for the M-19. The two men defended their actions by explaining that they had not risen from their chairs in respect to the M-19, but because the Colombian national anthem was being played, and as patriots in good conscience, they felt they could not remain seated and dishonor their country. Nevertheless, the envoys did not rise from their seats during the second meeting.

Norma pressed for amnesty or for a presidential pardon for the 311 political prisoners. She cited a precedent in the actions of the Brazilian government during the kidnapping of American Ambassador Burke Elbrick some years before.

Zambrano and Jiménez responded that there were no provisions in the Colombian Constitution to allow such an action by the President without specific authorization by the Congress. When Norma alleged the illegality of the courts-martial proceedings against civilians, they pointed out that the decisions would be subject to review by the Supreme Court. That meant there was a recourse to ordinary justice to examine the legality of the military tribunals.

On the subject of ransom, the government reiterated that it would neither negotiate nor pay, but it would not oppose such actions by other governments, institutions, or private individuals who were "friends of the hostages." Further, it offered the guarantee of safe conduct of the terrorists out of the country.

At that time we had a mild expectation that the government might attempt to resolve the crisis before the midterm parliamentary elections. It was not to be, probably because the Administration was not willing to risk failure before the elections. We decided when it became apparent nothing was going to get accomplished before the elections that if the government won, it would try to settle the matter quickly. We were to be wrong about that too.

On the outside, the wives of the hostages weren't idle. Some of them decided to try to pressure the President to resolve the crisis quickly. The increasing gloom inside the Embassy generated counsels of despair and desperation. A group of hostages led by the Bolivian chargé d'affaires discussed with their families the possibility of the wives' staging a hunger strike. The guerrillas enthusiastically endorsed the idea as a means of bulldogging President Turbay. Fortunately, the plot never got off the ground, but the impulse transmuted itself into a scheme for a letter to be signed by all the wives and sent to Nydia Quintero de Turbay, the First Lady of Colombia, petitioning her to intervene with her husband on their behalf to seek a quick solution to the Embassy takeover. Nancy and I discussed the idea over the phone at some length and decided that she would not only refuse to sign such a document, but that she would actively lobby against the letter.

Nancy later told me that the language of the letter smacked of the letters begging for funds for charity that normally plague businesses abroad and that all the wives of the chiefs of missions encounter at one time or another in their contacts with local social activists. Oozing with sentimentality, the letter importuned Mrs. Turbay as a wife and a mother to intercede with her husband with their message.

Nancy started to lobby against sending the letter and called the nine wives who had already signed it. None of them, it turned out, really supported the letter but had signed it as a matter of expediency. Nobody wanted to be the only one who didn't sign, and so the letter had snow-balled from wife to wife. Nancy also called the wives of the Brazilian and Israeli ambassadors, who had refused to sign the document. They individually reinforced her objections and urged her to continue her efforts to stop it from being sent. As a result, Nancy met with the author of the letter over tea and discussed the matter with her in the true style of a diplomat.

Nancy gently questioned the timing of the letter with elections coming up and the inordinately tense political atmosphere. She also brought up the threat of a coup by the military and suggested that while the author was free to send the letter on her own initiative without the signatures of the wives of the American, Brazilian, and Israeli ambassadors, she might better wait until after the elections when all the wives could meet to decide on a more representative course of action. As it turned out, some of the other wives had already called the author of the letter and suggested something similar, so she accepted Nancy's advice. She agreed that the letter was too emotional and would probably have little influence, and nothing more ever came of it.

However, Nancy did speak privately with Nydia Turbay later. The First Lady graciously pledged her support for the hostages and said she was deeply moved by their plight. She assured Nancy that the President was tending to the problem personally. Mrs. Turbay emphasized her husband's measured good judgment and serenity as well as his lack of impulsiveness. Nancy and I both came to believe in the President's firm and steady hand.

Later, when President Turbay awarded me Colombia's highest honor, the Grand Cross of the Order of Boyacá, he insisted that half of the honor belonged to Nancy for her unflagging support and her active role in backing me. Graciously, he presented Nancy with the rosette that accompanied the decoration. It was an apt judgment on President Turbay's part because Nancy deserved both the honor and its recognition. Her support throughout the crisis was endless and tireless. She was always prepared to do what she could, either coordinating an effort to mobilize support for me in Washington, or keeping tabs on the children and keeping them informed, or making sure my material comforts were taken care of as best she could while I was being held hostage. Many of the other wives rallied behind Nancy during the weeks we were held captive, and several friends have remarked as to her steadfastness of purpose and the unflinching support for me and for our government. Nancy was as important as any other element in our daily routine. I relied on her, and she never let me or the other members of the American Embassy down. She is a woman of remarkable courage.

TEN

At the start of the takeover, I didn't see the faces of the terrorists, only the barrels of their guns. Their weapons were hypnotic: I watched them with morbid fascination as I would have the head of a rattlesnake threatening to strike. While Omar stood before me poking his carbine in my chest, I kept stone-still, my breath trapped inside me, resolved not to give Omar a reason — or an excuse — to shoot me.

Once Commander One and Omar felt the Embassy was as secure as it was likely to get, they stopped prodding us with their guns. Commander One was too busy being intoxicated with power: he knew the entire world was watching and listening to him. Bloated with rhetoric and self-importance, he kept the zealous media attentive as he got up on his soapbox and endlessly harped on the evils and abuses of the Colombian government. Not one to be outdone, Omar was an endless fount of venomous revolutionary jargon. The only difference between the two men was that Commander One let down his pompous facade in private; Omar never did.

By the end of the first week, I started to perceive the true character of the rank and file holding me prisoner. The terrorists became people with foibles, tastes, and varied views. My original impression of them as a group of reckless, scar-faced desperadoes became more realistic as I interacted with them day in and day out.

Generally, I found the terrorists to fit into three distinct categories, each considerably different from the next. The first group, which constituted the "officers" of the Command Staff, were hardened professional revolutionaries. They were difficult people to talk to or reason with because they were so doctrinaire. They were unalterably convinced they were the sole repositories of truth. Men such as Commander One and Omar saw themselves as defenders of the faith and models of the revolutionary hero.

On the average, they were young — between the ages of thirty and thirty-three — intelligent and intense. Besides Commander One and Omar, the Command Staff also included Norma; Alfredo, Number Seven; and Number Five, a big, strapping, athletically built fellow whose ideological purity was leavened somewhat by a certain *bonhomie*. His dark complexion earned him the nickname of El Negro. Alfredo and Norma tended to be less recalcitrant than the others. Even though they were difficult to deal with, Norma and Alfredo were susceptible to sound argument and persuasion. Despite their tough stance, however, the people in this group came to rely on the ambassadorial committee for advice and assistance during our talks with the Colombian government.

The second group was composed of bright, young, idealistic and articulate university students. They were in the stage of life when they were searching for and examining "answers," so they were anxious to justify their actions to us. Jorge, a tall, mustachioed political science major, was probably the best educated of his group. He was apparently from a good middle-class family and had told his parents he was going to Europe for a few months. María, Jorge's "revolutionary spouse," was a psychology major. She was an attractive, promiscuous woman who spent much of her time flirting with anyone who caught her fancy. There was also La Negra, a dark girl from Palmira in the Cauca Valley near Cali, who surprised me one day by asking for a copy of a House Foreign Relations Committee study on the United States' policy toward Latin America. Alfredo was her "revolutionary husband." La Doctora, the woman who had been standing sentry outside the bathroom door when I found Commander One's .45, took her job as medical officer seriously and saw to the health needs of hostages and terrorists alike. She made it a practice to monitor our general health carefully by checking our vital signs regularly. As some of the hostages began to deteriorate physically, she did what little she could and kept Commander One informed of our general medical status. Lastly, there was Renata, a slow-witted and literal-minded country girl, she of the head-wound from the initial shoot-out. I don't think she really understood what she was involved in, but she was sweet and kind to us all.

Ambassador Diego Asencio chats up terrorist La Negra. Photo by Luis Guzmán.

The third, more nondescript, group was made up of adventurers who were hardly political. If they hadn't been with the M-19, they would have been out holding up banks or stealing cars. El Flaco ("Skinny") combined a cheerful disposition with a devil-may-care attitude. Napo, short for "Napoleon," was notable for having memorized a remarkable repertoire of tangos and *rancheras* even though he had a tin ear. There were two other young men, who were unusually taciturn and uncommunicative, and another young woman, who alternated her flirtatiousness with blatant hostility. Later, when one of the hostages made a daring escape during her watch, she was reduced in grade in their hierarchy.

From time to time, psychologists have tried to plumb the terrorist personality in an attempt to understand the true nature of his motivation. Some cogent interpretations have evolved, particularly that of Henry Murray of the Harvard Medical School, the creator of the Thematic Apperception Test. Dr. Murray discovered a strange group of unrealistic young men among the students at Harvard who seemed unable to be objective. These students were inadequate to the tasks and responsibilities facing them at the university. They were failure-oriented and had over active fantasy lives. Moreover, these same men had a singularly intense desire to be admired and loved universally. They dreamed of cynosural adoration, a loving world casting itself at their feet.

For them it wasn't unrealistic to expect that, at a moment's notice, they would rise from their current obscurity and unimportance to become international figures of importance and respect. Paradoxically, their rise was to be instantaneous, without the customary hard work it normally takes to achieve such status. The students in Dr. Murray's sample also dreamed of overcoming gravity, or, as he said, "to stand erect, grow tall, dance on tip-toe, leap in the air, climb, fly or shoot through space in a rocket." Like Peter Pan, these young men fantasized that they had the ability to fly.

Another psychiatrist, Dr. David G. Hubbard of Dallas, Texas, discovered another group of men with the same attitudes. Skyjackers apparently experience similar difficulties in their relationship with gravity; they too dream of flying unaided. To the skyjacker who can't hold down a simple job, it doesn't impress him as illogical that the country would stand up and applaud him wildly the next day for his daring feat of pirating an airplane.

Follow-up research at the Behavior Research Center in Dallas has demonstrated the same personality traits in kidnappers and terrorists. Interviews with Arab terrorists in Tel Aviv revealed that these biologically mature men also fantasize about being able to "fly like a bird." The men had not yet surrendered this fantasy, common in five- to eight-year-olds but rare in mature adults. The majority of terrorists are probably similar to these impractical, dreamy, ascensionist groups.

This rebellious, antigravitational drive in terrorists contrasts sharply with the psychology of the normal adult. Many of the terrorists at the Dominican Embassy demonstrated what Dr. Murray called "the Icarus Syndrome," named after the mythical man who spurned his father's warning not to fly too close to the sun lest it melt the wax that held the feathers of his makeshift wings in place. The starry-eyed Icarus, of course, lost his wings and plunged ignobly to his death.

Always, in the backs of their minds, Icarian terrorists, such as Commander One, Omar, and Norma, imagine the public rising up to support them against the authorities. Inevitably, however, they are disillusioned when their zealous call to rebellion doesn't lead to revolution. The terrorists who ramrodded the takeover of the Dominican Embassy expected to be supported, borne up, lifted above the crowd by some elevating force. The M-19's startling exploit was designed to make each of them stand out, as Dr. Murray describes, "as a unique person, that he startle, surprise, astonish, amuse, enchant, or enthrall others, that he leave in their minds an enduring imprint of the spectacle of himself."

Freudians see the Icarus Syndrome as an expression of arrested development in the reality training of childhood. A mother endlessly warns her child, between the ages of two and three, of the presence of an invisible, demonic force that threatens the well-being of the child and could destroy all his good works. The mother screams, "Don't put your glass on the edge of the table," and, "Don't stand on the back of that chair." In each of these angry, repetitive warnings, the mother tells the child there is an invisible, evil, entropic force in the room with him. These experiences with gravity constitute a glimpse of reality about us all. The mother's angry imprecations are an attempt to warn the child against the tendency to daydream. Freudians believe that certain children, for biological and social reasons, reject this pessimistic concept. Like Peter Pan, they say, "I won't grow up!" The terrorist symbolically tries to defy the laws of gravity. One might be tempted to say that these dreamers fail to appreciate the gravity of the moment, that their heads are "in the clouds."

As Icarians, the Commander and his Command Staff were singularly attentive to the media because they constituted the system by which the world learned of their exploits. Commander One was careful to groom an image of himself as a no-nonsense Marxist who had put his own personal safety behind what he perceived as his duty to take on a corrupt, democratically insensitive and brutal government. Being in the limelight was important to Commander One because he believed it validated him as an individual and his attendant cause.

Paradoxically, I found the terrorists were not very well informed about the social and political realities surrounding them. Typically of Icarians, the terrorists were steeped in their own ideological cant. The more unbending revolutionaries such as Omar steadfastly adhered to their ignorance, but some of the other terrorists had open minds and were willing to listen to "the other side" and then correlate the information.

This faulty perception of their country became painfully apparent when the Colombian government changed the telephone lines into the Embassy to spare us from the barrage of telephone calls that had kept us tied up nonstop for days. Journalists had insisted on harassing us all hours of the day and night. Although we'd been anxious to talk to reporters during the first couple of days, the endless repetition of the M-19's demands and our feelings became a psychic drain.

At first I welcomed the relative peace, but soon we began discussing politics with our captors. Our encounters gradually evolved into something akin to a lecture series. Ambassador Lovera spoke on Venezuelan history and on the university's role in the Latin American integration process; Ambassador Nascimento e Silva spoke on international law; the Ambassador from Haiti gave a capsule summary of his country's history; and I discussed my favorite topics, futurology and science fiction. Omar, in typical fashion, held forth on the class struggle and damned the middle class and its works. Generally, the terrorists were attentive and inquisitive except for those who claimed to "know better." These intractable souls tried to refute everything that was said, and I was often amazed by the fallacies and misinformation that guided their thinking. One such debate centered on what the students condemned as "the monopoly and political control of Colombia by U.S. multinationals."

Their accusations not only startled me because they were so blatantly cliché-ridden and simplistic but also frightened me because the terrorists were so removed from reality and an understanding of the issues involved. "You could make a much better case for the United States' neglect," I told them. Alfredo asked me what I meant. "Everyone in Colombia would be better off if American capital investment was greater," I started my explanation. Their thesis that U.S. interests were controlling Colombia was reminiscent of other, earlier times, a glittering example of politically induced paranoia. I even had the economic staff in our Embassy prepare statistics to show the actual rate of investment by U.S. concerns compared with the investment from other foreign countries and, more important, with investment from purely Colombian domestic sources. Both comparisons showed a declining level of U.S. investment. I passed the fact sheets out to the terrorists and asked them to study the statistics for our continuing debate. "It's a sorry state of affairs," I told them, "when you believe your own propaganda."

To my surprise, Alfredo agreed with me. "If the M-19 ever comes to power," he proposed grandiloquently, "we will encourage U.S. investment in order to expand our industrial base, and then nationalize!"

I spent time talking with some of the terrorists about their concept of a socialist state. As I'd suspected, their thinking was immature, incomplete, and quite eclectic, not to say unorthodox. Fortunately, I found many of them highly impressionable and willing to listen and reconsider their own views in the light of new information. At one point, I brought up the Club of Rome report on the future of the world and argued that social problems revolved not around ideology, but around the unchecked increase in world population, the anticipated peaking of the so-called Green Revolution in food production by the end of the century, environmental contamination, and the depletion of nonrenewable resources such as fossil fuels. These were the real problems that needed to be addressed, I insisted. I presented an equation I'd used in some of my speeches that a capital investment of no less than three quadrillion dollars in the year 2020 would bring the world up to the technological level of the United States today. This figure was based on increasing costs for energy and on an estimate that it takes $30,000 to create a single job in an industrial society. On this basis, I said, the only hope for the future was a breakthrough in technology to cheaper, more efficient, alternative energy sources. If they accepted these premises, then these social problems were susceptible only to technological solutions. Ideologies were only secondarily important. While their brand of Marxism might be useful for mobilizing opposition to an established government in some societies, it was useless for providing answers to the critical problems currently facing all societies. To highlight my point, I observed that writers behind the Iron Curtain had produced little quality Marxist science fiction. Even the inveterate Communist understood at least intuitively that answers for the future lie in technology, not in rhetoric. Needless to say, I stirred some heated debate.

The terrorists' ignorance surfaced repeatedly, and each time it did, we were obliged to clarify the facts as best we could. When the terrorists tried to justify the death of Nicolas Escobar on the grounds that Texaco was an exploitive multinational guilty of stealing Colombia's surplus petroleum, I nearly choked. I pointed out that Colombia had no petroleum surplus; in fact, the country had a deficit and was importing nearly 25 percent of its needs. There was nothing to steal! In addition, foreign oil companies were investing heavily in Colombia in search of oil reserves — an enterprise that was bringing millions of dollars into the economy. I told them as gently as I could that it was important for an aspiring political organization to base its allegations on sturdier grounds. They couldn't afford to make irresponsible charges. Fortunately, as students, they were predisposed toward Socratic inquiry, and they responded to it. Often times, they would seek me out to test different theses, and if I was able to counter their arguments effectively, they would regroup and come back with new formulations.

The group discussed other issues that were more difficult to address: starving children, dramatically disparate income distribution, and the homeless. We also discussed one of the primary issues in Colombia today, an issue that profoundly affects the United States: the drug Mafia.

The illegal drug trade, which affects a broad stratum of Colombian society, produces as much as three billion dollars in annual income and thus rivals Colombia's primary cash crop, coffee. Because of the high stakes — Colombia provides as much as 70 percent of all the marijuana and cocaine in the United States — the drug underworld is predictably sophisticated and particularly brutal. Informers are routinely murdered. In August 1980, a woman from Bogotá was arrested at Miami International Airport carrying hermetically sealed Monopoly games that hid $1.5 million

83

in cash. After María Lilia Rojas served a year in prison, prosecutors offered her immunity if she would divulge the names of her contacts. The woman decided to stay in prison and keep quiet rather than risk reprisal against herself or her family. She took her clue from Robert Walker, an alleged narcotics broker who had agreed to testify in return for leniency. The day before Walker was scheduled to testify, police found his mutilated body in a field. Such incidents are relatively common in Florida, a primary connection point to Colombia.

The stakes are astronomically high. In Miami, where 70 percent of our nation's drug trade originates, federal authorities estimate a cash influx of between seven and ten billion dollars yearly. The impact of these "narcobucks" in Florida's economy has been profound: real estate values, for instance, have skyrocketed. There is a network of middlemen in Florida who launder and invest these monies, and they maintain close ties with all elements of the industry. There are dozens of smuggling rings, such as the infamous Black Tuna, named for the radio code that links it with Colombia. At one time, the Black Tuna accounted for 8 percent of the United States' drug stock of illegal cocaine and marijuana.

Authorities in the Justice and Treasury Departments have launched a major counteroffensive in the United States through an operation known as Greenback. Operation Greenback is focusing on the money rather than the drugs and is conducting major investigations of such men as Isaac Kattan. A former Colombian travel agent, Kattan is a central figure in the drug network that extends from Colombia to the United States and Switzerland. Kattan alone is supposed to be responsible for laundering one hundred million dollars a year on behalf of a dozen different rings. Operation Greenback grand jury investigations in Tampa and Miami are presently looking into the activities of over a hundred drug smugglers, their money-men, and the banks that transact their deals. This new generation of computer-oriented businessmen has created an electronic grid in which to conduct business. When Kattan was arrested in July 1981, federal agents found a sophisticated home computer, a Western Union telex machine, and five high-speed money counters with special equipment to detect counterfeit bills. When they arrested Kattan in the street as he watched two associates transfer a red suitcase containing forty-four pounds of uncut cocaine, they also found in his pockets $17,098 in cash, another $330,000 in cashier's checks, and a letter from his brokerage firm reiterating the terms of a $1.2 million wire transfer to Switzerland.

The United States also has often tried to attack the drug problem at its source: in the countries where the drugs are grown. Mexico, for instance, has its own program for spraying marijuana crops with the herbicide paraquat. A 1978 law prohibits the United States from offering financial aid for these spraying operations, so we have had to concentrate more on the points of entry rather than the sources themselves.

I'd spent a great deal of time and energy during the last two years as Ambassador to Colombia developing a massive narcotics interdiction program in Colombia with the full support of

84

President Turbay. The President decreed sections of the north coast of Colombia off limits to aircraft without special flight clearance because the Guajira Peninsula is the principal growing and staging area for the transshipment of marijuana and cocaine to the United States, The President created a judicial police force attached to the Attorney General's office, which the United States helped arm, equip, and train. In order to put teeth in his threat, President Turbay mobilized an army brigade complete with air and naval support to patrol the north coast.

The United States, anxious for the President's ambitious program to succeed, donated helicopters, ground vehicles, and two Korean War—vintage radar units, along with funds to pay for fuel and rations for the national troops. The American Embassy staff was augmented with cadres of Drug Enforcement Agency, Customs, and special State Department personnel to handle the equipment and training of the Colombians involved in the operation.

At the height of the operation, we seized three times the rate of marijuana and six times the rate of cocaine normally captured in the United States. More than a hundred aircraft with American registry were seized, some in the DC-7 class, and dozens of ships of every shape and size. Within a few weeks, the price of marijuana in the United States tripled, and the cost of cocaine went through the roof. Until the drug underground established new sources and routes of supply, there were distinct short ages of both drugs in the United States.

These attempts stood me in good stead with the M-19. I was able to state unequivocally that the United States government, in cooperation with Colombia, had been making a major effort to halt illicit drug traffic. I even jokingly suggested to Commander One that we arrange an alliance with the M-19 in which they could target major drug traffickers rather than kidnap relatively inoffensive diplomats.

Some of the guerrillas talked about their personal lives. They avoided revealing too much of their identities, but most of the terrorists claimed to have been arrested at one time or another, and they complained bitterly about torture and heavy-handed interrogation techniques by the Colombian police. Their enmity for the system was more passionate than logical; they reacted with their glands rather than with their brains. They hadn't thought out the ramifications of their acts, nor had they made essential plans, such as one for their escape. I later found out that Icarians rarely plan their way through a terrorist act completely; rather, they provide the first two acts of their drama and leave the last act to Providence and good luck. Commander One and Omar flaunted their disaffection with the Colombian political system every chance they got. Others of their band were more indulgent, but all of them bore a grudge of one sort or another. In one conversation, I tried to make them understand that all societies had their injustices, and it seemed infinitely more practical to me for them to work from within the system rather than to try to subvert it from the outside. This seemed particularly true because Colombia, while suffering from a widespread political apathy known as "the politics of anesthesia," had an open political process. The terrorists were not in the mood to listen, however, because they had already committed themselves and were beyond the point of no return.

The real tragedy of these young people was that their strenuous and youthful idealism was being perverted by a radical political organization for its own ends. I told them that if they were serious about their slogan "Democracy and Liberty," the United States had better models for them to study than the stale ideological jargon to which they were pledging their allegiance. Ironically, in the week before my capture, I'd met with the rector of the National University, who had argued it was time for the United States International Communications Agency to return to its campus. In the late 1960s, we'd retreated from most of the national universities in Latin America in the face of radical violence. Once we had sponsored exchange professors, courses, and cultural events, and had financed teaching aids and equipment. Our abdication created an immense gap of understanding between Latin America and the United States, and I was now suffering the effect of that ignorance. I sensed that several of the terrorists suspected their own beliefs about America because of their willingness to listen to me. I got the distinct impression these youngsters weren't all that set in their political biases and could be converted to a more humane and legitimate political and economic system. When I gave these impressions to a left-wing journalist some weeks later, he burst out laughing.

"What's so funny?" I asked, somewhat irritated by his unexpected behavior.

"I just finished interviewing one of the guerrillas," he said gleefully, "and he said the same thing about you!" The terrorist had told the journalist I wasn't such a bad fellow after all, and I was definitely convertible.

I tried to understand why such a haphazard organization as the M-19 was able to recruit, establish, and maintain an iron grip over such otherwise attractive people. The traditional rebelliousness of youth and the "generation gap" were weak reasons. The organizational structure of the M-19 capitalizes on conditions common to any club or secret society. It has a central philosophy that cements its leadership, but the philosophy is as thin as the mumbo-jumbo of any college fraternity. What the M-19 did offer was a goal to strive toward for those unhappy with society. The faction lent a sympathetic ear and showered camaraderie on its members. J. Bowyer Bell characterized the M-19 perfectly when he described radical groups in Assassin: "They are part cult, part radical conspiracy and most of all a means of group therapy. They could work at revolution, support each other's fantasies, lead lives not of private but public desperation."

The M-19 endeavored to be father, mother, companion, and confessor to its constituency. It took care of the members' intellectual needs by providing discussion groups on almost any topic. One woman who was aware of my interest in the subject told me the M-19 even provided a science fiction forum group. Those in severe financial need were able to draw on the considerable resources of the group, which had raised kidnapping for profit to an art form. The system of "revolutionary spouses" took care of their sexual needs. They even had a compulsory summer camp system for their military training. The Colombian government's proscription of the M-19 reinforced the bonds of membership; as outlaws, they could trust only one another. The M-19 is a classic case of the application of ordinary and sometimes even noble organizational techniques for political purposes. As Bell wrote: "…they have sought out and found comfort in a symbiotic relationship with others," They were a closely knit group of desperate men and women. But they were terribly alone, and they knew it.

ELEVEN

The third negotiating session took place in the van on the tenth day. Norma and Ambassador Galán attended. The government's official negotiators, Zambrano and Jiménez, continued to resist demands for the liberation of prisoners. They took the line that the juridical framework of the Colombian Constitution would not allow such a possibility. The phrase "juridical framework" became a standard invocation — we eventually learned to grow sick of it.

Norma tried to get around their obdurate stance by suggesting to Zambrano and Jiménez they lift the state of siege which had been enforced almost continuously during the past thirty years. This tack, which President Alfonso López Michelsen had tried briefly in 1974, would have the automatic effect of vacating all charges pending against civilians facing courts-martial. That translated into the effective release of most of the prisoners the M-19 demanded.

Norma's proposition was clever, but it wasn't realistic. I never believed her plan had much chance. If President Turbay lifted the siege in order to accommodate the M-19, the security and military forces would create a murderous backlash that would reverberate throughout Central and South America. President Turbay wasn't about to toy with that kind of political dynamite if he could help it. Norma's proposal, which was certainly prompted by Commander One and Omar, was politically artless, typically Icarian. What Icarians and terrorists fail to realize — what might be termed their tragic flaw — is that governments will not jeopardize certain principles, at least not while there are viable alternatives. In our case, the safety and well-being of Colombia would supersede our safety and well-being. The government's question was never "How do we get the hostages out?" but "How do we get the hostages out without compromising certain political exigencies?" Commander One and his cohort were slow to understand the reality of the situation in which they had embroiled themselves.

Zambrano and Jiménez gave Norma some leeway concerning the payment of ransom. Technically, the payment of ransom is illegal in Colombia, but by applying the concept of extraterritoriality to the Dominican Embassy, the government said it would not oppose the payment of ransom by "friends of the hostages on the grounds of the Embassy." It also tried to convince Norma that the M-19 had already achieved several enviable objectives: the M-19 was now at the forefront of subversive organizations around the world, and it was benefiting immensely from the worldwide publicity resulting from the event.

Shortly before the meeting ended, the Colombian negotiators offhandedly suggested the authorities might be willing to accelerate the judicial reviews of pending cases to determine which prisoners might be acquitted so that they might leave Colombia with the terrorists when the time came.

Norma didn't respond to Zambrano's suggestion; I don't think she understood its implications. Instead, she told the two men she was tired of hearing about juridical matters. She didn't care how the government solved its problems, just so long as it solved them. Logistics were their problem, not hers. The M-19's sole objective, she lectured, was the liberation of its comrades. Her people were sworn not to leave the Embassy empty-handed, especially after the sacrifice of Camilo, who had been raised to the status of martyr. Then Norma launched into melodramatic oratory: Camilo's death would not be in vain. She was sworn to give her life to the cause, if it became necessary, and so were her compatriots. She was not afraid to die, she insisted, if the Colombian government wanted to see the hostages come out alive, then it had better talk, she warned, and talk sense, not all this legalistic gobbledygook. With that, Norma stormed out of the van and returned to the Embassy, leaving behind two startled negotiators.

Commander One gathered us all together once Norma got back and made Ambassador Galán give us a detailed summary of the dialogue in the van. When Commander One heard the Mexican's account of what had happened, he turned choleric. He accused Zambrano and Jiménez of intentionally stalling. As far as he was concerned, Commander One threatened, the time was coming to start executing hostages. Then, he reasoned, Turbay would take him seriously. Obviously, Commander One had expected significant progress toward a reconciliation in the van, but when he didn't get it, he began an endless tirade accusing the government of everything vile and deceitful. What they had to do, Commander One finally concluded, was break off dialogue with the government.

Emotions flared. Commander One felt he was butting his head against a brick wall. He was angry and disappointed. He was not prepared, despite his claim to the contrary, to stay in the Embassy "one or two months if necessary." Commander One thought he had the Colombians over a barrel, but he did not; in fact, the President and the Foreign Minister were working hard to get M-19 over a barrel through the use of coordinated delay and subterfuge. Unfortunately for us, however, these tactics generated volatile emotions in the terrorist leaders. Commander One fancied himself "a man of action," and he had become frustrated and dangerously impatient. I was afraid he would act rashly. None of his fellow terrorists tried to restrain him, and I think Omar even enjoyed it.

For all the homework Commander One claimed to have done in preparation for the seizure, he was ignorant about the rules and rhythm of diplomacy. Rather than understand the complexity of the Gordian knot he had created for the Colombians, Commander One was having a temper tantrum.

Some of the hostages watched him with disbelief, while others were frightened. Emotion was snowballing into hysteria. Instinctively, I took the floor.

"It's too early to take that attitude." I tried to sound convincing. "You've got to give the government time to figure out these problems. You can't expect them to do a complete turn-around and comply with your demands. You've got to give them some leeway."

"Why?" came a snide voice from the crowd.

With that question, I realized for the first time the terrorists really believed the government would stop dead in its tracks and do their every bidding.

"Look," I said as I started to feel my frustration burning in my cheeks, "I've been dealing with these people for two years, and it takes them three meetings just to say hello, if you're going to get emotional now, then we're all in serious trouble."

Rather than the automatic refutation that customarily came with everything I said, there was a pervasive silence. I thought perhaps they were listening to me, and this gave me the courage to continue. Zambrano and Jiménez were mouthpieces, not decision-makers, I said. They were glorified messengers. It didn't make sense to focus on their conduct or to expect them to have the authority to decide what the government should or should not do. What Commander One wanted to do was a classic case of shooting the messenger because he bears bad news. The real decisions were being made at a much higher level, and the Command Staff had to learn to study those reactions carefully. "There are no easy solutions," I tried to explain emphatically. "If you're going to play a big game for big stakes, then you've got to play by the rules."

I sprinkled my little speech liberally with the references to the art of getting along with *pendejos*, a broad term, obscene in some Hispanic societies and just plain vulgar in others like Colombia. The word originally referred to pubic hair, but in common parlance it means "jerk" or "moron." Aside from its semi-obscene character, I had earlier discovered its power to defuse a tense situation.

A few months before, two Houston firemen had violated Colombian airspace and landed on a clandestine airstrip in the Guajira Peninsula. They were picked up by national troops and the aircraft was seized, the prevalent assumption being, of course, that the firemen were planning to smuggle out narcotics. But the Houston Fire Department and the mayor's office were outraged by the arrest. The mayor of Houston publicly called for the marines to invade Colombia to rescue the two wayward firemen.

The mayor's thoughtless remark accomplished little but to rub salt into old Latin American wounds and incite the Colombian press, which didn't waste time returning the insult. While the situation escalated, a group of journalists ferreted me out and asked me to comment on the mayor's remark. I told them that it proved conclusively that one could also say *pendejadas* (idiocies) in the United States.

My remark made page-one headlines nationally and was quoted approvingly on television and radio. The additional fillip that the word had come from the mouth of the American Ambassador guaranteed the matter would get lost in good humor. Whenever I ran into President Turbay during the next few months, he would chuckle and say, "So it's *pendejadas*, is it?"

When the terrorists heard me use the word, it had the same effect. There was some laughing and jibing. The tension and strain of one minute were defused in the nervous laughter of the next. I didn't know if they'd understood what I was trying to tell them, but I felt good because I felt involved in the decision-making process.

I quickly learned that my speech managed only to lower the tension of the moment and did little to mitigate Commander One's aggressive stance. He still intended to pursue a hard line with the government even though he must have known his relentless insistence could only backfire. As soon as we found out that Commander One was going to continue his frontal assault, the ambassadorial negotiating committee met in an emergency session. We agreed we had to try to insert the voice of reason if possible. If we couldn't calm down the Commander and Omar, their attitudes were bound to lead to violence. We asked Commander One if he would meet with us, and he agreed.

The situation, we argued, was becoming critical. I went back to my original argument: if the talks were going to progress, then he had to give the Colombians a chance to handle the M-19's demands in an appropriate political context. The government could not act arbitrarily and unilaterally release over three hundred prisoners on the President's whim. President Turbay and his aides might, however, come up with a legal expedient that would let the government grant the M-19's demands without breaking the law. I reminded Commander One the Colombians had found a way around the sticky problem of paying ransom by employing the concept of extraterritoriality to the Dominican Embassy. If the Commander would give President Turbay some thinking room, he might very well find the solution to this problem as well.

Commander One listened, but he didn't buy our argument. He said he was tired of hearing about the "juridical framework," which was nothing more than a token of a bourgeois society, If the negotiators didn't come across during the next session, he was going to break off the negotiations.

In diplomatic parlance, "breaking off negotiations" has powerfully negative connotations. We explained that to him and advised him to use the softer, more acceptable phrase "suspend talks" instead. The Commander agreed to our suggestion, and we went to work preparing a statement for him to use if he had to: the M-19 would suspend all further talks until the government was ready to address the prisoner issue.

The climate was also reserved in the streets of Bogotá. Final preparations were being made for the elections. Nearly 50,000 voting booths were set up nationwide to fill 9,000 seats on municipal councils and departmental legislatures. The by-elections, known as *la mitaca* for the second, smaller harvest in Latin America, were the beginning of a process of sorting out party alignments for the next presidential elections. Citizens had 37,000 candidates to choose from, including a self-proclaimed witch, Regina Betancourt de Liski, whose party symbol was a broom and whose motto was "health, money, and love." A four-day curfew on liquor sales went into effect, and President Turbay went on television to urge the people not to let the terrorists intimidate them, but rather to show strength and courage and to vote. His party was concerned that voter turnout would be poor. During the 1978 Presidential election, only a third of the eligible voters had cast a ballot, If the voting public became any more apathetic, its attitude could jeopardize the democratic system in Colombia.

Unfortunately for all of us, the fourth negotiating session on the thirteenth day fared no better than the third. The Commander had given Norma explicit instructions to cut off the dialogue unless the government negotiators had something new to say about liberating the prisoners. True to form, Zambrano and Jiménez rehashed the old line. Nothing was accomplished. The only surprise was that Norma did not cut off the negotiations as she had been told to do.

Norma was not nearly as aggressive and inflexible as her lover or Omar. Ambassador Galán had confided to me that she was attentive and constructive during the negotiations. Even though she could be brash and impatient at times, she often gave Zambrano and Jiménez as much room as she could. Norma was acting on her own authority even though she had been instructed differently. Ambassador Galán was pleased with Norma as a negotiator, and he believed she was our best bet in the van. The terrorists really didn't know what was going on in the van or how Norma was conducting herself they accepted her appraisal at face value. But when Commander One found out she had not cut off the negotiations, he was furious.

Some of us tried to intercede on her behalf because we knew we couldn't afford to lose her as the M-19 negotiator. Her decision was for the best, we argued. The government was probably on the verge of making an offer.

Commander One rejected this idea out of hand. But when we urged him to meet with Zambrano and Jiménez at least one more time to explain his decision to suspend the talks, he agreed at least to do that.

Norma later told me the General Staff had disciplined her for not obeying instructions. Her punishment was to complete several hours of ideological exercises. I told Norma I found the assignment ironic. I'd never heard of an organization that assigned ideological study as punishment. All that would accomplish was a distaste for the central philosophy of the group.

The fifth negotiation session, on March 13, again confronted the prisoner stumbling-block. Zambrano insisted that any solution beyond that which could be justified under the Colombian law implied serious criminal and political responsibilities for the President and his Cabinet. He went back to his casual comment in the third session and pointed out that the government was trying to accelerate the courts-martial proceedings. But the Supreme Court had declared that procedure unconstitutional. President Turbay then appointed a blue-ribbon commission of jurists to explore the possibility of abbreviating the trials. But this would take time, Zambrano pointed out, because the jurists would have to read the entire, often voluminous record at the trials. The only ray of hope the Colombians offered was a proposal to invite the International Red Cross and the Human Rights Commission of the Organization of American States to watchdog the investigations of human rights violations. It didn't sound like much at the time, but this proposal ultimately would save our lives.

Predictably, Norma was enraged and "suspended" the talks. She accused Zambrano and Jiménez of being dogmatic and legalistic. As she left the van, she shouted, "Liberty for all our *compañeros* who have been tortured and are being judged!" She flashed the V-for-Victory sign to nearby journalists. "It is our final word! We are holding firm. Our mission is to win or die!" With a grim Ambassador Galán at her side, she disappeared into the Embassy.

The government, incensed by the break in the talks, fired off a fierce communiqué relating its version of what had happened. The communiqué challenged the terrorists with the responsibility of restarting the talks. Omar was unimpressed.

Actually, the government's proposal was an ingenious solution to its dilemma. By hastening the trials and sentencing those who were charged under the subversion act, some prisoners would have been acquitted and others would have been freed if their sentences matched the time they'd already spent in prison. Yet other prisoners would have been moved from military to civilian jurisdiction where they would probably get lighter sentences. It was a clever way around the Constitution without jeopardizing President Turbay's principles. Unfortunately, the terrorists didn't respond to the idea. I don't think they understood it, and if they did, they were too impatient to accept it. They expected miracles.

The mood inside the Embassy was solemn. Depression was a heavy fog. In the quiet of our own personal thoughts and dashed hopes for a resolution, a Mirage fighter jet buzzed the Embassy. Its raw power was a rude reminder of the forces lurking outside.

TWELVE

Once Norma withdrew from the negotiations, our hopes for progress towards a reconciliation evaporated. Commander One and Omar settled back into the beds of ideological jargon that had spawned them. Anything less than their original demands was compromise, and as far as the two of them were concerned, compromise was a sign of weakness. Armed with their homegrown versions of right and wrong, Commander One and Omar clung tenaciously to their original script. The curtain had fallen on Act II and there was no script for Act III. The Commander and his strategists planned their entrance carefully, but they hadn't thought of their exit. In the classic attitude of the terrorist, they would "cross that bridge" when they came to it. And here it was.

Commander One's adamant pose had a sobering effect on all of us. Some of the hostages became depressed; they had been relying too heavily on progress in the talks. It was hard not to believe something would break our way. But when the negotiations fell apart, discouragement rippled through the Embassy with deadly effect.

The Venezuelan Ambassador, Mr. Lovera, was particularly hard hit. His health had been failing him steadily. La Doctora recorded dramatic fluctuations in his blood pressure, and so we were afraid that the Ambassador's heart might be giving out. I urged Commander One to let a doctor come in to look at Mr. Lovera. I reminded him of the President's threat if anything happened to the hostages, and I appealed to him on the grounds of humanitarianism. If the Ambassador's heart gave out while he was a prisoner, I warned the Commander he might have to face the moral outrage of Venezuela and the possible creation of a martyr. With the additional urging of the ambassadorial committee, the Commander agreed to let a specialist come to the Embassy to check the Ambassador.

The incident was the first time I had seen the effects of captivity so dramatically revealed. The strain was taking its toll on all of us, having been denied the thin hope of progress, and it now expressed itself openly. The Colombian Red Cross sent in a nurse with an electrocardiograph.

The nurse nervously set up her equipment and balked while connecting Ambassador Lovera to the electrodes. I first assumed her nervousness was the result of having masked terrorists with guns at her elbow, but it became increasingly apparent she had another more cogent reason for being nervous: she had only a vague idea of how to operate the machine. After much fidgeting with the device, the nurse finally managed to get a reading, but her technique was so unsatisfactory that it proved inconclusive. I later wondered if the woman was an intelligence agent disguised as a nurse and given a crash course on the EKG so she could take an inside look at the Embassy. But I ultimately had to dismiss the thought. I didn't believe the Colombians would jeopardize the Ambassador's health just to gather intelligence. But then I couldn't understand why they would send in such an obviously incompetent woman to do such an important job. Trained volunteers, I decided, were in drastically short supply.

The Venezuelan, a choleric man by nature, started to lose equilibrium. He called Foreign Minister Uribe Vargas and argued violently that human law and international law were above the Colombian Constitution. Mr. Lovera damned the Colombian "juridical framework" much as Norma had. He insisted the government's appeals to legality were nonsense, and he badgered the Foreign Minister no end.

To underscore his point, Ambassador Lovera repeated his argument with full emotional force on national television after an enterprising film crew sneaked through the police cordon and onto the roof of a house next door. The Ambassador stood at a second-story window and delivered his appeal with all the passion he could muster. The guerrillas were tickled by the opportunity to have the Ambassador's appeal for humane consideration broadcast on television, and they stood by off-camera, smiling. But underneath the Ambassador's impassioned appeal was the clarion note of desperation, something we all felt.

Commander One was busy giving his own interviews. The suspension of talks was big news, and the newsmen were scrambling to get a story. Commander One even called one major weekly magazine in Colombia, *Cromos*, and tendered his side of the argument. He attacked the President and the Foreign Minister for their dilatory tactics.

Commander One had another, more curious reason for calling *Cromos*. One of his hostages was a freelance photographer who scratched out a career taking pictures of the guests at diplomatic functions. Luis Guzmán would sell these photos to magazines and newspapers for a few cents a frame. Being a prisoner didn't slow Guzmán down; he became the semiofficial photographer of the crisis, the man with the inside exclusive. He was always busy flitting around the Embassy taking pictures of us. The Commander liked Guzmán because he saw him as a simple workingman, "a humble man," Commander One described him, "a true representative of the proletariat." Acting as Guzmán's agent, Commander One twisted the arm of the managing editor of *Cromos* and got her to cough up $25,000 for two rolls of Guzmán's film.

One of Guzmán's shots was of me on scullery detail in the kitchen. I was wearing an apron and washing pots and pans. The picture caught on and later appeared in *Time*, the *Washington Post*, and other periodicals around the world. Guzmán, who felt protected by the good graces of the Commander, was the only hostage who actually enjoyed his captivity. He was always underfoot, clicking away with his camera.

Ambassador Diego Asencio on kitchen detail.

The editor of *Cromos* also interviewed me. She asked if I was afraid to die, a question I was getting used to. I adopted the typically Latin macho stance and told her, "Spaniards are never afraid to die. We are fascinated with death." I also told her I was heavily engaged in debate with the terrorists, and if the siege went on much longer, I'd probably convert them to my thinking.

When the government caught wind of the Commander's acerbic interview with *Cromos*, it reacted with the fury of an avenging angel: in a serious tactical error, it retaliated by cutting off all the telephones and besieging us with silence.

The effect was devastating. We were already down because of the suspension of the talks, but when our only means of staying in touch with our families and governments was rudely severed, we plunged into a dangerous depression. I relied heavily on my daily conversation with my wife, who was instrumental in keeping up my morale. Commander One had been tolerant by allowing us telephone privileges, and we quickly had become emotionally dependent on them.

A hostage's greatest fear is that he has been abandoned, that he is alone and without support. Our daily telephone calls had helped us to overcome those fears by keeping us in touch. After we spoke to our wives and our embassies, we knew they were working diligently on our behalf. That knowledge kept the lid on fear, but when the phone lines were cut, the immediate result was to multiply our fears by isolating us. We had been cut off as much as the phones. I felt the door had been slammed shut on me. I was left in the dark without Nancy to reassure me and without Frank Crigler to advise me of progress. I was left with an awful, deadening silence. I can't express the terribleness of that sudden, unexpected isolation, nor the pall that fell over us. Even the most optimistic among us questioned our chances for survival. Our lifelines had been cut.

I later found out the Colombians' decision to sever the phones had been based on standard procedure in such cases. The effect of the action, it was reasoned, would punish the terrorists and increase their sense of isolation. The procedure was tragically shortsighted. The terrorists didn't need outside lines. They had already given their interviews and made their speeches. if they were concerned at all, it was because of what was happening to us. What the crisis managers had managed to do was punish us and increase our sense of despair.

Some of the prisoners became crabbed and mean; they hoarded their personal possessions and aggressively defended their little corners in a perverted manifestation of territorial imperative. A larger number became thoroughly passive and withdrawn. They did little but complain about the conditions and lived for the moment when they could again speak to their families. One colleague, reacting strongly to our dilemma, attempted to eat himself into a diabetic coma. Others went on eating and drinking binges. Disorientation, insomnia, and irritability became commonplace.

The spiraling physical deterioration of the Venezuelan Ambassador was an apparent reaction to unremitting stress. By now, Mr. Lovera's condition had degenerated so dramatically that a doctor had to come into the Embassy to examine him. The doctor reserved his diagnosis, but he did tell us Mr. Lovera's heart was not the problem.

The Venezuelan's desperation was painfully evident. Before the Colombians turned off the phones, he had called any journalist who would listen to him and made an impassioned plea for the government to capitulate to the M-19. "This is not a legal problem," he told one magazine. "This is a human problem that should be resolved in concordance with the law of God to preserve human life. We hostages are what is called in Caracas the ham in the sandwich." It hurt me to see my old friend wading in deep water, and it frustrated me that there was nothing I could do to console him. He directed some of his anger against me because of the United States' noninterference policy. He became increasingly difficult to talk to. Rather than antagonize him, I remained as cordial as possible, but he was inconsolable. The Ambassador was frantic for his immediate, unconditional release.

The hostages progressively lost solidarity. Once it became clear there were informers among us, the main body of captives splintered into protective, even secretive cliques. At first I thought a couple of the psychologically weakest hostages had turned informers out of fear and an inner need to please their captors. I'd already seen some of the hostages trying to curry favor with the terrorists, so it wasn't implausible to think one or two of them had gone "underground." The ambassadorial negotiating group kept its own counsel. We also kept an unwavering eye on those we either knew or suspected of being snitches, and we avoided taking them into our confidence when we could help it.

THIRTEEN

The presence of informers and the currying of favors among the hostages brought me forcibly into encounter with the Stockholm Syndrome. In a hostage crisis, the Stockholm Syndrome is included almost as a given. The syndrome was originally coined to commemorate a bank robber, an impressionable young woman hostage, and their overnight stay in a Stockholm bank vault. Ultimately, the term came to describe the special relationships that develop between captor and captive in moments of crisis.

The process has been variously described as "brainwashing," "conversion," "turning," or "going over to the other side." The popular conception of the Stockholm Syndrome in most political and military circles is so distorted that crisis managers' confused reaction to it often causes as many problems as the syndrome itself.

Unknown to me at first, a faceless jury of peers in Washington, with no other evidence than the fact that I was being held hostage, assumed I had fallen victim to the Stockholm Syndrome. The label subsequently caused me endless problems by interfering drastically with the effective reconciliation of our crisis. Washington's interpretation of the syndrome and its assumption about its effects created a nearly impenetrable barrier of misunderstanding. Before the phones had been cut off, I had started to notice an insidious but subtle change of attitude on the part of my staff and my government, which apparently questioned the soundness of my thinking. They believed, I suppose, that my capacity to make sound judgments had been compromised by my captivity. My statements, desires, and evaluations appeared to be screened carefully on the premise that since I was no longer a free agent, anything I said was suspect at best, and distorted or invalid at worst.

The fact that I and several colleagues were active participants in the negotiating process — indeed, we were to become major parties to it — and were allowed the relative freedom of acting on our own behalf did not seem to carry much weight. Never before had hostages been actively involved in the negotiation process, and this new twist undoubtedly complicated our role. Still, I was disappointed that my input to the American Embassy in Bogotá and to the State Department seemed to be almost automatically discounted. As far as they were concerned, I was an unknown quantity and therefore unreliable as a witness, an observer, and as an active participant in the negotiations. This attitude by my own people was an endless source of frustration, and it served to increase my anxiety when I believed they weren't listening, and they wouldn't trust me when I had to ask them to trust me. It was a compromising situation to be in, and I understood the State Department's concerns, but that didn't make it any less frustrating.

I assumed their thinking was guided by their perceptions of the Stockholm Syndrome, a concept I was familiar with through work on other kidnappings. The Stockholm Syndrome is a new name for a basic but rather sophisticated human dynamic. In its simplest terms, one dominant person influences another submissive person's thinking. The authority of the dominant figure convinces the submissive figure consciously or unconsciously to accept the attitudes of his superior. The passive figure oftentimes develops a trusting, affectionate relationship with the authority figure, and the authority figure, in turn, usually either accidentally or skillfully manipulates the dependence for his own ends.

The United States was first shocked by a handful of American prisoners of war in the mid-1950s who came forward and said they would rather stay in North Korea than come home. In most cases, the POWs who wanted to stay had adopted the social and political views of their captors. Public reaction in the United States was intolerant. We branded the soldiers as traitors — "turncoats," we called them — and we accused the Koreans of brainwashing them.

When the North Koreans seized the USS Pueblo, a navy intelligence ship, off the coast of North Korea on January 23, 1968, the crew was held prisoner nearly a year before international negotiations secured their release. Some of the eighty-two crew members signed "confessions" during their captivity that were later disavowed. Again, the American public was intolerant of those crew members' compliance with the demands of the persuasive North Koreans. The popular assumption was (and still is) that healthy strong men — true red-blooded Americans — would rather die than comply with the enemy.

But the notion, as some have learned, is naive. Experience has emphasized the point. Officers and enlisted men in the Hanoi "Hilton" broke under torture. A very few later declined opportunities to return to freedom. The sensational court-martial of Marine Private First Class Robert Garwood in 1980 was precisely over this issue. Garwood, originally a prisoner of war, spent fourteen years in North Vietnam before returning to the States, even though he had ample opportunities to do so before then. Branded as a traitor, Garwood was received in the States with hostility. There was no sympathy, nor any intent to understand the man who had apparently forsaken his country for the enemy's.

Until the war in Vietnam, Americans had a grossly unrealistic optimism about free will and human endurance. But as accounts of men under torture began to leak out of Vietnam, as we learned about tiger cages and *punji* sticks, we became faintly sympathetic.

Even with the end of the war in Vietnam, the problem has not been reconciled. To this day, our society is constantly troubled by manifestations of the same process. Newspapers regale us daily with stories of the seduction of unsuspecting youths by Scientologists, Moonies, and numerous other quasi-religious conversion groups. And we read about parents who pay men to kidnap back their children and "deprogram" them. We have been alternately repelled and fascinated by fringe sects headed by charismatic people such as the Reverend Jim Jones, who led his faithful congregation in a mass ritual suicide in the jungles of Guyana.

The applications of the Stockholm Syndrome are not always nefarious, however. Identification with a stronger force as a consequence of an affectionate, dependent relationship is not new. This same state of individual persuasion is common to all young humans (with the exception of very ill, emotionally disturbed children) in their relationships with their parents. The mind of the child is filled with awe at the omnipotence of his parents. His heart is full of terror at the possibility that a displeased parent will abandon or punish him. These fears cause children to be obedient to parent figures and willing to acquire their ways. Without this remarkable relationship, the children born among us would remain unconverted from their undisciplined behavior. It is through "identification with the aggressor," or being "brainwashed," if you will, that children are woven into the social fabric.

Subsequently, children often form similar relationships with their teachers, coaches, scoutmasters, and their more respected peers. In each instance, the child is directed by an urge to comply with the behavior of his friend or mentor.

These same principles often guide an adult's thinking. Canny politicians have long identified the relationship between political extinction and some failure on their part to conform to the public will. The late Lyndon Johnson used to say that a smart politician should, when necessary, modify his course. "If you can't lick'em, join'em," is the same as identifying with the opposition.

Johnson's mentor, Sam Rayburn, had taught him a lesson with the same message phrased differently: "You've got to go along to get along."

The distinction between becoming "brainwashed" and "socially responsible" is entirely subjective. Society normally has a positive attitude toward the training of its own; however, training outside its embrace is usually condemned. An example of acceptable training occurs when the Marine Corps takes an eighteen-year-old, pink-cheeked Iowa farm boy with no apparent propensity for violence, and spirits him away to boot camp for intensive indoctrination. The process includes being separated from those he loves and upon whom he normally counts for support. His body image is altered dramatically by barbers who unceremoniously shave his head and by the supply sergeant who purposefully gives him ill-fitting clothing. The recruit is quickly given to understand that "your ass belongs to the sergeant."

A healthy young male, given these influences, will metamorphose into a crackerjack marine within ninety days. By then, he'll be pure spit and polish. He will say, "Yes, Sir," and "No, Sir," and will be the image of the sergeant who converted him into a Marine. This approved behavior is called indoctrination. If a marine who has been through indoctrination is sent on patrol and several squad members move forward on point, he is expected to support them. If they get into trouble, he is expected to put a burst of weapon-fire over their heads to aid their retreat. If he does this well, he may be rewarded with a commendation.

On the other hand, when Patty Hearst was kidnapped from her family and forced to stay in a closet by Commander Cinque of the Symbionese Liberation Army, she was abused. Her body image was sharply modified, and she eventually began to see herself in a new light. Patty responded obediently the same way a Marine recruit would have. Later, when the Harrises were on point and got into trouble at a sporting goods Store, Patty put a burst of weapon-fire over their heads to help cover their retreat. At her trial, Patty's defense argued she had been brain-washed, but the court declared her guilty and sentenced her to prison.

The Marine gets a medal. Patty Hearst gets a prison sentence. There is no essential difference between the methods employed either by the Marine sergeant or by Commander Cinque. Patty Hearst was a victim of the Stockholm Syndrome, a term that would never be applied to a boot-camp recruit even though the process is the same.

I also found out there is a chemical side to this phenomenon. Nature, in her all-knowing way, provides most vertebrates with a complex chemical transmission system that is communicated through the bloodstream during the body's reaction to danger. One of the principal chemicals that modify behavior is norepinephrine, an adrenaline-like hormone. Norepinephrine is the chemical agent an animal secretes to mobilize itself for fight or flight — survival through action. The chemical affects the body in manifold ways: the pulse rate, blood pressure, and blood sugar all go up. The animal thus becomes prepared for maximum physical response to a threat.

There is a reciprocal chemical agent that is an antagonist to norepinephrine. Acetylcholine is a chemical compound characteristic of biological surrender. This is the agent found in large doses in a hibernating bear's bloodstream. It can also be found in the bloodstreams of opossums when they play "dead." Like norepinephrine, acetylcholine affects the body in manifold but opposite ways: the pulse rate, blood pressure, and blood sugar all go down. With its blood full of acetylcholine, the animal thus becomes biologically prepared for surrender.

Recent research suggests that the perpetrators of violent crimes have large doses of norepinephrine circulating in their blood. Hostages, on the other hand, having been thrust into a submissive role, may have large amounts of acetylcholine circulating in their blood. The chemical balances between these two agents apparently seesaws, depending on circumstances and the individual. During certain moments, offenders are chemically charged toward violence and victims are chemically forced toward surrender. The prisoner's identification with the aggressor can occur during just such times. But research has also shown that some prisoners have the capacity to reverse these roles and force identification on a captor.

Herein lies the rub. The reactions of prisoners vary significantly. Some are likely to become submissive and, in their changed state, become susceptible to the Stockholm Syndrome. Others, however, are much more resistant. Washington's response to my captivity was inflexible because it wrongly assumed that all prisoners fall into the former category. Observers assumed I had surrendered to my captors, and as a prisoner in a submissive role, had compromised my capacity for objectivity and decision-making. Their assumption was much too simplistic. They did not take into account my previous experiences, my individual personality, and the unique characteristics of this hostage situation as compared with others, such as the Teheran crisis.

A comparison between the hostages in Bogotá and those in Teheran reveals how dissimilar the situations in fact were. We were in a friendly nation; they were not. Our group was barricaded and surrounded by friendly troops; they were surrounded by hostile people everywhere. I was in a group that stayed together and was not only allowed to organize but was encouraged by our captors to assume leadership; they were disbanded from the beginning, their leadership was ruptured, and the prisoners were broken up into isolated groups. I talked to the American Embassy and to Nancy almost daily until the phones were cut off; they, except for the chargé d'affaires, were denied communication with the outside except on rare occasions. Nancy was nearby and supporting me: the Iranian hostages were thousands of miles away from their families. In every case, my situation was better than the alternative situation in Iran. I was near freedom, so near I often felt I could touch it. Freedom was outside the window where people were waiting to help me. My colleagues worked hard to support me, as I worked hard to support them. Even my captors respected me and offered me every courtesy they could afford. The hostages in Iran were not allowed much courtesy, and freedom was so distant, it must have seemed unattainable even at the best of times.

With all these benefits, and with my aggressive attitude, I hoped that Washington could place more faith in my abilities. But the conventional wisdom of hostage situations is not to allow the hostages to take part in the negotiating process. This is probably good advice in the majority of instances, but when conditions are as highly variable as they were in my case, there should have been greater flexibility and willingness to consider the alternatives.

The actual incidence of classic Stockholm Syndrome symptoms in our group was, in fact, quite low. With mutual support and periodic contact with the outside world, we were able to keep our balance and good judgment. A few of the hostages manifested differing physical and psychological symptoms, mostly the result of unremitting stress, but with a couple of exceptions, no one went "over to the other side." We took care of our own. We understood from the beginning that these were the matters of survival.

FOURTEEN

Without warning, the terrorists started to rip up the dining room floor. The normally reserved quiet of the Embassy gave way to the splintering of boards and the unsettling sound of the rhythmic bite of a shovel into the earth beneath the floor. We wondered aloud what Commander One was up to, but the terrorists refused to say anything other than that they would shoot anyone who went near the dining room. Their threat was so categorical it frightened all of us. The seismic needle recording our anxiety must have jumped over to the far side of the tape, and our tension increased markedly. Some of us gently prodded the terrorists we thought most likely to give us a clue to what they were doing, but they remained adamantly secretive. The sound of the shovel was maddeningly insistent: in the lull of dusk or late at night, it haunted us.

We developed theories. Some of the hostages said the terrorists were replanting their explosives. None of us had ever seen any explosives, or the fuses or wires that normally attend them, other than their fragmentation grenade. I was suspicious of their claim to have rigged the building for detonation. There was a chance, however, that the terrorists could have brought plastique or dynamite with them in their gym bags and were now strategically planting it around the house. The only chink in the theory was why they would have waited so long — more than two weeks — to do it. If they intended to rig the mansion with explosives, they probably would have done it within the first few days while the threat of invasion was the greatest.

One of the hostages had an intriguing angle. He thought he remembered that General Rojas Pinilla had had a tunnel dug under his house many years before. As a former dictator, Rojas Pinilla had more than the usual share of enemies, and he was the kind of man who would have taken the precaution of having an escape route handy if someone ever tried to get even. The theory sounded a bit farfetched, but reasonable. If the terrorists knew about the tunnel, they might themselves be looking for it.

The most ominous theory, which was favored by the majority of hostages, was that the terrorists were digging an escape route for themselves if they ever felt obliged to blow up the Embassy with us in it. The M-19 had used the same tactic when government troops inadvertently stumbled in on the "people's prison" where terrorists were holding the kidnapped general manager of Texaco, Nicolas Escobar. The idea of the terrorists digging an escape tunnel struck me as supremely ironic: usually prisoners were the ones to dig tunnels, not their captors.

With all our speculation, we had too little evidence to make a reasonable assumption as to which of our theories, if any, was the most likely. Whenever the shoveling started again, we would look at one another and wonder, "What were they planning?"

As it turned out, the theory about the old tunnel was true. After my release, I met friends who told me they had seen the original construction plans for the General's house. The architect had made provisions for an escape tunnel, but it apparently had never been dug. The M-19, also having heard a rumor of the existence of such a tunnel, was trying to find it. I also asked about the M-19's threat to have wired the Embassy for detonation. No explosives were ever found; the M-19 had been bluffing. But the Colombians had been virtually certain from the beginning that the M-19 was bluffing, so the truth came as no surprise to them. Early on in the negotiations, one of the government arbitrators asked Norma how much explosive they had planted and how it had been wired. Norma ducked the question. "Don't worry," she told him, "We've got more than enough."

"How much is that?" the negotiator prodded.

"Oh, about thirty pounds," Norma bragged.

Thirty pounds of dynamite might sound like a lot, but explosives experts concluded it was not enough to blow the Embassy to bits as the terrorists had claimed. The dynamite would have been dangerous to anyone in the house, however, and even though officials felt they saw "bluff" written all over this threat, they proceeded with caution.

Inside the Embassy, we had no indication the M-19 was bluffing, and to us, the threat was very real. Until the terrorists started tearing apart the dining room, I had been able to suppress their claim; after all, I hadn't seen anything concrete to convince me the threat was real. But once the Commander began his secretive excavations, the possibility preyed on my mind.

With tension compounding, we tried our best to keep our minds off our setbacks. We found a rallying point — food, strangely enough — and gave over our energy to solving our dining and culinary problems. Food was one of our few sources of pleasure. We were without refrigeration and had to improvise from one meal to the next. At first our diet was atrocious, and we had to scavenge what we could between the Embassy's pantry and the haphazard offerings of the Colombian Red Cross. Once our families were permitted to send us CARE packages, however, we started to eat better, but our kitchen was totally disorganized and incapable of serving forty people three meals a day. After the release of the reception caterer and his waiter, we had to fall on our own questionable talents as cooks. Mario Guzmán (no relation to Luis, the photographer) was a relative of the President of the Dominican Republic and a congenial, easygoing man who enjoyed puttering around the kitchen. Mario fancied himself an amateur cook and volunteered to cook most of our meals; unfortunately for us, his idea of cuisine ran heavily toward Caribbean cooking. It didn't take us long to tire of a steady diet of beans, rice, and fried plantains. Some of the hostages complained, so I decided to see what contribution I could make to the culinary arts. It was a mistake from the beginning.

Nancy had sent me some homemade spaghetti sauce along with jars of anchovies, clams, and olives. The Red Cross donated a supply of pasta, and I went to work. One of my favorite dishes is a delicacy called spaghetti *alla putanesca*, which supposedly gets its name from the street-walkers of Rome who come home after a long night's work and throw whatever is in the icebox into a pot along with some pasta, which is exactly what I did: in went the anchovies, clams, olives, and anything else I could get my hands on. I made four disastrous mistakes: first, I'd forgotten how lousy Colombian pasta is to begin with; second, it didn't occur to me that to combine these ingredients willy-nilly might be unpalatable; and third, I forgot that our kitchen didn't have a colander. I produced what can only be charitably described as a soggy, soupy mess. My fourth and fatal mistake was serving this insult to my fellow hostages. At first they tried to be polite and swallowed a couple of forkfuls, but there is a limit to being polite. Someone lamented the sad fact there wasn't even any Parmesan cheese with which to disguise the flavor. I was unceremoniously banished from the kitchen and never allowed to pick up a pan again except to wash it.

My bunkmate, Eliahu Barak, the Ambassador from Israel, chided me for not consulting with him beforehand because he said he knew a simple field expedient he had learned about in the Sinai desert that would replace a colander. We used his clever technique the next time we made spaghetti, which turned out to be a success because it was supervised by Bishop Acerbi, who had both Italy and God on his side. Hortensia, the charming wife of the Brazilian Ambassador, sent in the sauce; our families sent in some grade-A pasta; the Ambassadors from Brazil and Mexico performed the scut-work; and the Ambassador from Israel supplied the makeshift colander made out of gauze bandages. My contribution was a promise to stay out of the kitchen.

We followed the spaghetti course with ten Spanish omelets, which Nancy had cooked with 120 eggs. If that wasn't enough, we later had 150 Cuban tamales mass-produced under the direction of Melba Zavala with the help of her Cuban and Colombian friends. The tamales, which were wrapped in corn husks and made with chicken or pork filling, kept us fed for days. The thoughtful women even put strings on the pork tamales so I could avoid the chicken tamales (I don't like fowl), and so the Ambassadors from Egypt and Israel could avoid the pork ones. Despite some casualties in the kitchen, we eventually learned to fend for ourselves.

Meanwhile, we were still trying to cope with the communications blackout. There was no one to whom we could appeal and nothing we could do but wait and hope the government would realize the error of its ways. Despite our efforts to lighten the atmosphere, depression bottomed out during those days. In retrospect, it is easy to see our attempts at levity were too forced and self-conscious, but at least we made the effort.

The Ambassador from Uruguay, Fernando Gómez Fyns, was one of those who became increasingly distraught. I became aware of him when he muscled his way into the negotiating group's talks with the terrorists. Ambassador Gómez told us the other hostages had elected him to observe the talks and report back to the group; he insisted our briefings to our fellow hostages had been too sketchy. We reluctantly admitted the Ambassador because his claim to representation seemed legitimate. His sullen presence was disturbing, however, because he contributed nothing constructive. As a group we were exploring any avenue of mediation we could think of. It was a depressing venture to begin with because Commander One was so intractable. The terrorist leader had his "honor" to protect; he felt that giving in to any pressure would jeopardize that honor. Commander One was intent on holding fast until President Turbay made the first move. When Ambassador Gómez did say something, it was almost always critical. Before long, he was acting like a burr under our saddle irritating us and the terrorists alike.

When we found out that Ambassador Gómez was inciting the other hostages with patently false information, we knew we had to take corrective action. He had told the others, for instance, that the Red Cross was going to cease making deliveries. At that time, the Red Cross was our only link with the outside, our source of food, clothing, medical supplies, and messages from home. The idea that it was going to stop deliveries created what was tantamount to panic. If it actually happened, I believe we might have been psychologically crushed. I checked with the Red Cross to find out what the problem was, and the volunteers didn't know what I was talking about. No, they said, the deliveries were going to continue on schedule.

By this time Ambassador Galán had become suspicious of Ambassador Gómez's self-proclaimed proxy to join the negotiating committee on behalf of the hostages. He checked with the others only to find that Ambassador Gómez had made up the story. From that moment, the Ambassador was barred from all future meetings.

But Ambassador Gómez wasn't one to give up easily. He started skulking around and eavesdropping on our conversations. Then he would carry back distorted versions of what he'd heard to the other hostages, who became unsettled by what they heard. Finally, the situation became so unnecessarily chaotic we had to ask Commander One to keep Ambassador Gómez away from us.

Our attempts to exclude Mr. Gómez from the committee meetings were made more difficult by my determination to include the Ambassador from Brazil in the group. With the possibility that the Human Rights Commission of the OAS might become involved, I realized that Mr. Nascimento e Silva's experience in the inter-American system and his expertise as an international lawyer might become critical to our effort. The Commander had no objections to the Brazilian's inclusion, and because he was already bunking with us in the master bedroom, we were able to slide him in without creating an uproar. The Ambassador from Uruguay, however, was slighted by our move.

We finally got some sorely needed good news. The Foreign Minister opened a direct telephone line between the Dominican Embassy and the Foreign Ministry. The Colombians apparently realized that a total blackout was counterproductive and that limited communication was better than none.

The news was a great relief at the moment — a little window of light in the overwhelming dark. Exchanges between the terrorists and the government could begin again. Hope regenerated itself spontaneously. I felt as though a crushing weight had been lifted off my back. For a diplomat, dialogue is everything. Without dialogue, we were shut in a soundproof vacuum. Denied any chance of understanding, we were left to stagnate. Those days were among the worst.

Once the line was established, we were allowed to speak only with the Foreign Ministry, which, in turn, would convey our messages to our families and embassies. It was an awkward and impersonal process. My first call was from Foreign Minister Uribe Vargas, who had heard yet another nasty rumor that I'd been shot. I reassured him I didn't have any holes in me. There had been many such virulent rumors circulating about the condition of the hostages during the blackout. One rumor exaggerated the Brazilian's minor leg wound by intimating the terrorists had sadistically crippled him by intentionally shooting him in each leg.

I also heard a piece of intriguing news: Fidel Castro had officially offered sanctuary to the terrorists and protection to the hostages. The message, which had been delivered by way of the Colombian Ambassador to Havana, was accepted by President Turbay with mixed reaction. Castro's offer was not rejected out of hand; rather, it was accepted under advisement with a hesitant but polite "thank you."

Within the next couple of days Uribe Vargas decided to let our families use his telephone. They had to troop down to the Foreign Ministry and stand in line and wait their turn to use the phone. On March 16, the nineteenth day of captivity, I again spoke to Nancy.

It was a reunion for us. The sound of her reassuring voice gave me fresh confidence. We were only able to chat briefly — "Hello, how are you?" — because others were impatiently waiting their turns to use the phone. I realized how much I had missed talking to her and how much my morale had depended on those daily talks. I felt relieved that I was talking to her again — there was an intimacy between us despite the commonplace words — and I was angry with the Foreign Minister for making her have to go downtown and stand in line with the others.

Until that trip downtown, Nancy had not left the residence since the day I'd been taken hostage. She had shut herself up in the compound and dedicated herself to organizing support for me. Bettie Crigler, the Deputy Chief of Mission's wife, and other friends came by frequently to tend to the details of running the residence while Nancy concentrated her efforts on my release. When her frustration got to be too much, Nancy would put on her roller-skates and skate furiously up and down the residence drive and around the flagpole. Fortunately, the press never caught her at it, but it would have been something to see, the wife of the American Ambassador skating with a vengeance around the flagpole.

When the invitation to speak to me came from the Foreign Minister, Nancy accepted immediately, though she was reluctant to go out into the streets of Bogotá. Some of her closest and dearest friends were Colombians, and yet Colombians were holding me prisoner and threatening to execute me in the name of the people. She became aware of this animosity en route to the Ministry when she saw young people on the streets wearing warm-up suits similar to the ones the terrorists were wearing. After the takeover, the suits came into fashion as a soft-spoken symbol of support for the M-19. Nancy couldn't help but react emotionally. Her hostility was all the more torturing because our Colombian friends had gone out of their way to support Nancy and me during the crisis. Our second son, Charlie, was engaged to a beautiful Colombian woman and we were close to our future daughter-in-law's family. They were always ready to do what they could for us before and after the incident, and for that we will always be grateful.

When Nancy arrived at the Foreign Ministry, she hid her feelings under a mantle of optimism. Some of the other wives were also there, and they were visibly upset. The atmosphere at the Ministry was strained and very uncomfortable. When Nancy got her turn, she picked up the direct line to the Dominican Embassy only to be startled by a woman's sharp voice shouting, "Democracy and Liberty! May I help you?" The absurdity of the situation came slamming down on Nancy, and she later told me she had to exercise every ounce of her self-control to keep from laughing aloud. "Yes…" she started to answer, but then she quickly restrained herself and, after a pause during which all kinds of snide replies flashed through her head, Nancy simply asked to speak to me.

Our depression was only partially relieved by the good news. Although we were jubilant for the moment when we got to speak to our families, even if only for a minute or two, we were still facing the negotiations deadlock. The lack of sessions was taking its toll. Some of the hostages, always impatient for progress, blamed the negotiating committee for fouling the works. I thought this criticism unwarranted and unfair. The committee had, over the days, slowly insinuated itself into the mind of Commander One, who was leaning on us for advice more and more even though he didn't always accept it. His reason for refusing our advice was often specious: he didn't want to appear to be beholden to us. I argued we were all in this jam together, and that their lives were in as much danger as ours. We needed to work our way out of the dilemma by combining forces and seeking alternatives acceptable to all parties. The Commander agreed in principle, but he would at times perversely reject our earnest advice only to remind us he was the boss, the chief honcho making the decisions.

During one of my conversations with Uribe Vargas, I suggested that if he would let me know when the government was ready to return to the van, I would do my best to convince Commander One to reopen the dialogue. Much to my surprise, the Foreign Minister turned down my offer. I assumed he was reluctant to go along with the plan either because of his own suspicions about my competence (the Stockholm Syndrome again) or because he was intent on wearing the terrorists down to a frazzle.

If his plan was to overwhelm Commander One and his soldiers with frustration and the unresolved tension of waiting, then his plan was working. The terrorists often squabbled among themselves, some in favor of reinitiating discussion, others dead set against it. Norma was showing signs of restlessness, and Ambassador Galán knew she was ready for a negotiated settlement. Commander One, however, was reluctant to take the first step toward the resumption of dialogue for fear it would be construed as a sign of weakness, and so only Commander One and Omar refused to budge from their stance.

As a consequence, we were left with no alternatives other than to kill time by playing games of chess, checkers, and backgammon, and listening to the endless grousing of the malcontents.

In the early morning hours of March 17, I was violently startled out of my sleep by gunfire a few feet away from where I was lying. I felt the sharp report of the sentry's carbine go through me as though it were a bullet. For the moment while I was struggling to consciousness, I thought I might have been shot. I realized I hadn't been only when I saw the sentry cautiously peering out the window into the street. Throughout the house around me I could hear the other terrorists deploy and take up their positions. Someone in the distance was shouting — I couldn't place the voice. The other hostages were sitting or standing up with drawn, tired faces trying to understand what was happening. My mouth was sour with the familiar taste of fear. My second immediate thought was the military had launched an invasion. I could hear activity in the street: a car starting up, some urgent voices.

I'd been awakened by gunfire in the middle of the night before. The experience wasn't new, but it was always frightening. Usually, however, the weapon-fire came from the troops outside who were shooting at trespassers. Now and then, late night *Bogotanos*, mostly drunk, would make a wrong turn and crash through the barricades near the Embassy. The government, wary of an M-19 attempt to save its barricaded comrades, had little patience for those who invaded the security area and fired on them. Six local citizens were shot and killed making this tragically careless mistake. The troops' command directive was clear: shoot first, ask questions later.

From time to time the Colombians tested the alertness and the location of the sentries by smashing empty bottles against the walls of the Embassy late at night. I assumed they were playing a psychological game of cat and mouse with the terrorists by constantly and unexpectedly increasing the tension and then lowering it. The theory is based on the premise that strain would ultimately incapacitate the terrorists. The only trouble with the theory is that the tension made the terrorists edgy and more likely to commit an error in judgment that could cost

110

us our lives. I began to understand the true nature of terror when I was brutally awakened by that gunfire in the middle of the night.

I was afraid the troops might be losing their patience. If the soldiers were trigger-happy and waiting for the chance to show the public how they could clean up the mess, any small incident could set off a massive explosion of violence. I hoped the leaders had tight control of their itchy troops; it seemed the height of lunacy to take the Embassy by storm so long as there was any possibility of a settlement through negotiations.

Of course, there were gaping holes in my thinking: the government might try to take advantage of the lull and order its troops to attack when the terrorists least expected a raid. The element of surprise had worked well in Entebbe and Mogadishu; the army might think it would work in Bogotá.

Worse was the thought the government might believe the stalemate had no reasonable possibility of being resolved. That left force as the only practical alternative. The possibility of a raid depressed me particularly: the Commander and Omar had made a point of reminding me that I would be the first man shot if there was one.

The terrorists were as nervous as we, perhaps even more so. Rumors on the Colombian radio hinted that Israeli commandos or U.S. Marines were being deployed around the mission. There was also news that an El Al jetliner and a Hercules transport plane were parked on a guarded runway at El Dorado Airport. We deviled the terrorists with our own ploys by telling them, "Don't worry, if it's commandos or Marines, you won't know which until it's too late." Commander One and Omar did worry. So did we. We were playing a dangerous game.

The shots that startled me out of my sleep in the middle of the night on the seventeenth were intended for a man zigzagging for cover near the front door. The half-dressed man turned out to be Uruguayan Ambassador Gómez, who was apparently fed up with being a hostage. He had lowered himself out of a second-story window on a blanket tied to his belt and then jumped the remaining distance to the concrete. He was dashing toward the front street, about 120 feet away from where he had landed on the sidewalk, when a soldier spotted his shadowy figure and fired a warning shot that lodged in the roof of my car. Another soldier opened fire on the Ambassador without thinking he might be an escaped hostage. About this time the sentry spotted Mr. Gómez and fired at him, thinking he was an infiltrator. Exasperated, Mr. Gómez threw himself under one of the cars parked at the curb and shouted, "Don't shoot! Don't shoot! It's the Uruguayan Ambassador!"

Fortunately, the soldier and the sentry both missed him, but he was still in danger of being shot by the terrorists once he identified himself. The police took defensive positions and trained their weapons on the windows of the Embassy while a colonel screamed, "Get the car started!" A black Mercedes staff car with officers aboard careened to the Ambassador's rescue. The officers managed to yank Mr. Gómez into the car and sped off to the hospital.

As it turned out, Mr. Gómez had been planning his escape for some time. He had been feigning attacks of dysentery in order to accustom the guards to his frequent late-night trips to the bathroom. He waited until one of the sentries was inattentive and slipped unnoticed into the wing next to the library. From the window of the Dominican Consul's office — a window which wasn't under the M-19's watch — the Ambassador made his escape. He did not, however, get away uninjured. The Ambassador fractured his spine jumping to the ground from the window. Still, he was a lucky man and, in a sense, so were we. I hesitate to think what might have happened if he'd been shot since the Colombians' promise not to attack was predicated on the hostages' safety.

Ambassador Gómez had been very unpopular with both sides during his captivity. When news of his escape circulated among the hostages, several people became very emotional. Ambassador Lovera insisted we were bound by a tacit agreement that all would leave the Embassy together or not at all. Other hostages declared him an errant coward for deserting his colleagues and leaving them in the lurch. He had unfairly jeopardized our lives with his daring, breakneck escape. As far as these hostages were concerned, Mr. Gómez's escape was an act of treachery. Commander One was beside himself. He ordered tighter security and increased our restrictions. As of that day, we had to conform to a 9:00 P.M. curfew. Anyone who wished to use the bathroom had to ask permission from the watch commander. All future telephone conversations would be subject to complete monitoring. The wing from which Mr. Gómez escaped was closed off, and all the windows in the mansion were wired shut. Our freedom of movement was severely curtailed. Anyone who broke these rules, the Commander warned, would be shot.

Commander One later told us that Ambassador Gómez had petitioned him for his release on the grounds that he was an undercover *Tupamaro* agent. The other terrorists had voted Ambassador Gómez the hostage they would most like to execute.

I myself didn't judge Ambassador Gómez harshly because I knew he had personal problems and was hard hit by captivity. While I didn't feel particularly charitable toward him for leaving us at the mercy of the M-19, my overriding reaction was one of envy. Mr. Gómez understandably found himself in an untenable position both in and outside the Embassy: his government had taken a tough stance, he was alienated from his fellow prisoners, and he must have been aware of the terrorists' feelings about him.

During the next few days, Ambassador Gómez started to call the wives of the other hostages, who told him in plain language what they thought about his escapade. I advised Nancy not to accept the Ambassador's calls in order to avoid what was becoming an unseemly spectacle.

A few hours after Ambassador Gómez's dramatic escape, Ambassador Lovera's health gave way. He started to suffer sudden dizzy spells and fell to the floor, complained of numbness in his limbs, and finally suffered a complete physical collapse. We tried to call the Foreign Ministry, but it was lunchtime and no one answered the phone. Exasperated, the Mexican Ambassador, who was certain Mr. Lovera was having a heart attack, went to the front door and began shouting at the troops for a doctor. When a troop commander finally said he'd send for an ambulance, Ambassador Galán demanded a doctor and said that if anything happened to the Venezuelan, it would be the Colombian government's responsibility. Mr. Galán was so infuriated he told the troops in no uncertain terms that they had handled the entire situation irresponsibly. He unloaded all his frustration on the bewildered troops, who didn't really understand what was going on.

Fortunately, however, the Ambassador got his point across, and within minutes a cardiologist came bounding into the Embassy. After he examined Ambassador Lovera, he assured us again that Mr. Lovera was not suffering from a heart condition; he diagnosed his ailment as labyrinthitis, an awkward but not serious affliction of the middle ear, probably the result of stress.

Commander One, certain that Ambassador Gómez would brief the authorities on the M-19's security arrangements, started a campaign to contradict all the intelligence Mr. Gómez might relate. He started moving us around from room to room; the occupants of the master bedroom were shuffled into another bedroom next to the library. The Commander also moved the Haitian Ambassador and the Venezuelan Consul General into the bedroom with us — the Consul General so he could attend his ailing superior. I wound up on a pallet in a corner with the Israeli and Mexican ambassadors. Our new room was overcrowded with the addition of the new people, so we had to ask Commander One to move the Haitian into another room. He agreed, but we were still terribly cramped. The bath was smaller too, and the toilet lacked a seat, but at least we didn't have to share the facilities with the terrorists anymore. The only good that came from our move was that we escaped the constant surveillance of the sentry. From then on we were subject only to a roving patrol that checked on us from time to time. It wasn't privacy, but it was breathing room.

In captivity the trivial and the mundane become critically important, at times even overshadowing truly relevant considerations. We often were preoccupied with matters we wouldn't have noticed in our everyday lives. But given so much time, we ended up examining and overanalyzing everything. Some hostages would fret or sulk for hours over some small, perhaps unintentional slight by a colleague or by one of the terrorists. Others would rage and carry on interminably, collaring anyone foolish enough to listen to their complaints. We had to work hard to maintain a balanced perspective. It was remarkably easy to lose it, and there were many times I feared I had lost it myself. Fortunately, I shared my thoughts, fears, and hopes with those I trusted. We reinforced one another: our combined courage was greater than any individual's, and we rose to meet the challenge. That, combined with our innate sense for the absurdity of our dilemma, kept us reasonably healthy and sane.

But it didn't keep us from worrying about not having a seat for our toilet. We sent out an urgent call to our embassies to rustle one up. Ingrid Stegelmann, my personal assistant at the Embassy, sent us an objet d'art decorated with butterflies and Peanuts and Snoopy stickers, one of which read: "Love is where you find it; I'll be here all day." Overjoyed with our gift, Albert Byfield, the Honorary Consul General from Jamaica, spent the next hour and a half installing the seat with the help of some gun oil we borrowed from the terrorists. "Swords into plowshares," someone remarked snidely. With our new hardware in place, we toasted Ingrid and inaugurated our seat.

We spent our time plugging up holes in the ceiling and accommodating ourselves to our new quarters. With the omnipresent sentry gone, some of us began to consider the necessity of creating a workable escape route in case of an emergency. One of our bedroom windows looked out over the front doorway of the Embassy. A portico extended to a point just below the window, if we had to, we decided we could batter down the window with the coffee table in our room and jump out the window onto the portico. From there we could jump to the ground and hope for covering fire from the troops. The sentry who watched the front of the building would have to lean out the window to get a clear shot at us, and by so doing, would expose himself to sniper fire. Once we were on the ground, the canopy would shield us from further danger. It was a short run to the cars parked curbside, or we could jump over the containing wall to freedom. The plan was risky, one not to be undertaken lightly, and we filed it away for future reference in case the situation got desperate. Meanwhile, downstairs in the dining room, we could hear the terrorists shoveling dirt.

FIFTEEN

The Colombian government decided to go on television and bring the crisis out of the cellar. Even though the media had been having a field day since the beginning of the takeover, there had been no real official line except a few obvious, obligatory statements from time to time. President Turbay, it seemed, was taking pains to develop his strategies behind closed doors.

When I heard the announcement that Foreign Minister Uribe Vargas was going to address the nation himself, I grabbed what I saw was a prime opportunity to knock Commander One out of his catbird seat. I'd been looking for some way to cash in on the stalemate between him and the Colombians. Even though the Commander held the guns to our heads, the real power belonged with President Turbay. Commander One was beginning to understand that he wasn't in as advantageous a position as he'd first thought. After his initial derring-do, the political realities of his ambitious adventure began to figure in the Commander's pipedream. The wax on his wings was softening. This was a game with two different sets of rules: the deadlock was now working against him, not for him, as he'd first supposed. Time allowed his enemy to formulate a sounder counteroffensive, and the Colombians could afford time when he could not. Day in and day out the terrorists had to try to second-guess the government.

I sensed Commander One was primed to accept a good argument because he was at a loss. He knew what he wanted to do, but he didn't know how to do it without losing face. The Commander was acutely sensitive to the M-19 High Command, who were certainly monitoring his leadership carefully; he was like a teenager trying too hard to please his parents. The Commander was terrified of showing any weakness or lack of resolve, and that fear made him outwardly obdurate.

The Colombians had an equal problem: they were too anxious about tarnishing their image of effectiveness, strength, and an iron hold on the political exigencies involved. If there was going to be any resolution between the two groups, it had to be on middle ground, on the no-man's-land between the M-19 and the Colombian government. We, the hostages, were obviously the ones in the middle, and we had the ears of both sides — a rare position for any hostage to be in — so we formulated a simple approach that would antagonize neither side and thus, we hoped, be acceptable to both.

With these thoughts in mind, I approached Commander One with a series of rhetorical questions that I thought might make him more receptive to reopening talks with the Foreign Minister. What would happen, I baited the Commander, if the Foreign Minister got on television and declared a hopeless impasse? Wouldn't it be to his advantage if he, the Commander, cracked the door a bit to let in a little light so Uribe couldn't justifiably make such an announcement? In this chess game, it was the Commander's move, and if he didn't move quickly and confidently, he might forfeit a critical turn.

I could see Commander One was worried and that my questions were getting through to him. What I needed to do then, I realized, was give him the out he needed that wouldn't compromise his self-esteem. Let the hostages act as neutral arbitrators, I suggested. Let us make the appeal — on our own — to restart the talks; we could make a simple bilateral appeal to his people and to the government's people in the interest of reconciliation. The Commander liked the idea and responded to it readily. Once we got his "official sanction" we rang up the Foreign Minister and tried our pitch on him. He too agreed, although I noticed a marked lack of enthusiasm on his part. The Foreign Minister's acceptance was one of wearied capitulation, and it worried me. Still, the fact we were back on track overshadowed my concern about the Foreign Minister. A surge of solid optimism shot through the hostages when the committee members announced that both parties had agreed to sit down together again.

The Foreign Minister was on national television the next day. His speech was tough but not unreasonable. It seemed to leave some doors open for us. He said nothing of a hopeless impasse; rather, he expressed hope in a rather vague, unconvincing way.

What I found more disturbing was Mr. Uribe's on-camera demeanor. The Foreign Minister is an eloquent, confident orator in a country in which politicians pride themselves on their oratorical panache. But Uribe Vargas looked tired and acted ill at ease during his televised speech. He stumbled occasionally over the words in his prepared speech. This wasn't the brash, consummate politician I knew. The pressure was obviously taking its toll on him. My heart went out to the man because I understood that he had to deal not only with his own government, but with the fourteen other governments, which were clamoring for a quick, practical yet peaceful solution. If that wasn't enough, the Foreign Minister was being endlessly goaded by the wives of the hostages and by some of the hostages themselves, especially Ambassador Lovera, who was constantly harassing him and at times even abusing him. Everyone wanted an answer — soon.

I later found out that the Foreign Minister's speech had been taped before our call to him urging the resumption of talks. My gambit had worked; if Commander One had seen the broadcast first, I doubt he would have gone along with my plan.

One of our happiest moments came when the government restored our telephone lines. My blood was still boiling that the lines had been cutoff for such specious reasons, and when I thought they were reinstalling them as a reward for getting the talks going again, my dander started up again. Privately, however, it meant the world to me to be back in touch with my family, and when word came that the phones were on again, I was prepared to forgive the Foreign Ministry for its folly.

116

Ironically, the first calls we made only jeopardized the reinstated privilege. The government had issued a communiqué to the media claiming the terrorists were the ones who had asked (implication, "begged") to resume the negotiations. Realizing how that kind of blatantly false information could permanently damage our credibility and even our role as intermediators, we took to the phones with a vengeance "to set the record straight." We knew the Colombians might take umbrage at our "truth" campaign and cut off our phones again, but we really had no choice. We had to prove to the terrorists that our efforts were sincere and that our advice was legitimate. We weren't protecting the terrorists' interests so much as we were protecting our own. When our interests were the same, and when a plan of action did not unreasonably compromise the Colombians, we actively pursued that end, even if it meant losing our most cherished possession the telephone.

The terrorists were grateful for our voluntary entrée into their diplomatic affairs. Their attitude and treatment of us as prisoners changed materially. Whereas the women had been friendly before, they were now openly flirtatious, going out of their way to tease and play coy with certain prisoners. The terrorist men even made a point of stopping by off-duty now and then to chat and share a glass of wine. Even dour Omar lightened up.

Commander One also started feeling his oats. He decided to get the old lecture series cranked up again and headed the bill with an interminable and insane account of the history and aims of the M-19. While he spoke, he referred to notes he'd scribbled out beforehand and droned on and on so, that he confirmed my original impression of him: the man was a dreadful bore. He inveighed against his chosen nemesis — cursed Yankee Imperialism — and used the record of the old United Fruit Company as a "sterling" example of the subversive activities of modern-day multinationals. He mercifully ended his monologue but not without some sweeping pseudo-Marxist slogans in the worst tradition of a Latin demagogue. Finally, he took a parting shot at the Colombians for their brutal treatment of prisoners and their repudiation of the basic principles of human rights.

I took Commander One aside after his little performance and told him his attack on United Fruit was blatant demagoguery unworthy of his intellectual pretensions. United Fruit, after all, was a thirty-year-old skeleton and an irrelevant example of what multinationals were today. He was playing up to the deep-seated hostilities of Latins for United Fruit with his rabble-rousing.

I also barbed him about his observations on the violations of human rights. What's fair for the goose was fair for the gander, I insisted. Why weren't our rights important? The Commander only chuckled and then walked away without further comment. I didn't really expect much else from him: I was happy for the chance to vent some steam.

Undaunted, the Commander later hinted he might let the families of the hostages visit the Embassy. Ambassador Barak jumped at the chance. It was said that his daughter, Judith, was leaving for Israel to get married and he wanted to say goodbye and give her his blessings. Commander One was touched and enthusiastically agreed to arrange the reunion as quickly as possible. We all witnessed the moving, highly emotional meeting between father and daughter. Watching them, I thought of my own two daughters of marriageable age and wished I could embrace Anne and Mary and tell them of my confidence in and love for them. All of us who had families were hurt by the scene; we never felt the cruel separation more than at the moment when Judith said goodbye to her father, not sure she would ever see him again.

The Venezuelan was next to queue up in the visitation line and asked Commander One if his wife could visit him on his birthday, a few days later. The Commander, tickled with the favorable press he got after Judith's visit, suggested a birthday party for all the hostages and the wives that would come.

The thought of seeing Nancy thrilled me. I wanted to see her more than anything else, but after some judicious reflection, I realized how unfair it was to subject Nancy to reckless danger. I knew Nancy, given half a chance, would spurn any danger and show up at the front door demanding to be let in. Even though Commander One said he would guarantee our visitors' safety, I knew how brittle that safety was. There were too many unpredictables that might rear up. I don't mind taking an occasional chance with my own life when duty calls for it — it is one of the occupational hazards in my job description that, as my youngest son likes to point out, "goes with the territory" — but I wasn't about to risk the lives of my family without good reason.

The Foreign Ministry also objected to visits from the hostages' families when it got wind of the Commander's intended birthday gala. Not only did it want to avoid endangering the lives of more people, it didn't want the Commander to pull off what was an obvious ploy for sympathetic press coverage. While some of the hostages had no reservations about having their loved ones visit, I was not the only one unsettled by the prospect. I talked the matter over with my Mexican and Brazilian colleagues and found they agreed with my way of thinking. The idea was nice, but it didn't make sense. Thus resolved, we called the Foreign Minister and told him that whatever his final decision, we didn't want our wives near the Embassy. I had a lump in my throat when I made the request, but we knew we had to endure.

I also didn't like the idea of being in the position of asking people like Commander One and Omar for favors that wouldn't contribute directly to my or my colleagues' release. The prospect of having Nancy frisked like a street criminal by the soldiers only to be subject to the same treatment by the terrorists infuriated me. I already had to put up with their searching my packages and eavesdropping on my telephone calls. Nancy and I had made a pact not to write each other because we couldn't countenance strangers' reading of our personal mail. Bringing Nancy up to the front lines and subjecting her to these indignities went against my grain, and even though I wanted — needed — to see and touch her, I let better judgment preside over the sway of emotions.

Fortunately, the decision became easier once the Foreign Minister nixed the idea of visits altogether. Ambassador Lovera was shattered as were the others who'd put great stock in the visits. Commander One and Omar were quick to accuse Mr. Uribe of being unreasonable and insensitive. I didn't feel kindly toward their false sympathy for us; I think Omar secretly gloated over our disappointment. I don't think the Commander or Omar was ever truly aware of our role in the refusal, and, looking back, it was just as well they weren't.

We celebrated the Ambassador's birthday among ourselves anyway, and it was a resounding success. We had three lovingly baked birthday cakes and several cases of wine to soften our disappointment. The terrorists joined in with us: the Commander and Norma regaled us with solos. We sang and drank and kidded one another. Guzmán took pictures. The Nuncio fretted like a mother hen for fear someone would get too drunk and create an incident. But we let loose, pulled out all stops, and celebrated into what was for us, the wee hours: nine o'clock. A few drank until they felt no pain: others, to the point of losing consciousness. For a few hours we tried to forget who we were and where we were. We almost succeeded, but the strain, barely perceptible at times, was always there.

SIXTEEN

I had been right about the pressure being mercilessly applied on Diego Uribe Vargas by other countries whose representatives were being held hostage. One foreign diplomat sent to Bogotá to advise the Colombians summarized the nature of that pressure by telling the press, "We've been reading an awful lot about the difficulty Colombia is having settling this within its own laws, and the diplomatic community now thinks some more attention ought to be paid to Colombian international obligations." It was a polite way of saying, "Let's get the show on the road."

President Turbay defended himself by saying that his government had speeded up the trials of the suspected terrorists in La Picota Prison by expediting the reading of nearly 30,000 pages of evidence compiled for use in the trial. Even so, the wheels of the government were moving much too slowly. Rumors circulated that the Colombians were going to capitulate and allow the governments of the hostages to negotiate for their emissaries independently. When Frank Crigler refused to deny the rumor, he gave it credence. Speculation ran rampant. The Colombian press is notorious for its impulsive behavior, and many is the time a paper went to press before any facts were carefully checked.

Some of the members of the Group of Fifteen — the name given to the delegates sent to Bogotá by each of the fifteen nations represented by the hostages — produced a statement (over the objections of the U.S. representative) that attempted to establish the primacy of international obligations over domestic law. Their gambit was intended to undermine the Colombian position by declaring the problem an international rather than internal matter. By citing the Vienna Convention of 1961, which obligates the receiving state to protect the lives, integrity, liberty, and dignity of diplomatic representatives, the Group of Fifteen stated that "within the framework of international law, as well as in the practice of relations between states, the obligation of a state to fulfill the norms contained in these articles [of the Vienna Convention] cannot be avoided by invoking the necessity of fulfilling certain dispositions of internal law." The statement called upon the Colombian government to "take the necessary measures to free the captive diplomats avoiding the use of force since this inevitably would place in jeopardy the life and personal integrity of the victims." The document concluded by stating, "If in a particular case like the one under consideration, the government acts in a manner consonant with international norms, this does not imply in any way the rupture of the internal juridical order. On the contrary, it exalts it, emphasizing its flexibility, generosity and equity."

The Group of Fifteen's plea may have been eloquent, but it didn't get any sympathy in Colombia. Besides, Colombia had a major trump card: the United States was backing the Colombian position entirely. President Turbay wasn't about to buckle under the pressure of the various governments, knowing the United States explicitly supported him to the extent of giving him a public vote of confidence.

The Group of Fifteen's petition had worked before. The Brazilian government had resorted to the same course after the kidnapping of American Ambassador Burke Elbrick. With a precedent established, several of the hostages believed (or wanted to believe) that the concerns expressed in the Group of Fifteen's document would supersede any Colombian interests and therefore open the gates for countries to negotiate independently with the M-19 for their officers.

While the debate continued in the Council of the Organization of American States, the Colombian government's reaction was clear and stridently negative. The Foreign Minister declared flatly in an interview that the other countries were aware that "we are eager to continue discussions and resolve this [crisis] peacefully." He, like President Turbay, was insulted by the implication that Colombia was putting the interests of the hostages second to its own political interests. The accusation stung, even though it was partially true.

Despite his claim to want to resolve the complicated issues, the Foreign Minister, in the same breath, continued to take a hard line on the release of the so-called nonnegotiable core of prisoners the M-19 wanted released. He openly referred to the prisoners as "common criminals" and "miscreants" guilty of "horrifying crimes" such as murder, kidnapping, extortion, armed assault, and weapons theft. The government could not and would not countenance the release of these prisoners under any circumstances, he insisted, because no one had the right or the leverage to make his government "act in a crazy manner."

While the Foreign Minister was busy making his emotional appeal to the people of Colombia and the other nations involved, the ambassadorial negotiating committee was busy on the inside. We were becoming more confident with our role as arbitrators, so in order to counter Commander One's claim that he wasn't making any headway, we drafted a fifteen-point document that specifically outlined the advances he had indeed made. The committee, now acting as a watchdog for both sides, mobilized its efforts in anticipation of predictable responses. We knew the terrorists were bound to complain about the lack of significant progress, so we took elaborate pains to ensure they understood the intricacies and nuances of their efforts: something they were incapable of perceiving because of their lack of experience in matters political. Little and often make much, we insisted as we outlined our carefully thought-out document.

Our "Fifteen-Point Memorandum" was an exercise in psychology. We went over each point with the Commander to make sure he understood all the implications of each item. By the time we were finished with him, he thought he was in the process of accomplishing the moon. Commander One wasn't so naive that we could stall him interminably, but we were effectively able to keep him thinking in positive and constructive terms.

The memorandum was an ingenious device as well as a necessary one because it put off a crisis in the Commander's confidence. These were its points:

1. The Government has accepted dialogue;
2. The Government has ordered the removal of its troops from the immediate vicinity of the Embassy;
3. The Government has offered not to storm the Embassy unless an act of violence occurred within;
4. The Government acceded to the publication of an M-19 communiqué;
5. The M-19 has obtained wide publicity on an international level;
6. The M-19 has moved to the head of subversive movements in Colombia;
7. The M-19 has obtained the recognition of the leader of the Palestine Liberation Organization, Yasir Arafat;
8. The Government has offered safe conduct to the occupiers of the Embassy in exchange for freedom for the hostages;
9. [The Government] has offered to permit and to make conditions favorable [so] that private institutions and friends of the hostages negotiate their liberation in exchange for ransom;
10. The Government has shown it wished a solution that was humanitarian and decorous within the legal framework;
11. The Government has taken general measures to speed up the trials;
12. The Government has agreed to the presence of representatives of the OAS Human Rights Commission and the International Red Cross at the trials;
13. The previous point assures the trials would be impartial and that neither arbitrary acts nor tortures would be committed;
14. These measures have permitted the release of fifteen people already;
15. The Council of the OAS is studying a resolution concerning the situation that has occurred in Colombia.

We got some unexpected help from the outside when Enriquito Santos, the left-wing son of the managing editor of the daily *El Tiempo*, reported an interview given to a Mexican magazine in which the leaders of the M-19 in Picota Prison had said that the occupation of the Dominican Embassy has been a success and had achieved major political publicity objectives. Enriquito Santos was one of the front men of the progressive political organization FIRMES. In the staid political atmosphere of Bogotá, Santos was considered a radical and a distinct contrast to his very pro-Establishment, conservative family. He edited the only political magazine of the left in the country; sadly, he published his last issue while we were being held captive. Santos also wrote a weekly column in his father's paper, one of the great and respected journals in Latin America.

With our fifteen-point memorandum and Enriquito Santos's column, we urged on Commander One the argument that time was on the government's side and was running out for the M-19. Any further delays would only increase the possibility of a fatal confrontation. The terrorists had to maintain the favorable public image they had created by releasing the Austrian Ambassador and letting the daughter of the Israeli Ambassador visit him. The public's attention was already starting to drift; the M-19 was in danger of becoming "old news."

Commander One replied by saying he was under the direct orders of his High Command and wasn't in a position to alter his instructions. His leaders had changed their hiding places once he began his mission so there was no way he could contact them. Neither were the prisoners in Picota authorized to intervene; for better or worse he was in it until the end. The Commander felt irrevocably committed to his original plan.

The ambassadors in our negotiating group went back to the drawing board and tried to hammer out a common position that would satisfy both the government and the terrorists. We had been heartened to hear news of the government's release of three M-19 sympathizers and the subsequent release of twelve Colombian Revolutionary Armed Forces (FARC) members. We interpreted their release as a gesture of bona fides by the government actively to meet the terrorists' demands. We thought the Commission of Jurists had at long last begun to function effectively. Ultimately, we were proved wrong, but we were anxious to seize any straw.

Angelo Acerbi, the Papal Nuncio, began pressing for separate negotiations for the ransom, hoping that a clergyman could lend an effort to this end. The Ambassador from Brazil came up with the idea of a banking consortium to seek public contributions to a ransom fund since it was certain none of us would be able to put up that kind of cash. We later dropped this idea when we were informed that the money for ransom wouldn't be a problem. What worried me was that Frank Crigler had told me that the official U.S. position on ransom had stiffened considerably since the Richard Starr kidnapping.

The U.S. government had made it clear it would make no concession to terrorist blackmail. It would neither pay ransom nor release prisoners. Moreover, the United States supported other governments that took a similar stance "since concessions encourage further attacks and put more people at risk." When an ambassador was abducted, the United States would look to the host government to exercise its responsibility under international law to protect all persons within its territory.

Despite this clearly stated refusal to pay ransom, the terrorists were equivocal about it. While they didn't really expect $50 million, there was little question they wanted some money. They tried to balance this desire for cash with a high-minded image as idealists because they didn't want to be dismissed as political mercenaries. The terrorists also believed, and rightly so, that their chances of getting prisoners released would be improved by emphasizing this point of their terms, thus avoiding the risk of being fobbed off with cash.

The Nuncio persisted with his idea about ransom, which caused the Mexican Ambassador to joke, "It's his European upbringing. They only think about money!" I urged the Nuncio to hold off insisting on separate ransom negotiations because Commander One had repeatedly told us he wasn't even going to consider ransom for at least another couple of negotiating sessions.

The long-awaited and greatly anticipated sixth negotiating session was scheduled for March 24, eleven days after the talks had been suspended and the twenty-seventh day of our captivity. In the morning Bishop Acerbi celebrated Mass, and Ambassador Nascimento e Silva suggested special prayers for "God to illuminate the negotiators so we may spend Easter with our families." His comment gave rise to some gallows humor to the effect that no one minded making an occasional sacrifice and abstaining for Lent, but this was ridiculous. We were in pretty good spirits and very optimistic.

Norma forsook her usual white woolen hood for a black one with "M-19" emblazoned on the forehead. She and Ambassador Galán marched out of the Embassy and into the van, where the two government negotiators were waiting patiently. There was some vigorous handshaking and a few broad smiles as if old friends were being reunited.

The session lasted for an hour and forty-five minutes. The tensions were reduced and the atmosphere was cordial. Norma began by introducing her research on the Colombian Constitution and proposing various articles under which it appeared President Turbay was authorized to grant pardons or amnesties, an idea which the Foreign Minister had earlier refuted. One of the stumbling-blocks that the government negotiators had pointed out in earlier sessions was that only the Congress could grant pardons or commute sentences with a two-thirds majority vote. Since the Congress was recessed until July, the issue would require a special session. Once convened, Congress would take at least another six days to pass a resolution, provided there was no debate — a situation that wasn't very likely. To say the least, it would be an awkward, unwieldy, and time-consuming affair.

Norma tried to answer their objections by quoting the law. She implied strongly that the number of people that would benefit from such consideration would be small. Furthermore, a few of the prisoners the M-19 was most interested in were in the last year or two of their prison terms; commuting their sentences seemed reasonable to her. Norma also told them that she and her cohorts were ready to await the results of the juridical process so they could leave with those comrades who were acquitted in the courts-martial or against whom no charges were pressed. Because the government claimed it was accelerating the trials, Norma saw it only as a matter of time.

Norma's message should have been clear: she wanted at least a token number of prisoners released along with the prisoners against whom the Colombians would not or could not make a case.

The Colombians, in return, raised procedural objections to Norma's presentation. They insisted they had no control over the actions of the judges in granting freedom to prisoners. There was no way to predict accurately what was going to happen, they cautioned. They could make no guarantees.

Norma was unsettled by their cautiousness and uncertainty. She then wondered aloud if the Colombians might not try to pull a fast one by releasing prisoners only to re-arrest them as soon as they hit the street. When Zambrano and Jiménez failed to react, she suggested that any prisoners who were going to be released be released en masse at the end of the negotiations as everyone was about to flee the country. She directed the negotiators to have the prisoners transported to the national airport and given the option, in the presence of herself and the other terrorists, of staying or leaving with the M-19.

The men quickly discounted Norma's suggestion and said that once the prisoners were acquitted, they were free men; the government had no authority to compel them to go to the airport. They also argued that the government wasn't a travel agency, and that it would be up to the terrorists to invite them along. In short, the two men said bluntly, no way.

And so the session ended, each side testing the other, trying to appear and sound amenable but with an undercurrent of hostility that rippled the surface from time to time. The stumbling-blocks were still all there, and it didn't take much insight to see that the two sides would soon be butting heads again. Just the same, in the face of the obvious, hostage and terrorist alike were intent on believing in the possibility of progress, on believing, despite everything, that the end was near.

SEVENTEEN

Commander One became an underground hero. Radicals from different continents called the Embassy to congratulate him on his coup and to urge him on in the best tradition of the macho revolutionary. Naturally, these calls bolstered his ego and confidence. Over the weekend, the Commander had had a call from extremist radicals in New York who belonged to the Armed Forces for National Liberation (FALN), which has been around in one form or another for decades. The self-styled guerrillas of the FALN claim to be fighting for the independence of Puerto Rico and have claimed responsibility for dozens of vicious bombings in the New York area that have killed and maimed victims indiscriminately. The callers passed along a message of solidarity and goodwill to the Commander in his bold struggle for freedom.

Again in the limelight, Commander One reacted by granting interviews to the press in which he re-pledged his and his comrades' efforts to eradicate what he vaguely referred to as "the social problem." The Commander then announced himself as a "liberal democrat" and offered what he considered were two paradigms of socialism for the Colombian government: Nicaragua and Austria. By the time the Commander finished gibbering about what socialism meant to him, no one knew what he was talking about.

Undaunted, Commander One carried over his goodwill and released three more hostages, all Colombian nationals. His ploy was transparent but not unreasonable: with the second negotiating session of the new round coming up the next day, he wanted to be respected as a flexible, sensitive, and intent partner in the negotiations. I was particularly pleased with his action because it meant that Commander One had implicitly accepted the role we had cast for him. I don't think his decision to act as we had suggested was entirely conscious on his part, but he had at least given us a vote of confidence, intentional or not.

On the twenty-ninth day of captivity — two days after the first talk of the second round — the negotiators climbed back into the van for a session that ran nearly three hours. Our optimism was still running high, especially because the session was taking so long, but when we saw the look on Norma's face as she stalked back into the Embassy, we knew the meeting had not gone well.

The government negotiators had used the opportunity to deliver a lecture on constitutional law, explaining why the government could not do the various things Norma had suggested two days before. They even went further and, referring to her remark of the previous meeting that the terrorists would accept the juridical framework as a potential solution, stated that it would also be necessary for them to accept the consequences of such a solution. If there was any question that the government was playing hardball, they laid it to rest by announcing that the governments of all fifteen countries represented in the Embassy takeover had refused to pay any ransom. They spent the rest of the session reading the records of the prisoners the M-19 wanted released.

Norma was furious. She angrily pointed out that the only reason the M-19 accepted the juridical framework was to give the government a way out of the impasse and not because they themselves believed in it. It was the end, not the means, in which they were interested.

I had to break the bad news to the other hostages because our usual spokesman, Ambassador Lovera, was crushed. Ambassador Galán was too tired after having taken notes in the van. The group was dramatically subdued even before I briefed them; afterward, their silence was deafening. We were back on square one. The roller coaster of hope and despair was more than we could take.

As a result of this unexpected defeat (a defeat that was, in fact, predictable, but one to which we blinded ourselves with hyperbolic enthusiasm), we began to sour into diehard cynics. This day marked the end of our pie-in-the-sky hopes: we were now grizzled veterans with hash-marks on our sleeves. The hostages retreated into their individual cliques, and the terrorists started to take stock of their situation and to decide what new strategies they needed to develop in order to counter the government's oppressive effort to squelch them.

At our next meeting with Commander One, he surprised us with allegations of a conspiracy among the hostages to overpower guards and escape. What was unsettling about the Commander's accusations was the fact they were true: there had been significant discussion among us to consider the alternative of escape and how we might reasonably accomplish it. Besides our original plan to escape through the bedroom window onto the portico, the ambassadors from Israel and Brazil developed an attack plan to overwhelm the lone sentry in the kitchen. The Brazilian had an unwieldy weapon — the small but heavy transformer for the kitchen hotplates — with which he intended to clobber the sentry over the head before taking his rifle. Since the small, scruffy kitchen was more or less isolated from the rest of the house, their scuffle would likely go unnoticed by the others. From the kitchen the armed ambassadors could then storm the second floor by climbing the winding staircase to the second sentry's post in the corridor off the stairway. If they could surprise the other sentry and secure his weapon, the ambassadors reasoned they would be able to fight off the counterattack while they called for help from the outside.

Their plan was daring and probably a result of the setback in negotiations. What we didn't know, however, was that President Turbay had explicitly forbidden the army to intervene for any reason for at least six hours. The President instituted this restraining order as a precaution against hasty or reckless attacks. If the Israeli and Brazilian had carried through their plan, they might have found themselves stranded on the second floor trying to shoot it out with younger men and women much more inured to violence. Ambassadors, some of them advanced in years, are not particularly known for their commando instincts.

When Commander One confronted us with his allegations, we knew the informers were again bending the ears of the terrorists. The Commander was blunt: he told us he knew of our plans, and if necessary, he would tie us up to keep us from trying anything. If we did dare to act, he warned sternly, he had ordered his soldiers to shoot anyone acting suspiciously. His caveat had a sobering effect on us; our plans, for the moment anyway, turned to mist.

I tried to sidestep the issue by rationalizing our "rash talk" as nothing more than talk generated by our low spirits after the fiasco in the van. We needed some outlet for our frustration, I explained to the Commander. I asked his indulgence to allow us to fantasize. My argument wasn't very plausible, and the Commander rejected it outright by reiterating his threat to shoot first.

Most of us were more disturbed by the insidious and ever-present informers, if anyone had doubted their existence prior to Commander One's confrontation, there was no way of denying their presence any longer. The Commander was not second-guessing us — he had inside information and didn't mind intimidating us by letting us know he knew it.

We had already targeted our prime suspect, a small, black man of uncertain antecedents who went by the name of Tito Livio. Livio was acting as an employee at the Dominican Embassy when the siege occurred. One hostage reported he had seen Livio conferring with the Commander after he had overheard a compromising conversation among the hostages about escape plans. Another hostage had heard a rumor that Livio had been involved in an assassination plot against U.S. personnel in the Dominican Republic. Livio had apparently been around: he had been in political trouble in Mexico and had been expelled from Chile by the Pinochet government after the fall of Salvador Allende. There was some speculation that Livio was the M-19's "inside man" planted among us from the beginning to gather intelligence for Commander One. Several of us wondered how the terrorists had brought in their extensive equipment and supplies in their little gym bags. It was conceivable that, with the help of someone working on the inside, they had previously stockpiled material in the Embassy before the attack. There was considerable support for the theory that Livio was linked to the terrorists when one of the hostages remembered that the Embassy had received an unusual number of unordered crates just before the seizure. The Dominican Ambassador's wife had assumed that some local company had sent courtesy gifts in honor of their national day, so she didn't think too much about them.

We had no hard evidence against Livio, but the circumstantial evidence against him was mountainous. Nor was he the only informer among us. There was at least one other snitch and he, unfortunately, was one of our own, a member of the diplomatic corps. We assumed he was motivated by fear of the consequences of an escape attempt or was trying to curry favor with Commander One with the thought of getting himself an early release. The evidence against him is circumstantial, and it was a small comfort that he wasn't a professional diplomat. He happened to be a part of a particularly compromising conversation among several ambassadors prior to the Commander's threat warning us not to try to escape.

This same man "squealed" to the Commander that one of the hostages had lifted a butcher's knife from the kitchen. This provoked Commander One into conducting a massive shakedown of all the hostages. The terrorists frisked us and searched all our belongings, but they never found the knife. As far as I could tell, no one had taken the knife, and it was probably accidentally thrown out in the garbage. We tried to convince the Commander that that was what happened, but he was growing increasingly paranoid about us and our intentions. As a result, Commander One announced that unless the knife turned up, he wasn't going to release any hostages as a humanitarian gesture on the upcoming Easter Sunday. That wasn't the news we wanted to hear, but Commander One strenuously overruled our objections. Only the return of the knife would placate him; unfortunately, it never surfaced.

News from the outside was more encouraging. Nancy told me over the phone that Secretary of State Vance was sending former Assistant Secretary of State for Inter-American Affairs, Viron ("Pete") Vaky, to Bogotá to review the situation and report back to him. Pete had been my boss in Venezuela when he was Ambassador there, so I knew and trusted him well. Until Nancy gave me the news, I had been disconcerted by what I saw as the U.S. official nonchalance toward my plight. I knew the hostages in Teheran had priority — as they deserved — but I didn't expect to be treated almost as an afterthought. I perceived a notable lack of concern in Washington about my dilemma. I didn't believe the State Department was actually cultivating its lackadaisical attitude; rather, it was the result of being overworked and therefore overlooking. Still, every country represented by the hostages except the United States had sent a high-level envoy to participate in his end of the negotiations. Frank Crigler, a former Ambassador himself and a highly competent man, was trying to manage the crisis from his end at the U.S. Embassy in Bogotá. But Frank was himself too close to the crisis. He was upset when he found out Pete Vaky was being sent to Bogotá because he thought Washington was implying he wasn't managing the crisis effectively. The truth was that Pete's presence was the direct result of my children's strenuous lobbying at State.

My children were unhappy with the lack of progress in the Bogotá negotiations. They intuitively mistrusted the ability of the Colombian government to handle the matter, and they were equally dissatisfied with the U.S. government's role, which they characterized as "playing low." As a result, they began their own rigorous lobbying by bringing pressure to bear on the State Department and by urging congressmen and state leaders to make sure my case was getting its fair share of high-level attention.

My two daughters and three sons, ranging in age from twenty to twenty-six, pushed for a meeting with the Secretary and wouldn't take no for an answer. Although the Desk Officer in charge of Colombia kept them informed from day to day, they pushed for action. They came up against one of the bureaucratic adages known to all Foreign Service veterans: there is an inverse relationship between the level of knowledge and the level of responsibility at the Department of State.

Usually the Desk Officer is the person who knows the most of what's going on in a particular country, but the Desk Officer has very little responsibility other than to stay informed. The Office Director has substantially more responsibility but has substantially less knowledge of any particular country. The Assistant Secretary has a great deal of responsibility but normally can recall only a few rudimentary facts about a country. The Secretary, of course, has all the responsibility but little specific knowledge. This is a matter of utility because the sheer weight of all the knowledge would smother any one person. One might expect the Secretary to know everything, but this is practically impossible. Upper-echelon officials are at the mercy of briefing memoranda prepared by their subordinates before a meeting. If everything goes as planned, it is an effective procedure. But if things get too complicated, the official has to punt. This is one of the drawbacks of gigantism in government.

Secretary Vance found his match in the concerted experience and knowledge of my children. One of my sons, Charlie, who is a lawyer, bluntly told Vance that he thought the Colombian government was mishandling the situation. When the Secretary asked why he thought that way, Charlie began point-by-point itemization of their grievances. He informed the Secretary that he would hold President Carter personally responsible if any harm came to me and asked that the message be relayed to the President accordingly. The Secretary responded cautiously and conservatively. He agreed to pass Charlie's message along to the President, but restated his belief that the United States should not interfere in the political affairs of democratic Colombia. The children, wise in the way of politics, knew his answer was too simplistic and bulldogged him: there are diplomatic channels, they reminded him, and we could exert pressure if we had a mind to.

Secretary Vance reacted as he should have. Rather than dismissing the children, he asked Pete Vaky, an experienced Latin American hand and a former Ambassador to Colombia, to leave on a fact-finding mission to Bogotá. No one knew it at the time, but Secretary Vance was already considering resigning as Secretary of State, and in fact he did so before the end of April. He could have palmed off the children's requests: instead, he acted honorably and sincerely.

Ambassador Vaky was the best possible choice for the job; he is not only fluent in Spanish and quick on his feet, but he was on familiar terms with practically the entire Colombian leadership, including President Turbay. When he arrived in Bogotá and I spoke to him on the phone, I felt reassured, although I had learned to temper my optimism by facing the realities and difficulties ahead of us. Ambassador Vaky told me he would be talking with many political contacts in the next few days and would give me an assessment of the situation when he was finished. I told him about my heartfelt confidence in him, and he said he hoped he would be deserving of it.

When Pete, a native of Corpus Christi, Texas, asked me how I was holding up, I told him I could stand up to anything as long as necessary, but what I really wanted to know was whether I was being abandoned to my fate as a matter of political expediency. This wasn't bravado on my part because it made an essential difference in how I reacted to the crisis I was facing, especially when it came to planning an escape. I knew U.S. policy was stiff, but I still didn't know how stiff. Ambassador Vaky was reassuring within the context of U.S. policy. He said there was a great deal of concern about my safety and that Washington's energies were fully engaged in finding a solution. I didn't know if what he was telling was truth or an artificial balm, but I put my trust in Pete because I knew that with his subtle mentality, if there was a solution he would find it.

My oldest daughter, Anne, spurned her mother's advice to all our children to stay in the States and came to Bogotá. Nancy told me she wanted to visit me, but I stuck to my sanction prohibiting those I loved from taking any unnecessary risks. The decision came hard because I wanted to see Anne badly, but Nancy supported my decision and we stuck to our guns. I spoke to Anne on the phone every day up to her last night in Colombia. I told her that l loved her very much, and I thought of telling her (and through her the other children) that if I'd ever been unjust with any of them, I wanted forgiveness. The sentence was on the tip of my tongue, and I had a strong urge to say it, but I checked myself for fear I would sound fatalistic. The moment was very emotional for me. I think Anne sensed my feelings without my having to verbalize them. The negotiations were going well, I told myself and I didn't want to chance communicating anything to my family that it might interpret negatively. When I hung up, I couldn't help but wonder if and when I'd be back with my family. I knew then what Ambassador Barak must have felt when he kissed his daughter goodbye; had he wondered, as I, if it would be the last time?

Even though Commander One had announced the cancellation of his plans to release hostages on Easter Sunday as a goodwill gesture after the kitchen knife mysteriously disappeared, some of us decided to push the issue and see if we couldn't get him to recant. In a predominately Catholic country such as Colombia, Easter Week takes on mammoth importance. The ideal of resurrection and rebirth is inherent in the spiritual, political, and social vision of Latins. Easter Week, perhaps more than any other single religious feast, enables the Latin to recharge his faith, not only in his religion but in his family and his country.

Easter had the same connotations for us hostages. Easter Day loomed ahead as a landmark for us, as though simply reaching the holiday in one piece was a sign of progress. We urged Commander One to release hostages to boost morale and to express confidence in his and the Colombians' ability to iron out their differences. It was an old line by now, but it worked, and was worth plugging until the option exhausted itself. About this time Bishop Acerbi got on the bandwagon and suggested we make a big production out of Holy Week. We could celebrate Mass with great ceremony, have an outside priest come in to hear confessions, and perhaps even get a rabbi for Ambassador Barak since Passover fell within Holy Week.

The Commander liked the idea, so we began to prepare for Easter with the same industriousness as children preparing for Christmas. When our embassies and families found out our plans, they swamped us with gifts and food. I got two wicker CARE baskets from Nancy, one for Palm Sunday and another for Easter, filled with all kinds of surprises. In my regular fix of crossword puzzles which Ingrid Stegelmann clipped from The New York Times, the Herald Tribune, and other papers (Ingrid even had the British Embassy clip the puzzles from the Manchester Guardian), Nancy had hidden some contraband articles about me. The police at the checkpoint barely inspected the bundle of puzzles anymore, so the bootleg clippings made it through uncensored. The police as part of standard procedure in these situations cut off all periodicals to enhance the feeling of isolation on the part of the terrorists and to eliminate all sources of current news that might be helpful in their deliberations.

One of the articles was by Daniel Samper, an articulate man and widely read columnist on the left, who characterized me as the antithesis of the Ugly American and not at all "the conceited and arrogant Gringo who comes here as if he were visiting his private farm. Asencio is basically a Latin man of Spanish blood who displays humor and a spark worthy of the sharpest Creole leg-puller. Modest and frank, he is closer to our temperament than to that of his chiefs in the North…I say all this in the event someone has thought that the person in the Embassy is a stereotypical *gringo* diplomat. They should be aware they are mistaken." Samper also spoke glowingly of Ambassador Galán, so I shared the column with him.

Samper also wrote a satire on our predicament as negotiations dragged on through the year 2008. Referring to a press story that I was beating Commander One regularly at dominoes, Samper projected my winnings at a shade over $50 million — coincidentally the ransom the terrorists were demanding.

I showed the clippings to the terrorists and they were impressed. I knew the M-19 respected Samper, and I wasn't above playing up to that respect. As a result of Samper's generous estimation of me, I noted a shift in their attitude about me: their stereotype of the *gringo* politician was dissolving.

Curiously, there were two other gifts in my baskets which also impressed them. One was a collage by a major Colombian artist, Alejandro Obregón, of a rather intent and fierce condor — the bird that has become his trademark — with a handwritten message of support. The condor imparted a feeling of resolve and courage with its broad wings half out stretched as though preparing to take flight. I pinned the work over the duty list of household chores where others could draw from its subtle but meaningful message.

Another national artist, David Manzur, sent me artwork, although it was much more surreal and disturbing. Manzur sent me a dozen Easter eggs in their own basket, each egg crawling with houseflies he'd painted on them.

The housefly is to Manzur what the condor is to Obregón. Manzur is famous for his beautiful works that are always marred by the insidious, ever-present housefly — a symbol of death, imperfection, and corruption. The imposition of the fly created an unsettling tension in his work: hope cautioned by reality. Manzur had been giving Nancy art lessons for the past two years, and we'd become fast friends, but his flies, as they were no doubt intended to do, always made my skin crawl. Manzur and my daughter Anne had spent a whole day at the American residence preparing the eggs for my bizarre but welcome gift.

Collage by Colombian artist Alejandro Obregon sent to Diego as a morale booster, the condor represents freedom, the ominous clouds to the right, terrorism. Photo by Javier Jimenez.

Later, La Negra admired one of my Manzur Easter eggs but accidentally dropped and cracked it. Norma felt bad about the accident and gave me a handmade Easter card in recompense. The card showed an egg with a fist clutching a rifle protruding at one end, and an American flag and Colombian treasury bonds dropping out the other end. On the front Norma wrote: "*Señor* Diego, I hope I never have to shoot you." And inside:

> My intention was to compensate you for the cracked egg. This card is not crackable, but for your solace it is destructible. I assure you, Mr. Ambassador, that it is an Easter egg and a sincere gift. A little strong perhaps but since I don't like flies since they can be crushed with a single blow, I prefer my M-19 carbine.

Your esteemed Norma

I had mixed feelings about Norma's sentiments, but I appreciated the thought.

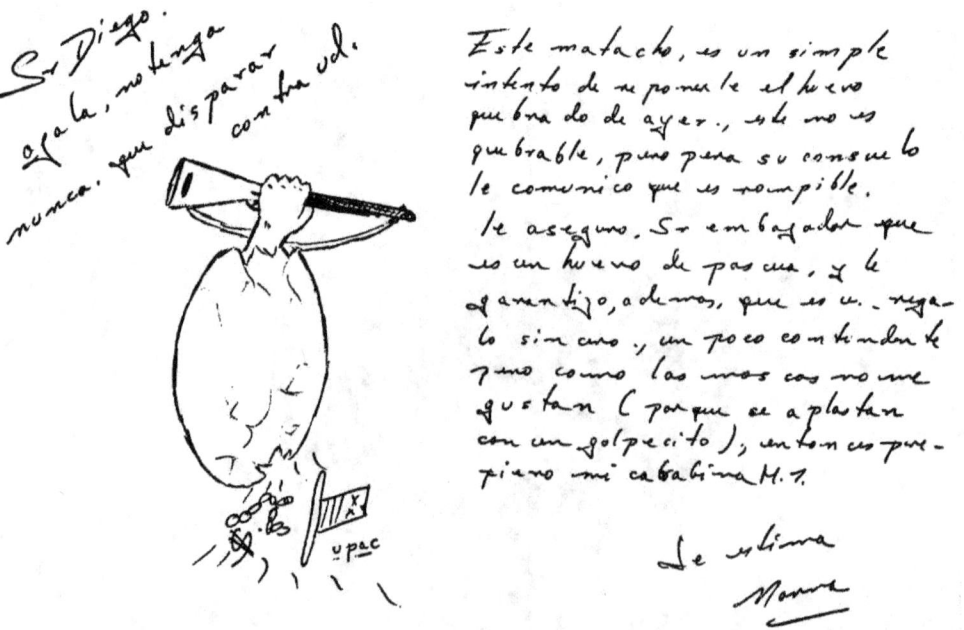

In the same package with the artwork were some welcome foodstuffs: Spanish sausage and ham from my favorite restaurant in Bogotá, La Barra, and a few loaves of *campesino* (country style) bread, which the chef at the Hilton baked for me. Topping off my first basket was a large bouquet of palms and a bottle of holy water from Father Bean, my parish priest, for our Palm Sunday Mass. The atmosphere in the Embassy relaxed in anticipation of the Holy Days. I did my puzzles, kidded with some of my colleagues, and read a novel by the Polish science fiction master, Stanislaw Lem. As I read the blurbs on the cover of the book, I saw one description of Lem's work that perfectly expressed my emotional state during those days: ". . . a lucid but serene despair."

There was also some low comedy to keep our minds off the obvious. The Dominican Ambassador, Mr. Mallol, had developed a quirk of going to bed wearing a ski cap complete with fuzzy pompom. He claimed it warded off the evening draft. The night after the shakedown for the knife, the Ambassador's cap mysteriously disappeared. The Ambassador was so upset that he insisted the terrorists undertake a second search for it, as though national security was at stake. The terrorists, amused by his fine frenzy, conducted a mock search for the wayward cap, but like the knife, it never surfaced. The Ambassador was terribly distressed by his loss; he reminded me of Charles Schulz's character Linus, and his security blanket. Finally, Mr. Mallol's family sent him a replacement, but it clearly wasn't the same to him. He wore a hangdog look for days.

Ambassador Mallol was also notorious among the hostages for his strange eating habits. He was the counterpart of the Paraguayan chargé, "La Metro," when it came to making noise. After eating, the Ambassador had the annoying habit of sucking his teeth clean in a symphony of weird slurping, sucking noises. After one meal, as he was gazing absentmindedly out a window near the Egyptian Ambassador's pallet and carrying on in his usual manner, the Egyptian Ambassador stared at him in disbelief and shouted in English, "Look! He's spitting on my bed!"

The Haitian Ambassador gave us a scare during our Easter follies. He had been uncharacteristically sullen and soon it became obvious he was becoming seriously ill; he had severe abdominal pains. Armchair doctors hazarded spot diagnoses: ulcers, appendicitis, gastritis. We called for a real doctor from the outside, who came quickly and examined him. His diagnosis was less dramatic: indigestion caused by overeating!

The terrorists weren't without their quirks either. They decided to commemorate Camilo's death during Holy Week with a military ceremony. In our tight quarters, they dutifully lined up in formation, dressed in full guerrilla regalia, and went through a series of close-order drills. They took turns making impassioned speeches about their martyred fellow soldier. Omar read some of his dreadful poems. Norma lectured on the dangers of attempting another escape; she was like a mother scolding her mischievous children. Together, they were a little, rather pathetic, bedraggled band: if they hadn't been so deadly, they would have been a comic bunch.

Commander One agreed to let an outside priest come in to hear confession. We got Father Xavier Nicolo, an Italian friar, who directed a relief program for the street urchins of Bogotá. The street children, who number around 10,000, are a pervasive presence in the city. These abandoned and runaway children, gamins mostly between eight and twelve, make a living stripping cars, snatching purses, and raiding merchants' stalls. They operate in loosely organized gangs called *galladas* and sleep in doorways or derelict buildings. In the mestizo culture of the

Bogotá highlands, the native Indians supposedly don't maintain strong family ties and clear out their children from the nest very early. By contrast, the mulatto culture of the coastal areas has stronger family ties, and abandoned children are quickly absorbed by other families. Father Nicolo ran a vocational school and dormitory in the inner city to try to integrate these lost children into society and keep them from becoming part of the swelling crime statistics of Bogotá.

When Father Nicolo arrived at the front door of the Embassy dressed in his flowing robes, he looked every inch the Italian friar: confident, a man of faith and conviction, a man of purpose. The terrorists received him formally and read more speeches. The friar, unflapped, read a letter from His Holiness Pope John Paul II, addressed to the Nuncio and praying for our safety and well-being. Several of us, including La Negra, went to confession. I told Father Nicolo that I hadn't gone to confession for twenty years because I objected to the Church's position on birth control. He replied with a twinkle in his eye that the trick was to find a confessor who was sympathetic. I also told him I'd accumulated quite a store of sins during all those recalcitrant years. Father Nicolo, without missing a beat, blamed my waywardness on my Hispanic heritage and told me not to worry — absolution was at hand.

Commander One retracted his decision not to let any hostages go and let two non-diplomatic prisoners leave. The gesture, of course, was well received even though we knew he was culling out the "nonessential" personnel, leaving only a nucleus of hostages comprised of ambassadors and Embassy officers. There were just a handful of non-diplomatic hostages left. Once they were gone, no one believed the Commander would start to release his trump cards. Those, we knew, he would keep close to his chest.

Since Passover began in Holy Week, we also received the High Rabbi of Bogotá, David Sharbani. Rabbi Sharbani, rotund, elderly, but ebullient and energetic, came to the Embassy in his ceremonial robes with a heavy gold Star of David studded with rubies around his neck. His unrestrained optimism and dégagé manner were contagious. He sang the Passover Seder for Ambassador Barak with a palpably joyous spirit. He blessed the wine and passed the cup for all to drink. The man was a breath of fresh air. He refused to be cowed by the somberness of our situation and went out of his way to make us all feel deserving of grace. When he came to me and asked if he could bless me, I asked him whether one had to be circumcised. He laughed heartily and said he would waive the requirement this one time. We embraced like two bears. He told me he was close to the Lord and was sure his prayers for us would be answered.

Rabbi Sharbani's robust cheerfulness was a dramatic contrast to the lugubriousness of others who had visited us. His personal magnetism and good will recharged us.

His charisma also captivated the terrorists. He freely joked and bantered with them but he didn't miss the chance to engage them in serious discussion either. The rabbi argued articulately that time was running out for them, and that they should take every step possible to accelerate the negotiations.

Commander One was so taken with the rabbi that he let two more hostages leave with him. With the Commander's unpredictable and whimsical sense of the dramatic, he surprised everyone by releasing the Dominican Consul, Mr. Sanchez. His release, considered by many as untimely, gave rise to speculation about his probable collusion with the terrorists. Even so, we were happy for their surprise release, and after an emotional farewell, we sent them on to freedom.

The rest of Bogotá was virtually deserted; *Bogotanos* traditionally escape the city during Holy Week. Everything, including the government, ground to a halt. Despite support from our families and friends on the outside, we were aware of the eerie, haunting quiet of the abandoned city. Stubbornly, we continued to believe our resurrection was imminent.

EIGHTEEN

A couple of days after his arrival, I spoke to Pete Vaky again. He told me the consensus of the Colombian political leadership was that there could be no prisoner exchange. President Turbay had insisted that the release of one prisoner was the same as the release of a thousand, and he intended to protect the juridical norms of his country at all costs. Whatever the risks, the Colombians would not undertake any action that might be construed as illegal within the terms of Colombian jurisprudence. But within a legal context, the President would do everything possible to resolve the crisis peaceably. The news was small comfort. The Colombians were not going to back down: that was clear. And neither would the terrorists.

Ambassador Vaky suggested that the ambassadorial committee emphasize the possible importance of the OAS Human Rights Committee to the M-19. I had been hoping against my better judgment that the government would make at least a token prisoner exchange, but that point, according to Pete, was now moot.

I took the idea to Commander One and insisted that if the M-19 truly considered itself a reasonable alternative to the Colombian government, and if he wanted to address himself seriously to his "social problem," then he would have to give up his Chinese-bandit mentality and begin to think in more statesmanlike terms. His original proposal of an exchange of prisoners and a payment of ransom might be considered a triumph in the short term if he could pull it off, but I doubted the long-term political impact would be anything but ephemeral. If, on the other hand, the M-19 was instrumental in bringing the Human Rights Commission to Colombia with the right to monitor the courts-martial proceedings against its members and to investigate human rights violations throughout the country, then the M-19 would be contributing a valuable service in transforming its society. If it would be remembered for anything, I told the Commander, it would be for this and not for his old-hat terrorist tactics.

The Commander told me he was open to the idea of having an international organization come to Colombia and take a close look at the human rights situation. As far as he knew, the M-19 had no objection to the original Colombian proposal of inviting the OAS into the country; in fact, it welcomed the idea.

We began to concentrate on the idea because it seemed like the only workable conciliation at the time. As soon as I got the chance, I called Frank Crigler at the U.S. Embassy and talked it over with him. Because Norma had already told the two government negotiators that the M-19 was willing to consider the involvement of the Human Rights Commission, I was not prepared to find out that the Colombian government had not moved off square one. Frank told me he did not think the Colombians had even called the OAS yet because it was their impression the M-19 had not accepted their original suggestion that the Human Rights Commission become involved in the trials.

I was so furious I broke out into a cold sweat. How could the Colombians be so derelict? They claimed to want to resolve the crisis, yet they did nothing to make it happen. I wondered if they were dragging their feet as a ploy to create expectations and to build up the participation of the OAS Commission as a great achievement in the minds of the terrorists. Whatever the reason, negligence or strategy, I decided to push the issue. We had been in captivity a full month. If we were ever going to get out, I wanted to know now how realistic a possibility it was. No more pointless waiting. If they were not going to move on their own accord, then I would move them myself.

Frank Crigler was startled when I called him back and told him that Commander One wanted to speak to him personally so he would know without doubt the M-19 wanted to pursue the angle with the Commission on Human Rights. I put the Commander on the line, and he reiterated what I had said. Then I got back on and told Frank to go immediately to the Foreign Ministry and tell Mr. Uribe of the Commander's decision. He should then ask the Foreign Minister to go ahead with an official invitation to the OAS. My message was intended to be clear; no more bureaucratic gobbledygook; we wanted action!

Frank later called me from the Foreign Ministry and told me the Colombian government was indeed anxious to settle the matter, but his words already sounded trite, even trying. "But what are they going to do?" I grilled him. Frank said they had agreed to allow the terrorists to leave with friends, family, and sympathizers if they wished. This included anyone with an outstanding arrest warrant. The Ministry had also agreed to invite the Human Rights Commission to sit in on the trials to ensure they were being conducted fairly. The Ministry predicted the majority of the prisoners would eventually go free, and the Commission would make sure they could leave Colombia without any further harassment. Under these circumstances, it would be unnecessary for the M-19 to wait for the end of the trials and then begin a mass exodus out of the country. At last, I sighed, something.

I sensed the hand of Pete Vaky in all this, and I was certain Frank was reflecting the sentiments of Mr. Uribe, which gave it additional, official weight. I countered by telling Frank that this was progress certainly, but that it would be hard to sell the idea to the M-19 unless the government would release at least a few token prisoners to leave with them. This did not seem such an unreasonable request since it was apparent that some of the prisoners were going to be acquitted, paroled, or have their sentences commuted anyway. I stressed that the terrorists were intent on not leaving empty-handed; if the government balked then it was sure to become a major stumbling-block. Camilo's death was always in the back of the Commander's mind.

The issue in my mind was whether the incredibly slow judicial process could produce some prisoners to accompany the terrorists within a short time. The slug's pace at which we were crawling now said "no" emphatically. Until we had something concrete to offer the M-19, we would have to rely on sleight of hand and our wits. So far, this was nothing but a dangerous shell game.

I prevailed on Commander One to give careful consideration to what I described cautiously as an important and serious proposal. I told him I had the sense, based on all my years of negotiation that we were close to a settlement. I tried to generate a sense of excitement and anticipation in him.

After a month of being mired in delays, official red tape, and the idiosyncrasies of erratic hostages, Commander One was more willing to listen. Yet his four weeks of experience had also taught him to be cautious. His caution, evenly tempered with his paranoia, conflicted with his anxiousness to come to some conclusion. I could see the effect of the tension in his face, especially around his tired eyes; I could hear it in his voice. The strain was a creeping vine that was slowly strangling him. He wanted to listen; he needed to generate hope for himself and his people. I decided, for the time being since I had no other alternatives, to feed that hunger.

Unfortunately, the hostages did not respond with equal enthusiasm. Ambassador Lovera was particularly outraged by the slow pace of progress. He did not hesitate to voice his opinions loudly to anyone foolish or unfortunate enough to listen. He was convinced the Colombian government intended to sacrifice the hostages in the interest of political expediency. At first he was confident the Venezuelan government would come to his rescue by applying intolerable pressure on the Colombians to meet the M-19's demands. He sincerely believed his own personal standing with the President of Venezuela and his own political stature in his homeland would ensure a speedy deliverance. But it was not to be. As time passed, he began to feel abandoned. His sense of malaise was intensified by the seemingly indifferent staff at his own Embassy, which was often not in when he called. His physical deterioration under the harsh conditions and stresses of captivity was taking a toll, and he would blow up on the telephone, often damning the Colombian government and all its works. When he heard that El Tiempo had published an editorial criticizing the international diplomatic pressures that were being applied against the Colombian government, it was the last straw for Ambassador Lovera. He had, until then, considered Enrique Santos a close friend. The Ambassador called him on the phone and had a violent argument with Santos only to suffer a physical collapse at the end of it.

Ambassador Galán also called the Foreign Minister to make certain the invitation to the OAS was going to be made. Mr. Galán became adamant on the telephone and pointed out that the hostage situation was a Colombian problem, but that we were the victims. Calm and patience were not infinite virtues, he warned, and several of the hostages were sick and desperate. Morale was at an all-time low. The media were no longer treating the crisis with the seriousness it deserved. Ambassador Galán also pointed out to Minister Uribe that the longer our captivity lasted, the greater the effect on bilateral relations. He stressed that the failure to issue an invitation to the OAS was a prime example of the stalling tactics of the government. The Ambassador from Mexico called for action, and he wanted it quickly.

The Foreign Minister promised to invite the OAS promptly. All of us felt better once we had extracted that promise. Some wags among us accused the Foreign Minister of gross procrastination and dubbed him "Diego the Bad" in order to distinguish him from me, who became known, charitably, as "Diego the Good."

With everything at quarter speed during the pre-Easter season, we devoted our attention to improving our living conditions. After a month we were still roughing it and yearned for some creature comforts such as hot water. Bathing was still an act of sheer masochism.

I routinely woke up around five in the morning while Ambassador Galán was doing his calisthenics before cooking our breakfast. With the unflinching resolve of an ascetic, I would take a shower while there was still some water pressure. I would meet the onslaught of frigid water with a cacophony of shouts, yelps, and groans in order to stem the numbing cold. The first time I tried this technique, three terrorists came storming into the bedroom with their weapons drawn. When they found out all the screaming was only the American Ambassador taking his shower, they left somewhat disappointed. Ambassador Barak gave it a try, encouraged by my technique, only to announce solemnly afterward that it was a bust.

The Red Cross took pity on our suffering and presented us with a heating coil for the showerhead. The electric shower is a standard fixture in most tropical societies. Installation is generally a simple procedure, and once we got ours in, we celebrated — luxuriated — in our first warm showers. A number of my colleagues took their first full bath that day.

The heating coil was not without a hitch, however. If the water pressure dropped (as it did often, especially after you were soaped up), the coil would burn out as soon as the water stopped. If you were wet and tried to turn off the coil, you were flirting dangerously with electrocution. Because our water pressure was so erratic, we were concerned about losing one of our colleagues as well as the heater.

Ambassador Barak solved the problem with another one of his ingenious field expedients. He attached a string to a knife switch next to the shower stall and ran the end of the string over the curtain rod. A quick pull of the string would cut off the electricity without endangering the bather.

Taking a shower became a slapstick comedy. First you had to turn on the shower only long enough to get wet, lest you lose all the water pressure. Then you soaped up. Fully lathered, you then turned the water on again to rinse yourself while holding the string in one hand in anticipation of the inevitable sudden drop in water pressure. If all went well you might get clean; but rarely has bathing been fraught with such suspense and drama.

April 1, however, was not a carefree day of pranks and good humor. April 1 was a trying day — a day that tended to smother what last vestiges of optimism were trying to sprout in the litter of broken promises and hopes. In El Salvador, where revolution was fulminating, five terrorists ambushed Ambassador Lemus from Guatemala and shot thirty-seven rounds into his car. The Ambassador had had the foresight to wear a bullet-resistant vest, which saved his life; he escaped with only minor cuts and bruises. Not one to give in without a fight, Ambassador Lemus pulled his own machine gun from under the seat of his car and returned fire, chasing off the startled ambushers.

In Teheran, the American hostages were entering their hundred and fiftieth day of captivity; in Bogotá, we were entering our thirty-fifth. Citizens in the States marked the anniversaries solemnly. Commander One was quoted in a newspaper interview as saying he was prepared to stay in the Embassy as long as or longer than the Iranian militants if he had to in order to achieve his goals. Naturally, the Colombian government responded in kind: it too would hold out as long as necessary. We could become old waiting for a resolution — we were already turning gray.

The eighth negotiating session was also scheduled for April 1. Norma and Ricardo Galán dutifully trooped out into the van, expecting to hear the government negotiators confirm the invitation to the Human Rights Commission. This information was going to be our glitter of gold in the dust.

The session went on for nearly two hours — an omen we cautiously interpreted as encouraging. Our ambassadorial negotiating committee and Commander One and his staff waited anxiously for Norma and Ambassador Galán in the downstairs reception room.

The pair stormed in scowling. It was not unusual to see Norma return from the van making faces — she was always upset about something — but it was disheartening to see Ambassador Galán so riled. Norma threw a document — the government's position paper, it turned out — onto a coffee table and launched into a heated description of the meeting. Ricardo Galán joined her in a joint diatribe against the inanity of the session. Immediately, Commander One began muttering about cutting off the negotiations again. Everything was going to hell in a hand-basket.

It was hard not to be disappointed after I heard about what had gone on in the van. To Norma's and Ambassador Galán's dumbfounded surprise, the two delegates opened the session by arguing whether or not the terrorists had agreed to the participation of the OAS. Our demarches to the Foreign Minister had been all for naught. Zambrano and Jiménez also insisted that any invitation to the OAS would have to await the publication of a report by Amnesty International, the London-based, sometimes partisan, self-appointed guardian of human rights, which had visited Colombia prior to the takeover. Amnesty International's report, everyone suspected, would be highly critical of human rights violations and would damage President Turbay's credibility as a champion of democracy. Such a report, needless to say, would not be received hospitably.

Ambassador Galán was overwhelmed by Zambrano and Jiménez' position. He retorted sharply to both men; their position, he charged, was contrary to what the Foreign Minister had told him on the phone the day before. What was going on? What kind of tricks were they trying to pull? Zambrano and Jiménez were both startled by Ambassador Galán's sudden fury and they reacted defensively. Both sides bristled. Then Ambassador Galán corked it off by suggesting that because the Embassy takeover was an international matter, as the government was insisting, the government should exchange the foreign diplomatic hostages for Colombian cabinet ministers. Then they could futz around all they wanted. Even though I personally thought his proposal sounded like a grand idea, Zambrano and Jiménez were not amused.

Ambassador Galán felt gravely insulted by the Colombians' double-talk. He told them in no uncertain terms how he felt about the way they were handling the crisis. Even Norma was shocked, although pleased, by his violent response. When I spoke to President Turbay after my release, he told me the government negotiators had excused the Ambassador's behavior because they understood the strain he was under. Nonetheless, Ambassador Galán knew he was being patronized in the worst sort of way. He felt that Zambrano and Jiménez had implied he was insane or just totally incompetent. Until then, Ambassador Galán had been an important restraining influence in the negotiations. Norma often looked to him for help. Now his guiding influence was in jeopardy.

The Colombian delegates spent the rest of the session rehashing what they could and could not do judicially. Finally, as if to add insult to injury, they presented Norma with a position paper.

I picked up the discarded paper Norma had thrown rudely on the coffee table and read it while the terrorists caviled. I found one passage particularly intriguing:

It is hoped that the persons in whom you have special interest will be freed of any guilt in which case they could travel with you. But the Government of Colombia is not in a position to announce this because it can have no knowledge of who will be sentenced or absolved — even the judges cannot know this. Similarly, there does not exist a legal procedure which would permit some of the prisoners who are standing trial at courts martial to have announced to them beforehand the decision of the court, since this would be a juridical impossibility. The trial will end for all at the same time but obviously those individuals against whom charges are not formulated will be granted liberty…If a quick juridical, humanitarian, decorous departure is preferred, you could benefit from the Colombian Government's decision to invite the Red Cross,

Amnesty International, the Human Rights Commission of the OAS, etc., to observe the end of the courts martial…We are not interested in prolonging indefinitely the present situation since it is bad for the Colombian Government, for the country, for the hostages and for all.

The poor presentation by Zambrano and Jiménez had not only provoked violent reaction in Norma and Ambassador Galán, it threatened the existence of the negotiations themselves. Yet here in the position paper was a crack of light, and no one had noticed it.

"Now, just a minute," I interrupted. "Instead of getting excited about the atmospherics and the ability or lack thereof of the government negotiators, let's study the Colombian position paper, which strikes me as supremely interesting." I started to read the paper aloud, hoping this would calm everyone down. I pointed out that I thought it was a serious proposal worthy of consideration and should not be the cause of a rupture. Even if it wasn't exactly what they were looking for, it at least merited a counterproposal.

Commander One refused. "No," he said. "They're playing us for fools. The only thing they understand is violence." I was watching the faces of the staff, however, and I noticed they were listening attentively, so I poured it on.

"If I had presented this document as the representative of the Colombian government, I would have done so in such a way that you would have kissed my hand or carried me out of the van on your shoulders," I said. "I would have emphasized the difficulties in getting the Cabinet to agree on this magnificent offer which, while short of what was being requested, still permits an honorable settlement for both sides. Negotiators can't afford to be swayed by emotion and must only react to the substantive content of what is being discussed."

At that point the other ambassadors chimed in with other positive observations about the paper, and I felt the tide turn. After talking it over with the terrorists for an hour and a half, I started to believe we were back on track. As the terrorists withdrew from the room to discuss the matter privately, El Negro, the big, strapping Number Five, whispered to me, "You have to understand the Commander is a very emotional man. Don't worry. It looks good."

A couple of months later I argued the relative merits of Zambrano and Jiménez with President Turbay. While he insisted they had carried out his instructions to the letter and gave them a ninety percent effectiveness rating, he had to admit that, in this instance, they had bumbled the presentation. The President considered our interjection at this point crucial to the eventual success of the negotiations; he was glad we had taken the initiative.

The next day Commander One called everyone into the library and read us a counterproposal he had drafted during the night. Indeed, he had kept me awake pecking away at the typewriter on the table in the upstairs landing next to our bedroom. I couldn't believe my ears when

Commander One read his document. The tone of his counterproposal was so tough and rhetorical, such an ideological screed, that my first reaction was that he was playing it for effect.

It didn't take long for me to realize Commander One was entirely serious. He finished reading the counterproposal by ending with a flourish of slogans such as "Win or Die" and "With Weapons, With the People, Into Power." As the negotiating group proceeded dispiritedly down the stairs to phone our embassies, I fell alongside the Commander.

"You can't be serious with that," I said. "You've gone too far. Your paper isn't suitable for negotiation. You're only giving the government an opportunity to proclaim publicly that you're a bunch of barbarians, incapable of participation in serious dialogue. They'll use it as an excuse to cut off the negotiations."

The Commander surprised me by not reacting defensively. "Do you think you can do better?" he asked simply. I said yes, I could. The Brazilian and Mexican ambassadors made similar arguments. We tried to convince him it was possible to draft a counterproposal with the same demands and arguments they were using, but without resorting to a confrontational style. "Go ahead," the Commander challenged, "give us an alternative."

I called Frank Crigler and read him both the government's position paper and the guerrillas' counterproposal, knowing they were being automatically recorded. I asked Frank to have both documents typed and distributed to the Group of Fifteen. I told him of our plans to modify the terrorists' paper so that it would be more palatable.

Ambassador Nascimento e Silva immediately started an outline while Ambassador Galán began to draft the actual paper in impeccable Spanish. I checked the final product and made observations as we went along. The Nuncio limited himself to his perennial request for a negotiation of the ransom demands.

We had some fun drafting the document since we tried to include traditional diplomatic parlance: "The Jorge Marcos Zambrano Column of the M-19 presents its compliments to the negotiators of the Colombian Government and has the honor…" and so forth. (This reminded me of an occasional feature in the Foreign Service Journal. Carefully selected Hollywood stills are captioned with an appropriate Foreign Service phrase under the title, "Lives and Loves in the Foreign Service." I recalled a photograph of Douglas Fairbanks gleefully piercing the gut of a villain with his epée. The caption was the traditional closing line of a diplomatic note: "Accept, Excellency, the assurances of my highest consideration.")

Without my knowledge, however, Frank Crigler was checking with Washington for authorization to type and distribute the documents to the other governments in the Group of Fifteen. In turn, the State Department mulled over the question of whether it was correct for officers of the American Embassy to be distributing political documents without the official sanction of Colombia, particularly considering the "subversive nature" of the counterproposal. The boys in Washington, ever cautious, decided it was not fitting for Crigler to act as a clearinghouse and denied him permission to carry out my instructions. Crigler then turned over the documents to the Foreign Minister.

Meanwhile, I thought the job was being done. I had no way of knowing I'd been cut off at the knees. Our committee was operating under the false assumption that the delegates of the Group of Fifteen all had copies of the new working document and were informed about the current state of affairs. What had happened, in fact, was that my Embassy had left me in the lurch. The State Department's immediate interests did not appear to coincide with my own, so my request was overruled "out of larger considerations." The problem was that all of the other hostage-diplomats had been counting on the dissemination of the documents when in truth they were locked up in the Foreign Minister's drawer.

Friction between Frank and me developed rather rapidly. I didn't feel he was cooperating with me as he should have, and I felt him resist some of my instructions. I nearly lost my patience with him entirely when he objected to questions I'd posed to the Embassy's lawyer in which I was exploring the different legal possibilities of transferring the courts-martial cases to civilian jurisdiction. Since the courts-martial proceedings appeared to be the primary focus of the terrorists' objections to Colombian justice, the negotiating group discussed the various possibilities of undercutting their argument by promoting the remanding of such cases to civilian courts. It would have virtually eliminated the terrorists' principal complaint and, at the same time, would allow indicted terrorists to go free. There were other possibilities, but none of them was politically viable. We were probably naive even to think the Colombians would consider such a move, but we wanted to investigate the option nonetheless.

Frank was treading carefully, as Washington had instructed him to do, and he balked at the notion of tampering with the "hands-off" doctrine we had thus far adopted with the Colombians. Retrospectively it's hard for me to fault Frank because he was in such an awkward position. He was hung up in the ancient dichotomy between headquarters and the field — a cross every Foreign Service officer must bear. On the one hand, he had received a request from his immediate superior (me) to perform a strictly mechanical task — that of distributing essential information to the parties concerned. We, as hostages, considered this material joint property and believed it should be available to the principal governments. My request was neither difficult nor unreasonable; I hardly believed Frank had to check with Washington to do it. But when Frank referred my request to State, they told him not to proceed. As far as they were concerned, Asencio was being too activist. They wanted me to lean back, relax, and await developments. That role was for me plainly impossible if not suicidal.

Representatives in the field are usually convinced they're being second-guessed by a bunch of fatheads sitting in the comfort of Washington, far removed from the realities of the problem. The people in the Department of State are equally convinced that if they don't watch those clunkheads in the field who are so immersed in the problem, they will disregard policy and get everyone in trouble. A good Washington staff will make observations to the field-men but will not bind their hands on the sensible theory that the man in the field is in a better position to judge the dimensions of the problem he or she is facing. A good ambassador will not brook instructions from Washington that interfere with his ability to resolve what he is facing. Heated exchanges between embassies and State are not uncommon. In fact, some old-line ambassadors cannily wait for Washington to say something stupid so they can land on the culprit with both feet.

This state of affairs makes for bureaucrats who are wary of treading on ambassadorial toes. It also has the effect of damping instructions lest they provoke a reaction that makes them look bad. One of my mentors in this type of song and dance was Pete Vaky.

We had come to know each other when I was his Deputy Chief of Mission in Venezuela. Later, when he became the Assistant Secretary for Latin American Affairs after I became the Ambassador to Colombia, I called him to say I disagreed violently with one of his instructions and was in the process of drafting a telegram telling him to stick it in his ear. Unperturbed, Ambassador Vaky said, "You can't tell your boss that. What you do is draft a response saying that you're studying the instructions to determine whether it's applicable to the conditions in the field. Then you do whatever it is you wanted to do in the first place. In the day-to-day pressure of Washington, we always forget what it was we asked you to do anyway."

But in this case, much more was at stake than a disagreement over procedure. I had carefully explained to Frank that some of us ambassadors were working together closely, trying to find a formula for our release. We assumed our delegates were doing something analogous on the outside. I expected, however wrongly, complete cooperation and loyalty from my own staff. After all, it was my neck on the block.

When I found out that Frank had not carried through my orders, I got mad. When my colleagues found out that Washington had squelched my orders, they too started acting crazy. Ambassador Nascimento e Silva was particularly upset and began talking about cutting me off from the discussions and deliberations of the negotiating group to avoid being second-guessed by Washington. Fortunately, they didn't deliver on their threats because they realized they needed me, but I was *persona non grata* at a dangerous moment in our deliberations. From then on, however, we laboriously dictated all documents to a stenographer at the Mexican Embassy, who would then make copies for the Group of Fifteen. I had to do some fast talking to get them to send a copy to my own Embassy.

The entire episode left me hanging with my colleagues and could have provoked a negative reaction from Commander One. As it was, he found it amusing and referred to the incident as a good example of "capitalist perfidy." At that moment, I was rather inclined to agree with him.

Later, I cleared the air with Frank. I told him I had little confidence in the government's ability to spring me alive, so I had no intention of sitting around doing nothing while the world came down around my ears. Washington and I were on entirely different wavelengths. If I could think of a way out, then I would pursue it unhesitatingly. I told Frank I expected his help, and I wanted to make that clear to Washington. I was emphatic: they were playing around with my life, so they had no right to expect me to acquiesce to the point of becoming a vegetable. I tried to make amends with Frank because I knew I was contributing to the pressures and whipsawing he was subjected to by the Group of Fifteen, the Colombian government, and Washington. I still feel unkindly toward the Washington second-guessers and, although it would never have occurred to me to ask permission to reproduce the two documents, I'm sure they would not have dared send me such a message.

I did learn an important lesson as a result of all this: I knew I was putting my career on the line by speaking out and acting on my own behalf. I knew I was being aggressive, but I was more convinced than ever that an offense was better than a defense. Better alive and out of a job than dead with one.

President Turbay later tried to convince me I was off base and, at that particular point, he had feared for my state of mind. All I could say, and unsatisfactorily at that, was that you had to be there to understand.

After bringing our combined experience in negotiation skills to bear, we managed to draft a palatable counterproposal, which Commander One ultimately presented to Zambrano and Jiménez — but not until he salted our smooth prose with some of his revolutionary jargon. Otherwise, it followed closely the draft we had prepared. The polished document (see Appendix) listed what the terrorists had achieved in the psycho-political aspects of the publicity they had garnered, and endorsed the proposal for international organizations to come to Colombia in order to verify the fairness of the trials at La Picota Prison and to look into the human rights situation. The paper also contained, at our insistence, a paragraph that indicated the terrorists might be reasonable about ransom if assurances of substantial social investment were made by the government. In all, the counterproposal was a balanced document except for the continued insistence on the liberation of the M-19 High Command.

There was little doubt in my mind that the rewritten paper provided a sufficient basis for a settlement if there was goodwill on the part of the Colombian government and not just a tactical stall. Frank Crigler agreed. I hoped he wasn't saying so out of consideration for my feelings, I often found myself becoming suspicious of what my own people were telling me because I wasn't sure whether they were telling me the truth or were merely humoring me. On their part I'm sure they had similar doubts, never really certain if I were truly a free agent or if I was being coerced.

NINETEEN

The meeting during which Norma presented the M-19's revised position paper was probably the shortest negotiating session on record anywhere: it lasted a total of twelve minutes. Norma delivered the draft without any amenities; Zambrano and Jiménez had nothing to say in response other than that they would study the document and respond accordingly. Their brief encounter reminded me of the old double-talk line the physician gives the patient who is inquiring the status of his health: "You're as well as could be expected under the circumstances." On the surface it sounds good, but it is not a line one would want to study carefully.

What was unusual about the session, however, was the change in the *dramatis personae*. After Ambassador Galán reported to his government that he had been gravely insulted by Zambrano and Jiménez, Mexico City immediately withdrew him from the discussions. The other ambassadors followed suit and refused to substitute for him out of a sense of solidarity. My staff had already told me that the people at State didn't want me to assume Ambassador Galán's position under any circumstances. That left us in a quandary. The withdrawal of the Mexican Ambassador from the negotiating sessions was a major setback because he had developed a rapport with Norma. In effect, Ricardo Galán was our "inside man." Norma relied heavily on him in the van. By a series of prearranged signals, he would either discourage a particular point she was making or truncate unpromising lines of arguments. For all intents, Ambassador Galán was directing the terrorists' half of the negotiations, at least while inside the van. When Galán reported the results of a session, he was careful to give the terrorists an edited version. Later, he would give the members of the negotiating group the complete details.

The reason for the censorship was important. For private reasons of her own, Norma was anxious to quit the Dominican Embassy and end the crisis. We knew, even though her own comrades didn't, that she was much more forthcoming and flexible in her discussions with the government in the van than was apparent from her reports to Commander One. We developed theories about her unexplained urgency. One was that after a long, hard life in the underground as a subversive, she was anxious to start a new life abroad with her lover, Commander One. Another less likely theory suggested that Norma was suffering from an incurable cancer and wanted out of the "revolutionary struggle." Whatever the reason, we were glad for it and were careful not to jeopardize Norma by being too explicit about what had happened in the van.

Ambassadors Nascimento e Silva and Galán agreed with me that it was critical for us to get him back into the mainstream of the negotiations, so we agreed to ask the Mexican government to reconsider its decision. We also asked other governments to intervene on our behalf with the Mexican Foreign Ministry to pressure it to reverse its decision. Unfortunately, we couldn't tell our staffs why it was important to get the Ambassador back into the negotiations without betraying Norma to the other terrorists. If they found out what she was doing, at best she would be relieved from her duty as chief negotiator. At worst…we were afraid to guess what they might do to her, but it was certain to be more severe than assigning ideological exercises. I asked Frank Crigler to tell the Department of State of my request on an urgent basis and to make the point that it was important. Trust me, I was telling them. Trust me on this one.

We solved the immediate problem of replacing Ambassador Galán by asking the Peruvian Consul General, Alfredo Tejeda, to take his place. Mr. Tejeda is a bright, congenial man. His mobility was handicapped by a cumbersome ankle-to-thigh cast as a result of a recent knee operation; we always knew where he was in the building by the sound of his clomping gait. While Mr. Tejeda was not as experienced or sophisticated as Ambassador Galán, we believed in him enough to let him be the temporary replacement.

I recall thinking at the time that we were making distinct progress. The terrorists were listening to our arguments and accepting our advice. Omar had lost his rough edges somewhat; Norma seemed to be working on our behalf. Progress was slow but definite. Our living conditions had improved: from the original fifty-eight hostages we were down to twenty. We were in daily contact with our families and our governments, and the Red Cross did its best to keep us comfortable.

The terrorists, however, weren't convinced of the good intentions of the Colombians. They feared the military particularly, and they were certain the army had undue influence over the direction of the country. They fretted over the possibility of a *coup d'etat* and wondered what would happen to them if a military government took over while they were still inside the Embassy.

Political violence is chronic in Latin America. It is the "Age of Caudillos," and in the past fifty years there have been over a hundred successful revolutions in eighteen of the twenty Latin republics, and many more failed attempts. This constant turmoil has often resulted in massive social and economic upheaval as countries suffered countless coups, juntas, revolutions, and civil wars in attempts to realize a workable, stable political state.

Karl Marx once postulated that violence was "the midwife of every old society which is pregnant with the new," and the statistics for Latin America seem to reinforce that view, at least outwardly. Colombia has had some twenty-seven civil wars, one that took 80,000 lives and another, 100,000. Nonetheless, because of my own personal exposure to the government and military officers during the narcotics interdiction program, I believed we were dealing with the military organization most inclined to civilian rule in Latin America. There had been only one military regime in Colombia during this century, and that one lasted only three years. As far as I was concerned, the democracy was comparatively stable, but I wasn't above exploiting the terrorists' fears of an incipient military coup. I decided to see what kind of mileage I could get out of playing up the possibility.

I portrayed the Minister of Defense, Luis Carlos Camacho Leyva, as a cross between Attila the Hun and the bogeyman. Ambassador Galán took his cue and chimed in. The easiest way to stage a coup would be to provoke a massacre at the Embassy, he chided. A rash act by the terrorists could lead to the "probable consequence" of the government's collapse as a result of its ineffectual management of the crisis. With the government unable to weather the severe political repercussions, the military would be in the perfect position to make its move.

The terrorists were not amused; they were worried. Any strange noise or change in the rhythm of routine to which we had become accustomed upset them. They spooked easily and would respond by taking up defensive positions at the smallest disturbance. The terrorist sentries tried to stay alert and would often spot men they assumed to be sharpshooters taking up positions on nearby rooftops. Occasionally even we would be startled by men waving to us from contiguous buildings and suggesting by their gestures that we should try to make a break for it. With the periodic shootings and other unsettling noises that plagued us day and night, we were never sure ourselves what could happen.

I was never able to get used to the burst of automatic weapon-fire or the loud crashes out in the street in the middle of the night. Neither could the terrorists. We didn't know about President Turbay's orders to the military for a mandatory six-hour moratorium before reacting to any provocation, but I don't think knowing would have helped anyway. The fate of the terrorists and hostages in the Spanish Embassy in Guatemala, which burned to the ground with everyone still inside, was a constant bitter reminder of what could happen to us. Colombian troops are tough and proud. I knew they were seething at the ignominy of having a leftist faction which they had proclaimed "broken" come back and seize an embassy in their capital. Only the strict discipline of the President and the commanders kept the troops from "evening the score" at our expense.

We certainly gave the army enough excuses to attack the Embassy had they been more inclined to do so. There were several close calls — accidents, really — that could have triggered a violent response from the troops. One of the most hair-raising incidents happened between Jorge and his "revolutionary wife," Maria.

Jorge was one of the best educated, most personable of the terrorists. He was particularly friendly to me and often came to trade amicable arguments or just shoot the breeze. Mariá, a bright young psychology student, was a coquette. She appeared to be on intimate terms with others of the terrorists, including Omar, but she was primarily devoted to Jorge.

The two would retire to the bathroom to bathe together and have their less-than-discreet trysts. The bathroom was about the only place in the building where one (or two) could have a modicum of privacy, so we were used to the rub-a-dub antics of the terrorists. One afternoon, while Jorge was in the bathroom fooling around with Maria, his shotgun accidentally fired. I was close by and the explosion petrified me. The Egyptian Ambassador leapt three feet into the air, and the Venezuelan Ambassador nearly collapsed. The Nuncio remained remarkably calm. I thought the shot was an accident almost immediately, but I was afraid it was the signal the army had been waiting for. Once I found some strength in my legs, I intercepted Alfredo, Number Seven, who was running here and there with everyone else, trying to figure out what had happened. Jorge and María emerged from the bathroom shaken: the shot had smashed the washbasin and ricocheting pellets had hit María in the hand. She held her bleeding hand outward and smiled sheepishly. Jorge explained what had happened. I urged Alfredo to use his walkie-talkie to inform the soldiers outside so they wouldn't make their own wrong interpretations. The Nuncio suggested we call the Foreign Minister to explain, but that didn't make sense to me; the army was outside and the Foreign Minister was miles away. Jorge and María were upset and didn't know what to do.

Ambassador Galán, fortunately, had the presence of mind to react quickly. He had been in the kitchen with the Ambassador from Brazil. When he found out what had happened, he ran to the front door, put on his most winning smile and nonchalant manner, and talked hard and fast to convince the troops that everything was fine, just a little accident. The army unit commander blustered a bit, but he eventually calmed down and returned to his business. There were a couple of minutes however, when I was sure the world was going to come crashing down around us.

A few days later we went through another traumatic heart-stopper. Most of the terrorists enjoyed themselves hugely carrying their guns and hand grenades and waving them around. I often found myself looking down the barrel of a gun, not purposely but accidentally. Gun safety was totally alien to them. They would walk around with their .45's cocked and would occasionally drop them. I never understood why there weren't more misfires.

The terrorists, particularly the women, wore hand grenades hanging from their belt loops. As one of the women was walking up the spiral staircase that led from the downstairs reception rooms to the bedrooms upstairs, one of her grenades tore away from her belt loop. I watched in sheer terror as the grenade bumped down the staircase step by step with a sickening thud-thud-thud until it hit the bottom stair and rolled clumsily to a stop. It was an incredibly ugly sound. Those of us nearby were soaked in sweat as we awaited the explosion.

After the longest seconds in my life, there was an explosion of laughter from the top of the steps. The terrorist woman thought the expressions on our faces were hilarious and roared. She retrieved the grenade and explained that it couldn't explode unless the pin was pulled: we weren't in any danger. Weak-kneed with relief, we shuffled away, expressing our gratitude in silent prayer. It wasn't funny then, and it still isn't funny.

Ambassador Lovera continued to deteriorate physically and emotionally to the point that he started babbling incoherently in our meetings with Commander One. After every incident I could see the devastating effect on him. At daily Mass Ambassador Lovera usually gave the first reading, and it was painful and piteous to watch him falter, lose his place in the missal, and fumble to find it. The contrast between this changed man and the vital and lively man I had respected and admired was one of the most difficult experiences of my captivity. He was shattered and resorted to alcohol and drugs. He became dependent on a daily diet of tranquilizers and sleeping pills, which he got from Ambassador Mallol, himself a doctor and something of a hypochondriac.

When we found Ambassador Lovera drinking his mouthwash, we began to worry about him seriously. His blood pressure continued to fluctuate erratically, and his dizzy spells kept him in a constant state of physical uncertainty.

La Doctora was also concerned for him. She knew she had to stop him from abusing drugs and alcohol so she searched his belongings and confiscated all his medication and his bottle of Listerine. In the future, she told Ambassador Lovera, if he wanted any medication, he would have to come to her. She also moved the Dominican Ambassador out of the same room so he wouldn't be tempted to prescribe any more medication. Slowly Mr. Lovera recovered some of his feistiness and stamina, although it would be some time before he returned to his former self.

Ambassador Lovera was not the only case. Other ambassadors were showing visible signs of strain. After La Doctora finished moving around the hostages, we also asked that the Venezuelan Consul General be moved out since he no longer needed to tend to his Ambassador. Once this was done, we were down to eight prisoners in the same room and had got rid of a virtuoso snorer. The Nuncio decided to move his foam-rubber bed to the space left vacant by the Consul since five of us were jammed against the front wall.

The Swiss Ambassador, Jean Bourgeois, had received huge quantities of food, wine, and beer from home, which he hoarded in boxes placed around his pallet. From his corner, he was gradually squeezing the Egyptian Ambassador toward Bishop Acerbi, who in turn squeezed the Israeli Ambassador. The domino effect had me mercilessly jammed into the opposite corner of the room. Since my bed began to fold in the middle as a result of this multilateral encroachment, I had to make a passionate plea to my bunkmates. The Nuncio then took the opportunity to move his camp to give us more space and to accommodate the creeping Swiss. Unfortunately for Acerbi, since Ambassador Lovera was no longer heavily drugged, he made an irritable bunkmate and would jostle the Nuncio in the middle of the night to keep him from snoring or get up and start talking to the sentries nearby. It wasn't long before the Nuncio returned to our side of the room. It might have been overcrowded, but it was quiet.

The Swiss Ambassador, however, was in a world of his own. He was often the butt of jokes about Swiss imperialism because of his sprawling territory of foodstuffs and wine, but the jokes were often lost on him because he was hard of hearing and didn't speak Spanish very well. Surrounded by his empire, he spent hour after hour playing solitaire. He apparently had insomnia because he would be sitting up in the middle of the night, chain-smoking cigarettes. In the morning he would give himself an alcohol sponge-bath under his bedclothes. He would then change clothes, go to the bathroom, and return to his corner as part of his rigid ritual. The only times he moved were when someone opened a bottle of wine and offered him some, or whenever someone offered to play Chinese Checkers with him. His passivity and withdrawal became his defense against the hard-edged realities around him. From time to time I briefed Ambassador Bourgeois on the status of the negotiations, but otherwise he kept entirely to himself.

At the beginning of the takeover, Ambassador Bourgeois had been openhanded and generous with his wealth of provisions. But as time passed, I noted a change in his attitude, and I began to worry if he would go the way of the Uruguayan Ambassador, Mr. Gómez. He had, in fact, been stopped from escaping during the early days of capture when he was spotted by one of the sentries as he crawled out of a second-story bathroom window. One of the terrorist women later told us that she'd heard Ambassador Bourgeois' wife object to his sharing with us.

We watched Ambassador Bourgeois with amusement as he furtively dug into his private stocks. He would scrunch down on his foam-rubber pad and — pfft! — lift the flip top of a beer can and sip from it surreptitiously. This aroused the devilish and mischievous character in some of the hostages who would then ostentatiously open a bottle of wine and share it conspicuously with everyone except him. It was a cheap shot really, and I suggested to my colleagues that sharing and generosity were their own rewards and not necessarily subject to reciprocity. I have to admit though, I did get a kick out of it. A couple of other ambassadors scowled and said he deserved it. Maybe they were right because Ambassador Bourgeois came around and again began to share. I will never forget, however, the look on his face when we poured ourselves wine and left him saddened, even though he had enough of his own wine and beer to open a liquor store.

TWENTY

On Easter Sunday, April 6, we celebrated Mass with great pomp; no congregation was ever more sincere and intent on cleansing their slightly soiled souls. And on Easter Sunday, Commander One released virtually the last of the non-diplomatic hostages. They included the Honorary Jamaican Consul General, a Colombian Foreign Ministry official, and the M-19's suspected inside man, Tito Livio. We gathered at the windows and wistfully waved goodbye as the released men push-started their cars once they found the batteries dead. The Colombian police, suspicious of Livio because of what turned out to be a lurid past, were waiting for him and picked him up the moment he hit the street, interrogated him, and subsequently deported him as an undesirable. The press then reported he had been arrested by the Dominican police when he arrived in Santo Domingo. It was later disclosed that Livio had contracted gonorrhea while he was inside the Embassy.

That fascinating bit of news brought all kinds of horror stories to mind. Had Livio been sleeping with one of the terrorist women? If so, which one? Renata? La Doctora? One rumor suggested Livio had not been having sex with any of the women; that his lover, in fact, was a male — a member of the Dominican Embassy staff. This theory gained considerable credence several months after the Dominican Consul had been released as a hostage. Mr. Sanchez, a smallish man with a mustache, murdered the newly appointed Dominican Ambassador, Eduardo García, supposedly after an argument over Mr. Sanchez's wife. Apparently, however, the Dominican Consul was more incensed by the Ambassador's snide comment about his sexual proclivities than about his wife's honor, so he pulled a revolver and shot his Ambassador dead. Worse, Mr. Sanchez dragged his body out of the house and tried to make the homicide look like the result of a robbery. He botched the ruse so badly the police immediately saw through the charade. Mr. Sanchez was protected by the conventions of diplomatic immunity, so all the Colombians could do was ask that he be recalled by his government.

I had been mildly suspicious of the Consul, Mr. Sanchez, when Commander One released him early for his "good behavior." I had suspected him as being one of the snitches, but now, I wonder if his involvement wasn't more pernicious. In the tiny Dominican Embassy he would have had to interact constantly with Tito Livio. There was also an unsubstantiated charge that his Ambassador, Mr. Mallol, had been ordered by his government to fire Livio the month before the takeover, but had failed to execute his order. Had the order been intentionally stalled? And if so, by whom? Why was the order to fire Livio given in the first place?

I also couldn't help wondering if the Embassy had sent Livio to the local precinct station to request police protection for the reception. If Livio had been assigned the task, had he in fact gone to the station house at all? All these questions were open to speculation. The answers were not forthcoming, but few of us doubted that Livio was the key man. I suspect the entire story will never be known about him. I found Livio to be a seedy little man, polite to the point of being obsequious. I don't know what will become of him, and I'm glad I didn't know he had gonorrhea while he was working in the kitchen.

Inside, the remaining hostages benefited from the reduction in our resident population. We were down to a critical core of fewer than twenty hostages. Access to the bathrooms became reasonable. Housekeeping chores became less onerous even though we had lost most of our amateur chefs. (This caused President Turbay to remark that it confirmed his suspicion that diplomats were much better at consuming food than preparing it.) As soon as a hostage left us, we would snap up his foam-rubber pad and whatever other treasures he left behind. We became a roving pack of scavengers ever ready to pirate anything to make our lives easier or more comfortable.

There were two hostages, however, who were offered their freedom but refused it. Both were Colombians. One man was the freelance photographer, Luis Guzmán, always taking his blasted candids. The other man was an even stranger bird and something of a celebrity in diplomatic circles.

Luis Valencia is the quintessential gate-crasher of Bogotá — the king of all of them in a city where gate-crashing has been elevated to the status of art. Valencia is the most infamous of the twenty-five or so professional *lagartos* in the capital city who sidle their way uninvited into the nearly three hundred yearly receptions at the embassies. Warren Hoge of The New York Times caricatured *lagartos* perfectly: "They pomade their hair, swing tightly rolled bumbershoots with practiced nonchalance and live off a diet of baby corns, cocktail sausages and freshly shucked prawns washed down with highballs." Valencia tried to justify himself by claiming to be the editor of a sometime magazine, *Le Monde Diplomatique*, which published with extreme irregularity.

One *Bogotana*, a woman whose husband and father had been ambassadors, vividly recalled Valencia's uncanny ability to crash even the most private affair. Valencia managed to get into her parents' fiftieth wedding anniversary party, which included among its few guests the President of Colombia. Security was strict, yet Valencia managed to get by the guard by telling him he was an executive of the hotel in which the reception was being held. "I looked up," she recalled with a sense of awe for Valencia's talent, "and there he was standing next to the President."

Daniel Samper wrote a column for *El Tiempo* in which he lampooned the *lagarto*: "Do you give society photographers cigarettes and address them with the familiar '*tu*'?...Have you attended at least three burials of people you never knew personally?...Do you send a telegram to each embassy on its national day?...Do you leave friends with the message, 'If the Minister calls, tell him I had to go'?" If you do any of these things, you qualify as a *lagarto*. Valencia attended any diplomatic gathering he was not forcibly ejected from. He was so well known that many diplomats considered a party incomplete if he wasn't there. It surprised no one then, when Valencia turned up as one of our group.

Falling back on his presumed profession as a journalist, Valencia took copious notes on the day-to-day affairs of the mission in the hopes of putting together a story.

Ambassador Galán loved to tease Valencia. He would say, "Valencia, you know you're going to be in trouble once we get out of here. The military is going to wonder why you didn't go when you had the chance, and you know their reputation for rough questioning."

Valencia whimpered, "But Ambassador, I'm a journalist, and the press corps would intervene for me. They can't do anything to me."

Ambassador Galán chuckled and said, "Don't be silly. They won't even know you're missing." With that, Valencia rolled his eyes and ran from the room.

Not long afterward, the Ambassador from Mexico began a crusade at the request of his special delegate to ask Commander One to evict both Guzmán and Valencia. The Group of Fifteen objected to their refusal to leave the Embassy and claimed they were the source of distasteful stories appearing in the yellow press. Ambassador Galán circulated a petition, which most hostages signed. When the Peruvian Consul General refused to sign the petition on the grounds that he was "without instructions" — polite diplomatic parlance for refusing to do something because your government has not specifically ordered you to do it — Ambassador Galán became outraged. Even when Galán retorted with the solid argument that, since the Group of Fifteen had requested the expulsion of Guzmán and Valencia (and Peru was a member of that group), that was plenty of "instruction." Still, Mr. Tejeda refused to sign. His real reason, I suspect, was that he didn't want to hurt the two men's feelings. Ambassador Galán stalked to the phone and called the Peruvian Ambassador to tell him the Consul no longer had our confidence and should be withdrawn from negotiating.

As a result of the squabble between Ambassador Galán and Mr. Tejeda, I realized how much the infighting and parochial bickering were affecting our judgment. As hostages we were becoming increasingly hostile to one another. Solidarity was breaking down. I tried to assure Mr. Tejeda and his friends that the issue should be settled after we got out, and that we should concentrate more on getting out than playing politics for no gain. I was only partially successful. Ambassador Galán also remained adamant despite our pleas for unity and calm. Several of us lobbied for an end to the backbiting, but grudges are difficult to overcome, especially in captivity. Emotions and reactions become exaggerated. We spent many unproductive hours smoothing ruffled feathers.

We solved the short-term problem of having a hostages' representative attend future negotiation sessions with Norma when Ambassador Lovera ordered his Consul General to replace Tejeda. But it was painfully apparent that it took us progressively more time to get anything done than when we were ambitious and aggressive at the beginning of the siege. We were fighting time and each other. We were barely controlling the urge to throw up our hands in disgust and crawl into a corner to wait until it was over, one way or another.

The arrival of Armin J. Kobel sidetracked our concerns for the moment. Kobel, a Swiss, was a high-level representative of the International Red Cross who wanted to talk to us and see what he could do to make our captivity more tolerable. He seemed a fine, upstanding, do-gooder type — all cheer and bustle. We were always ready for any visitor, so we greeted him as a welcome distraction.

Kobel's officiousness was mitigated by an underlying compassion for our predicament. He gave us a rather sonorous summary of his charter — to see to our well-being and comfort — and then met with us individually.

I asked Kobel privately to get involved in the negotiations because we were in danger of being whipsawed by internal political factors. The Teheran crisis was providing the Colombians with a perfect cover to give more weight to issues of political expediency rather than to the safe release of the hostages. I told Kobel that the important issue was not the juridical framework but that some of the politically unpalatable actions the President might have to take, such as remanding the courts-martial to civilian justice, lifting the state of siege, or accelerating the courts-martial proceedings, could be politically costly. I urged Kobel to bring up humanitarian concern for the hostages. We, as people, were getting lost in the shuffle.

Although Mr. Kobel politely took extensive notes during our conversation, he finally told me he wasn't in a position to intervene. All he was authorized to do was to see what he could do to improve our conditions. Later, one of the wags on my staff parodied our conversation:

KOBEL: How about a Ping-Pong table?

ASENCIO: Splendid, but the important thing is to help get us out of here.

KOBEL: Do you think you'd like a video cassette machine?

ASENCIO: Yes, but you should really try to get us out of here.

KOBEL: What about some new games?

ASENCIO: No! Listen, what we want to do is get the hell out of here!

Frank Crigler had told me that Kobel was a psychologist and was going to observe us to determine how we were holding up under stress. We joked among ourselves on how best to be declared insane so we could get out of the Embassy. My idea was voted best: I would insist to Kobel that I loved our confinement, that I was very comfortable and no, I really didn't want to leave. But after María, a psychology major, went to talk with Kobel to trade insights, she came back and told us Kobel wasn't a psychologist at all: he was an economist!

We asked Mr. Kobel to look in on his compatriot, Ambassador Bourgeois. He hadn't said more than a few words in the last several days and his immobility and withdrawal had us worried. Kobel sought Ambassador Bourgeois out and talked with him in French for a while. When he reported to the negotiating group, he said, "Look, you don't understand. He's all right. He's just Swiss."

Despite Kobel's glib response, the Swiss Ambassador's behavior was not normal. Those hostages who remained physically and mentally active fared much better than those who withdrew and became passive. The latter, in many cases, became virtual vegetables while those who helped in the negotiations, worked hard at their chores and at providing leadership, and tried to exercise on a regular basis, were in better all-around shape than when they first walked into the Dominican Embassy. I also noticed that those hostages who already had serious personal problems suffered more in confinement than those with secure families and jobs.

Kobel was also pressured by the ambassadorial negotiating group as a whole. We pressed him to help us get Ambassador Galán back into the van as the hostages' representative. Frank Crigler had already told me that the State Department had refused to intervene with the Mexican Foreign Office, presumably because it felt that the conduct of the negotiations was the responsibility of the Colombian government and no one else. The State Department didn't want the hostages, as representatives of other governments, to intervene or dilute that responsibility. I had asked Frank to express my objections to the State Department and to request reconsideration: it was applying absolute concepts to a complex situation it didn't fully understand. I told Frank to convince Washington that there were good and sufficient reasons for me to want Ambassador Galán back in the van, and that these reasons weren't just theoretical but eminently practical.

My demarche and request for the State Department people to trust me didn't go entirely unheeded. They replied that while they weren't ready to change their minds yet, they would entertain further argument. But I couldn't tell them my reasons for my passionate request while everyone and his mother was listening in on the telephones. All I could do was insist it was important, practical, and that they would have to trust me.

But with Kobel we had a chance to get the real story out in confidence. Ambassador Galán and I told Kobel about the extraordinary rapport between him and Norma. Ambassador Galán was exerting a critical moderating influence on the negotiations through her. I asked Kobel to relay the information to Frank so he could pass it on to the State Department, but Ambassador Nascimento e Silva objected violently. He reminded everyone of the incident of the dictated documents that Crigler had refused to distribute to the Group of Fifteen after receiving instructions from State not to get involved. Ambassador Nascimento e Silva felt that passing along this kind of sensitive information to the United States was dangerous. We had no way of knowing what use might be made of the information. We were jeopardizing our only ace in the hole, and we might be endangering Norma's life, he cautioned. We should proceed with more care. After some heated debate, we finally agreed that Kobel should approach only the Mexican Special Delegate of the Group of Fifteen.

I don't know if Kobel ever did this or, if he did, whether it made any difference. I got the distinct impression at my meeting with Kobel that he didn't understand many of the nuances of our dilemma and was determined to stick to his work of looking after our material comfort without getting involved in the larger issues. In any case, Ambassador Galán never returned to the negotiating van. Our effort deadened in failure again, which was a shame, because even if Ambassador Galán's return had shortened our captivity by one day, it would have been worth it. He might have been able to accomplish considerably more.

The only tangible result of Kobel's visit was an improvement in the quality of our meals. After he saw our kitchen and eating arrangements, he had box lunches delivered to us by the Colombian Red Cross. These were prepared by the caterers who service the Colombian national airline, Avianca. He had the Foreign Ministry underwrite the cost. At $2.88 per meal, it wasn't exactly gourmet fare. The meals usually consisted of a lump of mashed potatoes and a scoop of white rice with some nondescript and sometimes unidentifiable meat in the middle. Still, these meals relieved the tedium of scullery work and the often bizarre meals cooked by our indifferent chefs. The terrorists were suspicious of the food for fear it might be drugged, so they refrained from joining us. After having eaten those box lunches, I'm not sure the terrorists weren't right.

TWENTY-ONE

I looked forward to the tenth negotiating session. The government had enough time to study our revised counterproposal and respond to it. As far as I was concerned, the negotiation that day would be the acid test of the true nature of the Colombians' intentions. They would have to reveal themselves: no longer could they balk or duck, no longer could they sing songs or dance around the issues with well-coordinated delays. After more than forty days we had taken all the play out of the negotiations. We were now toe to toe, head to head. The terrorists' position was forthright and unambiguous; it was time for the Colombian government to do the same.

I understood the danger inherent in calling the Colombians' bluff; but the agonized game of second-guessing, coupled with uncertainty and suspicion, was too much to play any longer. We needed a concrete response, even if it was negative, so at least we knew where we stood and could reconcile ourselves to our fate. As it was we were in purgatory — the vestibule of Hell — but from time to time we would glimpse flashes of salvation only to have them occluded by the sinister machinations of the Colombians. Impatiently, I waited for Norma to return from the van. I held my breath and willed, as hard as I could, good news.

In the meantime I got hold of Frank Crigler and asked him to cable the American Embassy in London in order to have them urge Amnesty International to complete its report on Colombia so we wouldn't have another needless delay. I didn't expect Amnesty International's report to favor the Colombian government even though A.I. had originally come to Colombia at President Turbay's invitation. That previous January, a doctor working as part of the investigating team charged the army with harassment while he was in Bogotá. Dr. Edmundo Garcia claimed the army had placed taps on his phones and had agents watching the rooms in which he had been interviewing Colombians who alleged to have been tortured. García was quoted in the press as saying, "Our interviews with people who are making accusations of human rights violations are controlled by secret police agents." It wasn't clear whether the army was trying to intimidate the doctor or the people who were risking their security by visiting him. In any case, I assumed Amnesty International's report would be embarrassing to the government and only add fuel to the fire.

Then Norma returned to the Embassy. She wasn't exactly exuberant but she wasn't angry either. She briefed us. The government negotiators seemed to be saying that those prisoners against whom charges were not going to be pressed at the Picota trials could leave the country with Commander One. The other prisoners that were going to be bound over for trial would have the watchful eye of the OAS Human Rights Commission to look out for them. The Commission had been invited; Norma confirmed that. Zambrano and Jiménez implied that a limited number of prisoners being held by the military might be released in the near future, and the promise of fair trials would almost certainly result in freedom for an even greater number. After their release from Picota, the Human Rights Commission would then guarantee their safe conduct out of the country if they wished.

The Colombians made no outright guarantees, but the timbre of their negotiating song had clearly changed. We were no longer pushing air back and forth — there was substance in their offer. The fine points would have to be hammered out on the anvil of the negotiating table, but we now had the metal to shape.

Commander One was pleased within his limited context. He was always looking for the splendiferous solution which he expected to erupt full-blown like the phoenix from its ashes. But he was slowly learning the lesson of statesmanship; that solutions do not generate spontaneously but rather have to be cultivated from seed. He was also learning that his seeds did not have the germ of revolution.

We had a long talk with Commander One after the negotiating session so we could feel out his response and guide it accordingly. He insisted that four agencies monitor the trials: the International Red Cross, Amnesty International, the OAS, and Vásquez Carrizosa's Colombian Human Rights Commission. He would, however, negotiate on the number and composition of the group if need be, he confided. The Commander was trying to gain as much leverage as he could. He also proposed a rather screwy idea that the government should grant amnesty to the terrorists at large who were being tried *in absentia*. I told him I doubted any terrorist would come out of hiding to join our group on the way out of the country.

Our ambassadorial group then drafted another paper outlining the salient points we felt Norma needed to make to the government in the next session. We wanted to leave as little to chance as possible and didn't want Norma to make any impromptu demands that could suddenly jam the works. We weren't exactly rolling, but at least we had overcome initial inertia and were moving slowly toward reconciliation. Any small obstruction could bring the whole sensitive apparatus to a dead halt again, and we obviously wanted to avoid that. So we structured the terrorists' thinking and responses as much as they would allow us.

The major question in my mind was whether the Colombians could or would come up with four or five M-19 prisoners and not press charges against them. Since Colombian justice is notoriously slow, it would be a matter of sheer will on President Turbay's part to see the plan through, provided of course, that he wanted to see it through. I was certain such a token number would mean at least a symbolic victory for the M-19 and allow them to end the crisis quickly.

The next negotiating session went smoothly, and being on the heels of what I thought had been productive talks on the day before, I believed we were making significant progress. The government's representatives agreed to look into the possibility of accelerating the determination of those prisoners eligible for release. Neither did they quibble with the Commander's suggestion that the other humanitarian agencies sit in on the trials with the OAS — except for Vásquez Carrizosa's organization, which they objected to on political grounds. Most important of all, both sides agreed that two private negotiators could visit the Embassy and begin ransom negotiations. Optimism began to soar again, and although I wasn't sure I was justified in doing so, I did my best to fan the hopes of hostage and terrorist alike.

Many of the hostages conjectured wildly about the direction of the talks. Some — the perpetual optimists — thought we were certain to get out quickly since the basic terms were in the process of being met, while others — the perpetual pessimists — cast a jaundiced eye on the proceedings and reminded the others that nothing really substantive had been agreed upon so far, at least not in the immediate future. The middle road had yet to be found.

Our restlessness continued to increase. We saw light in the distance, but was it really the light at the end of the long, dark tunnel or just another illusion? Once you learn to become suspicious of hope and wait for it to justify itself, it takes a heavy psychic toll.

I could see a concentration-camp mentality developing among us. Individuals once gregarious, became crabbed and mean, withdrawn. On one occasion, the Guatemalan Ambassador, Aquiles Pinto Flores, urgently requested Commander One to let him make an important phone call. The phone was in a room where the negotiating group was calling our embassies about the course of negotiations and giving instructions on a particularly sensitive point we wanted our governments to pursue. The Commander interrupted us in the middle of making our reports so the Guatemalan could make his emergency call. As we stood around him wondering what was wrong, he called his home and asked that two ham sandwiches be sent for him in the next Red Cross shipment. We were startled but not really surprised. Our "united front" was disintegrating and each person started looking out for number one.

The problem as a whole came to a head with the great champagne controversy. The incident might have been funny if it wasn't for the savage undercurrent of fear and resentment that prompted it. The incident happened one evening while I was in conference with the Mexican and Brazilian ambassadors to prepare for a session with Commander One. In the middle of our concentration, the Costa Rican Consul General burst into the room with the expression of a man who'd just had his gold teeth stolen. He was a veteran of twenty years of Colombian politics. Mr. Blanco Solis was an elderly, mild-mannered habitué of the city's diplomatic cocktail circuit and had been chargé d'affaires for most of my tour in Colombia. He had distinguished himself to date as one of the most passive of the hostages and had devoted himself almost exclusively to eating and drinking. The word among the hostages was that it was dangerous to be in his way when lunch was served. Mr. Blanco barged into our meeting and announced without any introduction, "You're conducting yourselves very poorly." He then turned to Ambassador Galán and spat, "I've had forty-four years of diplomatic experience, and you're nothing but a snot-nosed kid."

We were surprised by his outburst. Once I regained my composure, I told Mr. Blanco that if he ever got out of the Embassy alive, he would owe a great deal to that "snot-nosed kid." The Costa Rican continued to rant, shouting that he wasn't just speaking for himself but for the rest of the hostages as well. With that he spun on his heels and stomped out of the room.

We were confounded. We were in deep trouble if we didn't have the backing of our own colleagues. We reviewed our strategies and tried to figure out where we'd gone wrong. It was obvious, I said, that we weren't being effective in our briefings with the others. Someone suggested we call a general meeting and have it out as far as our aims and purposes were concerned. This opportunity would give the others a chance to air their grievances and us the chance to present our case for our actions.

Ambassador Barak, listening to the whole brouhaha, offered "to scout the terrain," so we dispatched him to collect some preliminary intelligence. He came back five minutes later, chortling. "You and your tactics and strategy," he scoffed at me. The real problem had to do with a case of champagne the French Ambassador had sent earlier in the day. Our fellow diplomats were sure we were sitting by ourselves guzzling the champagne without sharing it with them.

So we solved the problem by hauling the case into the other room and dropping it on the floor with two words of advice: "Shove it!" Some of our colleagues were mortified by the incident and sheepishly told me they had nothing to do with the "rebellion." Others said nothing and took advantage of the windfall and drank the champagne.

I sensed the fractures between the hostages growing wider, and it troubled me because I didn't know how to counteract this disruptive influence. More and more energy was being spent on lesser and lesser things. Time was destroying us.

TWENTY-TWO

A new phase of negotiations was inaugurated when Victor Sasson and José Manuel Rivas Sacconi arrived at the Embassy to start ransom discussions with Commander One. Our morale perked up because we believed we might be entering the home stretch. Our prospects seemed bright. The Nuncio was beside himself with joy because his fondest wish was at long last being realized.

I already knew Victor Sasson, the sales manager of one of Colombia's largest textile mills and a widely respected civic leader. He is a super-salesman and one of the best private negotiators in Latin America; he is shrewd, tenacious, yet charming. I felt a profound sense of relief when I embraced Victor as he came trooping into the Dominican Embassy. He introduced me to Rivas Sacconi, a former Foreign Minister and a fine old gentleman whose role was to act as the political front man while Victor conducted the actual financial negotiations. We were never to be privy to their tête-à-têtes with Commander One, but I had faith in their abilities to strike a practical yet amicable deal with the terrorists. Later, when I telephoned Nancy, I told her I trusted Victor implicitly and hoped she would extend him that same consideration.

Norma went into the negotiating session confident of progress. Zambrano and Jiménez officially agreed to allow an International Red Cross representative to visit Colombian prisons and hospitals as part of a collaborative effort to improve institutional conditions. They also answered Commander One's demand for increased social investment by foxily pointing out the government planned to spend 600 billion pesos in various social programs in the near future.

Encouraged by their cooperation, Norma decided to test the water by bringing up the prisoner issue again. But here Zambrano and Jiménez balked. The man tactlessly blamed the defense attorneys for creating delays in the judicial process and suggested the terrorists try to coordinate their efforts with the defense counsels themselves. The ploy was an awkward sidestep. The government just did not want to release anyone, blackmail or no.

Then Norma shocked Zambrano by asking permission for her people to contact the number two man of the M-19 in La Picota, Felipe González. Norma said she would ask the defense attorneys to speed up the proceedings through González; after all, it had been their own suggestion.

No one really believed the government would allow Norma or Commander One to talk directly with González, yet here was Norma firmly pushing the issue. The only workable alternative was to have an intermediary — Armin Kobel, the Swiss from the Red Cross, was proposed — to relay the messages between the M-19 in the Embassy and González in jail. Zambrano and

Jiménez moved cautiously because they were suspicious of Norma's ulterior motives, but they finally agreed to have Kobel deliver a personal tape-recorded message to González at the Picota.

I could imagine the government's initial reaction when they heard Norma's request. The Foreign Ministry must have choked. I'm certain they worried that proposal to death and regretted agreeing to allow any communication with the M-19 High Command. To their credit however, they chanced the calculated risk in hopes of breaking the logjam.

That evening, while I was lying on my foam-rubber pad, I mulled over Norma's proposal. While getting in touch with González might make sense, there was still a slim chance the government might come up with a couple of prisoners who could leave the country with Commander One. Prudence demanded an alternative to blowing up the Embassy or having the army attack; we needed a middle ground on which we could overcome this relentless seesawing. We had accomplished too much to revert to a zero-sum game now. If contacting González could offer that new alternative, then it was worth exploring.

The new alternative could take the form of a guarantee assuring the M-19 that some of their comrades would, in fact, be released according to the promises made by the government. If Commander One could accept such a guarantee, then we wouldn't have to wait for the torturously slow wheels of justice to turn — we could all go home and await the results in safety. The guarantee itself would have to be valid and believable so Commander One could accept the notion comfortably.

I thought out a plan how I might accomplish this neat trick without compromising the confidence of the terrorists. The guarantee could be established by two or three attorneys the M-19 trusted. The lawyers themselves could be chosen by Enriquito Santos through the left-wing political organization FIRMES. These lawyers could then examine the record and, based on the promise of a fair trial, give Commander One a written opinion that would project which prisoners should be absolved and released. If the Commander worried about the Colombians' reneging on their promises, then the lawyers' opinions could be published in the press.

I tried the rudimentary idea on Ambassador Galán as he lay on the pallet next to me. Like two conspirators, we discussed the idea in whispers in the dark. I worried about the delicate way we would have to present the idea to the Commander. We couldn't afford to alienate him so he might provoke reprisals; we had to present the idea strongly enough at least to get him thinking. From our view, the actual form of the guarantee wasn't important — the details could be hashed out between Norma and the government negotiators. What we had to do was make the Commander believe he had completed his mission so he could leave the Embassy feeling a winner. Our argument was akin to the story of the dirty old man who asked the beautiful young woman if she would sleep with him for a million dollars. Once she said yes, it was only a matter of figuring out a realistic price.

As Ambassador Galán and I toyed with the idea, we grew progressively more excited. The plan was a long shot, but we had other forces working for us. Timing was becoming critical as the Teheran crisis worsened. Commander One *wanted* a way out of this maze. He now knew that the labyrinth of false trails and *culs-de-sac* was the home turf of the Minotaur, and that the Minotaur was indeed stalking him. Arm to arm, the best he could hope for was martyrdom. He was like Theseus; only his wits could guide him past the pitfalls that awaited him. The Commander had shown willingness to accept guarantees already, so if we could make this one attractive to the terrorists, we might be able to finesse our way out of captivity. Ricardo and I whispered through the night, hoping to create an offer the Commander could not refuse.

The next morning we were drained but enthusiastic as we tried out our idea on Commander One and Norma. They listened thoughtfully. I also lobbied the other terrorists before they met as a whole to discuss our proposal. I wanted to make sure the more moderate terrorists had the full benefit of my thinking rather than hearing it secondhand.

Our lobbying paid off: Commander One gave us the go-ahead. Our telephone squad took to the lines and called our embassies to push the plan. The stage was set for compromise. Norma made a formal presentation in the van the next day. We had done all we could and felt good about it as we sat back, sweetly exhausted, and awaited the Foreign Minister's response.

Meanwhile, Sasson and Rivas Sacconi were meeting with the Commander to talk about money. In contrast to the awkward, cramped conditions in the van, the ransom negotiators made themselves comfortable inside the Embassy. The three men always seemed to get on well with one another. They always met apart from us, but at the end of each of their talks, Sasson and Rivas Sacconi were allowed to visit with us. They had nearly free run of the Embassy and moved around comfortably. Victor would normally give us a rundown of his talk with Commander One and encourage us with signs of progress.

At one point, Victor suggested I talk up large sums of money to get Commander One enthusiastic. When I asked him about the status of our "bank account," he told me not to worry, there was plenty. He also told me he had assurance that he could get a token number of prisoners freed if it came down to that, but he asked me not to discuss it with anyone. His comments raised my spirits considerably, but once I started thinking about what he'd said, I wondered if he was merely humoring me. Perhaps mine was a classic case of paranoia, and then again, perhaps not. My greatest fear throughout captivity was that people on the outside weren't leveling with me. I don't know if they felt they were protecting me or if they felt my judgment had been compromised, but I wanted my government and my family to be straight with me. I didn't need the facts sugarcoated, and I didn't need to be protected; what I needed was the facts, the plain truth. When I felt I was being humored, it struck at my core and hurt more than anything the terrorists could have done to me. I felt abandoned by those who should have supported me.

Later, I talked to Norma privately, and she confided to me the real reason they wanted to contact Felipe González. Commander One wanted to get his blessing for something less than the complete fulfillment of his original objectives. For all his bravado, he didn't have sufficient rank to make a decision to modify his standing instructions.

I knew González could make a lot of trouble for us. He was in a fairly comfortable cell with a bed and his own bathroom. He received visitors, read newspapers, watched television, and was sought after for interviews. He even had a recreation area and a garden at his disposal. No one was standing outside his window hidden in the shadows waiting to get a clear shot at him, and he wasn't in danger of being blown up. His civil rights were being zealously guarded by his attorney, and he wasn't particularly threatened. Meanwhile, his comrades were under siege trying to free him. He could very well have a different opinion from those in the Embassy. He had nothing to lose by insisting that Commander One sustain his position and refuse any intermediate position other than the unencumbered release of all M-19 prisoners. Anything less, he might say, was not a success.

The Foreign Minister must have been equally troubled by Norma's gambit. If González wanted, he could stiffen the terrorists' resolve or even more dramatically order them to make the ultimate sacrifice in order to plunge the government into a truly severe crisis. The government took several days to reply to Norma's request, and I imagine they spent many late hours agonizing over the decision.

Foreign Minister Uribe finally agreed to allow Armin Kobel to carry a taped message to González, but with two conditions: the text of the message would be made available to him in written form, and he would have to agree to its content. He also indicated he liked the concept of verifying the courts-martial cases with attorneys acceptable to the M-19, but that the concept was still under review.

Any old political hand would have been ecstatic with the Foreign Minister's response. Our formula for success was simple: The Commander was looking for word from Felipe González and Felipe González was in the hands of the army. By exerting pressure on sensitive points, the army should have been able to engineer the "proper" response from González. I assumed that the authorities would approach González at Picota and tell him that his answers would have a strong bearing on his court-martial. If he gave a response that encouraged Commander One to resolve the takeover, his cooperation and foresight would gain him benevolent consideration at his trial. If, on the other hand, González gave a disruptive response, not only would his message be squelched, but he would needlessly aggravate his own legal problems. Any prosecutor worth his salt would do some plea bargaining to make sure the best response came out of Picota.

In fact, our solution seemed rather elegant. González would praise the terrorists in the Embassy for their accomplishments and heroism; he would tell Commander One he had achieved his prime directive and sanction the decision to quit the Embassy. No further concessions would be necessary. The prisoner issue would become moot, and we could all go home. Our solution left everyone happy: the M-19, the Colombian government, Felipe González, and not least, the hostages. No painful compromises, no coercion, no double jeopardy.

The Commander wrote a draft of his message to González and let us critique it. By now the negotiating group was acting more like an advisory board. We had earned Commander One's respect and trust, so we traded ideas freely. I argued strongly for the inclusion of a full description of our idea for lawyers to verify the status of the pending M-19 cases. Ambassador Galán volunteered to type the final draft of the document so he could surreptitiously tone down Commander One's coarse rhetoric. We managed to get a copy of the proposed message to the Foreign Minister before any of the terrorists noticed Ambassador Galán's editing. We sat back feeling we'd just accomplished a major step toward our freedom and waited for Foreign Minister Uribe's response.

For the first time since our capture, freedom seemed real and around the next bend of the long weary road we had traveled. I'd done everything I knew how to do. All of my effort and energy had gone toward a peaceful and honorable reconciliation between the M-19 and its antagonists. We had met the enemy face to face and weapon to weapon: his carbine against our statesmanship. The question "Will I live?" became "Will I endure with honor?" More than death, I feared dishonoring myself, my family, and my country. And yet I found I was basically alone, surrounded by lone men and women, left with nothing but self-esteem and a hard-boiled belief in the integrity of all life.

Even so, I sensed myself in defiance of Washington's instructions after a lifetime of enforcing them. I knew my actions were warranted, and I knew Washington was operating in the dark. For the first time in nearly thirty years, the bridge between Washington and me was down. Both sides were rebuilding from their respective shores, but it was clear from the beginning we wouldn't meet halfway.

The bridge between Nancy and me was never down nor damaged. If anything, it was strengthened by our adversity. The difference, of course, is that with Nancy I didn't have to be verbal to communicate. In Washington, everyone and everything depends on words. The important consideration however, was that I had not compromised myself or my country. I was not out to become a hero or a martyr — both prospects are alien to me. I was, as I am now, only a soldier in good conscience.

When Mr. Uribe called back, he made some nit-picking observation about the language (but not the content) of the text. When Commander One reread the draft to correlate it with the Minister's observations, he spotted Ambassador Galán's emendations and immediately restored the original language. His changes didn't tamper with the critical concept, but it was annoying nonetheless.

What was important was that the Foreign Minister had agreed to send the M-19's message to González. The rest, I was certain, would follow.

That night Commander One dictated the message onto tape. He included, as a safeguard against fraud, some personal questions that only González could answer. Our remarkable document:

Bogotá, 14 April 1980

Dear Comrades of the High Command,

For us it is cause for great happiness to have the opportunity of dialoguing with you, even though it may be through this channel which you may find a little irregular. We should like to inform you about the manner in which negotiations with the Government have been carried out, dealing with the matter of the takeover of the Dominican Embassy and the release of the hostages found therein.

Up to the moment fourteen conversations have been held during which we have presented our demands:

1. Withdrawal of the troops and the nonintervention of the troops in the Embassy.

2. Publication of the official communiqué of our organization.

3. Liberation of 311 comrades of our organization and others of the left, as well as of unions and guilds.

4. Payment of ransom of fifty million dollars.

Through these talks we consider that we have achieved the following:

1. Initiation and continuation of the dialogue.

2. Withdrawal of the troops and the promise of the Government not to attempt to take the Embassy by force unless we attempt to take action against the lives of the hostages.

3. Publication of our communiqué and national and international publicity, tending to demonstrate that in Colombia there are in fact torture and political prisoners.

4. The Government acceded to allowing friends of the hostages to start negotiations on the economic matter.

We are carrying out these conversations with persons designated by relatives of the hostages as their friends and who do not represent any particular Government, because the Government cannot in conformance with their internal legislation do so, under the argument of not fomenting a market in diplomats.

But the matter which most concerns us refers to you; that is, the liberty of the political prisoners. The Government's position has been the same as that expressed by President Julio César Turbay Ayala in his interview with the *Washington Post*. The Government has studied the legal procedures which might be employed and has not encountered in Colombian legislation any formula which authorizes it to free prisoners. It is for this reason, they say, that on more than one occasion they have stated it is not that the Government is refusing to negotiate on the matter, rather that it is refusing to commit a crime, since from the first negotiation and in all those following they have expressed the persistence of the Government in the defense of the juridical order.

Our position has been invariably that we have hostages and that we demand the freedom of 311 comrades in exchange for them, but what we do not consider negotiable is the non-debatable list on which appear the names of the High Command. With regard to this last point we have achieved the following:

1. That the Government take concrete measures to accelerate the trials by creating a commission of jurists for this purpose.

2. That the Government accede to inviting the Human Rights Commission of the Organization of American States, the International Red Cross, the Colombian Human Rights Association, and the Commission of Jurists to attend the public portion of the military trials and inform themselves of compliance with procedural guarantees of all those who are absolved in military trials and of those who do not have charges formulated against them.

On the preceding point, we should like to explain to you that our position has been that we desire to know the names of the persons against who charges will not be formulated and that the comrades of the High Command should be absolved and leave the country with us. The Government says that one of the problems it has encountered is that the defense lawyers have opposed the abbreviation of the processes and that they have become a general obstruction. We want you to explain this matter to us. Furthermore they state to us that the military trials are only in the private stage and there is still much time before this ends, and they do not accept defining the situation of the comrades of the High Command in advance, arguing that they will have to do the same with everyone at the end of the process. In this regard we have stated that you must be freed in advance in the same manner as María Cristina de Fais Borda, Miriam de Torrado, Tony López Oyuela and the farm workers who participated in the massive trials against the FARC which are being carried out in Medellin, or that the military trial which is being carried out in La Picota be declared null and void.

The position of the Government at all times has been that of not freeing one single political prisoner, but it seems that they may be able to accept, in order to get out of the impasse in which we find ourselves, a proposition formulated by the hostage Ambassadors in the sense that three eminent lawyers, of the full confidence of the M-19 in the quality of "friends of the court," gain access to the dossiers of those in the proceedings and be able to give us their opinion of who may be liable to be excepted from having charges formulated against them, or who could wind up being absolved at the end of the proceedings, so that in accordance with the Government's offer, these persons could then leave the country under the protection of the Human Rights Commission of the Organization of American States, the International Red Cross, and the Colombian Human Rights Association.

You, comrades, know our watchword, which is "Win or Die!" We hope this report gives you a general idea of the status of the negotiations and that you may give us your impressions via this same channel we are using. If it is necessary we will wait until the end of the trials, since what is clear is that we want to leave with our comrades. We are well in every respect and hope you are also.

Please answer the following questions at the beginning, the middle, and the end of your responses on the same cassette:

1. For Felipe: In what city and location did Don Carlos have his magazine stand?

2. For David: The last time we saw each other in Bogotá you invited me to lunch. What did we eat and who was with us?

3. To Gordo and El Cholo: There is a popular site in Cali where we went one time. What is the name of the owner and what song did he always play for us?

Attentively,

Commander One

Guerrilla Column Jorge Marcos Zambrano

TWENTY-THREE

The M-19 prides itself on being a highly trained and dedicated guerrilla action force. Part of its effectiveness has been predicated on its unpredictability. Latin revolutionary fervor has always expressed itself in surprising ways at surprising times. As we approached our fiftieth day as prisoners, we had developed a routine within the erratic framework of the negotiations. The M-19, like everyone else in the hemisphere, was waiting for the outcome of its Operation Democracy and Liberty. All else was on hold.

Or so we thought. While we prepared to tape-record Commander One's message to Felipe González, a small force of M-19 terrorists raided the Uruguayan Embassy across town. There they kidnapped the chargé d'affaires, Raul Lira, and spirited him to the cemetery where Camilo was buried, and sternly lectured him. A Colombian cemetery is not the friendliest of places. To Lira's dumbfounded surprise, the terrorists left him standing there and disappeared into the night. Their real mission, I suspect, was to scare Ambassador Gómez Fyns and punish him for his escape from the Dominican Embassy. The M-19 seemed to be saying, "We don't forget — and we don't want you to forget either."

The next day, April 15, Annin Kobel showed up at the front door to pick up the tape. I tried to brief Kobel as best I could without giving away our angle. I suggested to him that he give González a complete accounting of the atmospherics inside the Embassy. I touched all the bases for him: time was running out, the Teheran crisis was worsening, and with desperation came carelessness, thereby increasing the chances of a disaster. As before, however, I got the distinct impression that Kobel was only going through the motions by listening to me and that he was determined to act only as a messenger and nothing more come hell or high water. Still, I hoped for the best. Kobel was only the messenger; the Foreign Minister had the responsibility to make the ploy work.

Later that day I chanced to meet Victor Sasson after one of his sessions with Commander One. We went off to talk privately and I tested my thinking about the González affair on him. He scoffed at the idea. The plan itself was all right, he said, but he didn't think President Turbay would handle it the way we'd hoped. Victor had himself already approached Mr. Uribe to get his permission to meet with González as a private citizen who could be disavowed if the plan went askew. The Minister flatly refused. Victor was sure the government intended to play it one hundred percent: no gimmicks, no tricks, no pressure. We would have to wait to see, he advised, but he cautioned my putting too much stock in the gambit. Despite Victor's caveat, I found the prospect of at least talking to González in a friendly way too inviting to be ignored outright. Something was bound to come of it.

Victor also told me he had made an offer of $800,000 to the terrorists for our ransom and that he expected to reach a formal agreement with Commander One within the week. From $50 million to $800,000: it was quite a spread. What impressed me most was Victor's confidence about his ability to influence the terrorists and get them to agree to some sort of terms. As far as he was concerned, the negotiations in the van were a sham — a charade for public purposes. His were the real negotiations. In the long run, Victor, thought, he would end up doing the actual negotiating for the prisoners also. Victor had managed to create rapport where Jiménez and Zambrano could not; Victor had stimulated the terrorists' confidence and trust whereas the government negotiators created nothing but disgust and mistrust. Victor's dynamism was contagious, and he convinced the hostages of his strength too.

As soon as Victor left, the diplomats threw a party anticipating our freedom. We started a pool with a thousand pesos from each of us to go to the person who correctly guessed which day we would be released. The winner in turn would promise to throw a bash after we got out. In the excitement, I called Nancy and told her to hold off sending any supplies until the following week in the event we hit pay dirt.

Commander One was also optimistic. He joined our little soirée and told us for the first time he expected Felipe González to give him the go-ahead by declaring a victory. The Commander started talking about travel plans, which was to us a true sign of his belief we were about to end our vigil. He alluded to a final stop somewhere in the Middle East but we couldn't pry the destination out of him. Wherever it was, however, we knew we would have to make refueling stops along the way: Bogotá is 8,600 feet above sea-level and no jetliner can take on enough fuel to fly nonstop to the Middle East. There was some talk about stopping in Caracas, but the Venezuelan Special Delegate on instructions refused to allow the plane to land there. Panama and Cuba were possibilities. If we stopped in Havana, Commander One promised to let everyone off there; if we landed in Panama, however, we would have to stay for the entire flight. There was also some talk about stopping in Madrid or Vienna, where Commander One naively expected a friendly reception from Ambassador Selzer.

Then came the cold towel. Commander One told us he intended to keep a core of hostages with him until the very end. Everyone could go except the ambassadorial negotiating committee; we were committed for the duration. That way, he explained, if we stopped in Panama, he could then fly nonstop to the Middle East if he chose.

I much preferred going to Cuba. I had no intention of winding up some place like Libya or South Yemen where I might just trade one captivity for another. While U.S. relations with Cuba weren't the best, at least we had a Special Interests Section attached to the Swiss Embassy in Havana. Further, the Cubans were Latins. I could talk to them, argue with them if I had to; at least I knew where they were coming from. What could I say to one of Qaddafi's henchmen or to a Yemeni tribesman? I'd be entirely out of my element and at the mercy of forces I could not contend with reasonably.

When I spoke to Frank Crigler later about my possible travels, I tried to convey the thought subtly that if we hostages were ferried to some exotic but friendly locale and not released as Commander One promised, the security police of that country should flex some muscle and refuse to refuel the plane or let it take off until we were deplaned. Because I knew a terrorist was eavesdropping, I had to be obscure about my suggestion. Too obscure, apparently, because I later found out Frank couldn't make head or tail of my gibberish.

Frank also told me that President Turbay had played the González tape to the Group of Fifteen, and that the delegates felt there were considerable problems with it. He wouldn't elaborate because of our silent partner on the line. When I spoke to Nancy a little later, she conveyed the same message by implying broadly that she hoped we weren't banking all our hopes on González. It was important, she urged, for us to work on other alternatives.

Among Victor Sasson, Frank Crigler, and Nancy, the message was clear; González wasn't working out. I didn't understand why, and I was dissatisfied with their warnings.

I carried these impressions back to the negotiating committee, and it came as a splash of cold water. We still hadn't heard anything from the government and found ourselves hoping against hope that the delay was indicative of some activity on its part. We tried to console ourselves with the thought that the government could counterfeit an appropriate response if necessary, but that it would come through for us in the clutch. We tried to keep our doubts from the other hostages, but our long faces made it obvious something was wrong.

When we called the Foreign Minister to get clarification, he told us he "hadn't yet read the message." We interpreted this to mean he was still trying to negotiate a more favorable response. Finally, six days after we'd first proposed the idea, Foreign Minister Uribe called to say that González's reply would be delivered to the Embassy the next morning. He also suggested that if the terrorists interpreted the tape properly, they would find the message favorable.

This immediately gave us new hope. We assumed that if the Foreign Minister in his typically understated way had thought it was a favorable response, then it had to be a humdinger. Our exuberance was tempered by a little voice in the back of my mind that cautioned me about being too sanguine and Nancy's continued insistence that we should have alternatives in mind. What we didn't know was that the tapes had been leaked to the press, and complete versions of the exchange had already been published in all the papers. My little voice had been right.

That same day Amnesty International released its long-awaited report. The timing, for our part, couldn't have been worse. The forty-four page survey reached "the unequivocal conclusion that political prisoners were systematically tortured by Colombian military personnel." The report listed thirty-three centers within Colombia where torture had been conducted and fifty different types had been used, including beatings, burnings, electric shock, drugs, psychological abuse, and rape. The government tried to disqualify the claims by calling Amnesty International "a frivolous organization that appears and disappears by magic…It arrives with halos of social sensibility to respond to the calls of extremists but goes into hiding when these extremists are shown to be violators."

Among the recommendations that Amnesty International made was an appeal to limit strictly the powers of the military and the police. The abuse of authority resulted, as they saw it, from the almost continuous state of siege for thirty years, which resulted in "an almost permanent suspension of guarantees that protect human rights in the Colombian Constitution." Later in the year, Amnesty International would release a 258-page report citing 600 individual cases of torture along with twenty-seven in-depth interviews. Most of the victims were listed as peasants, Indians, and trade unionists, although white-collar professionals and "others who tried to uphold professional codes of conduct" had also been persecuted. Even though President Turbay had invited Amnesty International to come to Colombia, he clearly wasn't happy with the results. The report was dangerous ammunition that would be used against the government.

When the tape from González finally arrived, we gathered in the library to hear his answer. From the beginning, it was heartrendingly clear that González wasn't going to give us the quick solution we'd been praying for. The message was ambiguous; it was neither an invitation to leave nor a demand to stay. González praised his comrades for their actions but left open the option of what to do next.

He referred to the reform of the Colombian judicial system as the solution of the problem. The elimination of the courts-martial in favor of civilian jurisdiction and the lifting of the state of siege would provide the necessary elements for the government to arrive at a settlement with the M-19. All this was old hat. González clearly intended to lie low. We had little to go on except González's weak endorsement of my idea of lawyers to verify the status of cases pending against M-19 prisoners. González even recommended two possible candidates for consideration.

There we had it. Not what we'd hoped, but not as bad as it could have been. It was an opportunity missed and a blow to rising expectations, but not the end of the world.

Some weeks later I discussed the González tape with President Turbay. He said he was determined to be completely honest with the terrorists. He didn't want to be accused of chicanery at any point down the line. He also said that bargaining or even pressuring González would have been difficult. Plea bargaining was not possible in Colombian jurisprudence. Our tape gambit was clever, he agreed, but it never had a chance of succeeding.

TWENTY-FOUR

We were profoundly depressed. Within our negotiating group, the Brazilian and Israeli Ambassadors vented their disappointment. Ambassador Barak was beside himself with rage; the conduct of the Colombian government was, he complained, inexcusable. Escape plans again became rife. I finally told them to stop thinking with their balls. The other hostages and even the terrorists were looking to us for guidance and leadership. It wasn't the time to get tough; it was the time to get smart. We were professional diplomats and we had known the score from the beginning. Nobody ever said it was going to be easy, that all the pieces would fall into place conveniently. We'd explored a number of possibilities that might have proven to be the key to our dilemma; the tape had been one avenue to explore. It hadn't worked. We would seek others. We still had the prospect of the OAS Human Rights Commission and the other international organizations. I knew I sounded self-righteous lecturing to my friends — and it was all the more difficult because I felt the same disappointment — but they were mature, sensible men, and it took only a reminder to get them back on track. It could have been anyone of us saying the same thing: we shared a common conscience.

Ambassador Barak, in his trenchant military style, decided to take on the terrorists by himself. He marched up to the Commander and announced in his stentorian voice that he was giving him exactly one week to work out a solution. If he hadn't by then, he was going to walk out of the Embassy. No more flimflam, no more half-baked ideology, no indecision or stalling. The Commander could shoot him in the back if he wanted, but he'd had enough of this nonsense. That, he explained, was his resolution, and if the Commander had any sense left, he would make sure he stopped pussyfooting around and take a hard look at his options.

We knew Ambassador Barak's threat was no idle boast; he had both the capability and the *chutzpah* to break out. From the beginning when he'd threatened the terrorists with harm if any harm came to him, the terrorists considered him one of the most dangerous hostages. Now he was impatient, distressed, and on notice.

President Turbay later told me that the Ambassador's ultimatum was the beginning of the end for the terrorists. His stratagem brought intolerable pressure to bear on them. If Ambassador Barak tried to escape and they shot him, then the M-19 risked almost certain retaliation by the Army. If the M-19 let him go, then the door was virtually open for everyone else to leave. Either way, Ambassador Barak forced their hand.

Commander One reacted to the Ambassador's threat with a declamatory warning of his own: he would gag and bind the Israeli if he had to. Even so, Ambassador Barak would have managed to carry out his threat. He was too clever a man for the M-19, and they knew it.

The other members of the negotiating group took our cue from Ambassador Barak and dragooned Commander One's flank. We insisted on a meeting with him and began dogging him with demands that he make a solution. Waiting any longer was intolerable. A quick solution was imperative. We pushed him to take a long hard look at the possibility of leaving the Embassy with appropriate guarantees that the prisoners left behind would be treated fairly and humanely under the aegis of the different international agencies. The world was watching; the government wasn't about to double-cross them with every human rights agency in the hemisphere breathing down its neck. We gave Commander One a draft paper we'd written for him that detailed this concept and told him to study it.

We made sure Commander One heard us loud and clear. I could feel his resistance fraying with our constant verbal chafing. Suddenly we were demanding resolution rather than encouraging it. We were tired of all those weeks of feckless negotiations and the imposture of Zambrano and Jiménez. We had our fill of speechifying and descanting: we wanted manifest commitments from both sides. No more exiguous promises. No more legal feints. *The time was now.*

The next time I spoke to Victor Sasson, he told me his parlays with Commander One were going well. We commiserated about the way the tape had been handled and shook our heads in disbelief. I asked him to warn the Israeli Special Delegate about his Ambassador's last stand. We also discussed April 19, the upcoming anniversary of the M-19. I was afraid the terrorists on the outside might celebrate by doing something rash that would have fallout on our status. There were also reports that President Carter was considering military action against Iran, and that worried us. We were drowning in a whirlpool of concerns. Everything happening in the world around us seemed likely to affect us. It was a feeling of being crushed by the outside world. Our argument to Commander One was powerful because it was cogent: finesse of rhetoric gave way to blunt and timely admonition.

The next day, our fifty-second in captivity, and one day before the anniversary of the M-19 movement, we had another long talk with Commander One. I told him that, with President Turbay meeting with his Cabinet in the city of Melgar at that very moment, it behooved him to give something to the moderates to counterbalance the influence of the hard-liners and the military. And the Commander had to do it before the President addressed the nation the next evening. I goaded him as forcefully as I could without putting him on the defensive: he had to establish clearly and present the idea of having a group of sanctioned lawyers protect their interests during the trials so they could quit the Embassy without having to await the outcome.

Commander One hesitantly accepted my nudging and agreed to present our case to the government negotiators in depth. We incorporated the appropriate language in the draft paper we'd foisted on him earlier. This was a milestone for us, and I spread the news to the other hostages, who were all smiles.

I wasn't prepared for the shock when Commander One came back and told me that he'd talked it over with his staff and they were dead-set against my proposal. They continued to insist on having prisoners released to leave the country with them.

My patience, already worn to a frazzle, gave out. I told him he'd be better off to get tougher on the kind of guarantee they'd need to get them out of the Embassy alive rather than this other nonsense. It made no sense to backtrack to the first day of negotiations. We'd obviously been working under the mistaken assumption that their position had been evolving during the last seven weeks. All they were doing by being inflexible was inviting the hard-liners to say they were intransigent, and therefore could be dealt with only by force. He was asking for it, I warned. He was turning Operation Democracy and Liberty into a suicide mission for no purpose. He was the Commander, and I told him he had some tough command decisions to make.

This time I wasn't going to let go. I kept pounding away at the Commander until I felt his resistance begin to weaken. I realized he was looking for a solid line of reasoning to convince his own people. In a way, I had become his mentor. His leadership position was deteriorating, and he needed to regain control with a firm rebuttal.

We went over the plan carefully. With the arrival of the OAS Commission, I advised, he should demand an exchange of diplomatic notes between the Colombian government and the OAS that would define the responsibilities and obligations of each with regard to these judicial proceedings and investigations into human rights violations. Such an international agreement between the government and an international organization would be tantamount to a treaty and would have the force of law. Ambassador Nascimento e Silva concurred. The political implications of this accomplishment, for which they could claim credit, would make a prisoner exchange pale by comparison. They had the chance to create profound institutional change in their society, and if they meant what they said about the need for social change, then they were nothing more than self-centered hypocrites if they passed up that opportunity for the short-sighted goal of the release of their comrades in jail. They had to stop thinking small. We then offered to draft a potential agreement for the M-19 to consider as a negotiating point at the tables.

Commander One liked the idea of leaving behind an agreement of international stature that would stand as a monument to their cause. He carried the concept back to his general staff to talk it over with them. As he walked away, I was struck by the irony that the Commander had become a messenger boy running back and forth between the negotiating committee and his own staff. We were still upset by the Commander's unpredictability. He had lost a lot of his leadership capability once his own people understood that the true direction of the negotiations was being decided by the prisoners! We crossed our fingers and hoped for the best.

At the next session in the van, Norma didn't establish the possibility that the M-19 might leave the Embassy without prisoners. She did press for an answer on the lawyer verification issue; she also asked, at our insistence, that the OAS people visit the Embassy as soon as they got into town. The government turned around and flatly rejected the demand for lawyer intermediation without an explanation. The point quickly became academic, however, when Zambrano and Jiménez agreed to allow the OAS Commission to come to the Embassy.

Meanwhile I'd remembered Victor Sasson's off-the-cuff remark that he'd probably end up doing the real negotiating for our release. I'd taken his remark with a grain of salt when he first said it, but the possibility of its coming true looked continually more attractive. At this point in the negotiations, we would try anything that showed any promise, no matter how farfetched. We were desperate to resolve the crisis as expeditiously as we could, even though the sound of the word "expeditious" had an ironic ring to it.

After one of their many sessions with the Commander, I tested the water with Sasson and Rivas Sacconi by suggesting that they introduce the prisoner exchange question at their next meeting with Commander One. Victor agreed to represent us, but he wanted our governments to propose the idea first so he wouldn't be accused of trying to usurp authority. If the order for him to proceed didn't come directly from the Foreign Minister, then his hands were tied. So it was back to the telephones as we started our campaign to enlist Victor Sasson as a special delegate in the negotiations. Nothing ever came of this idea either. At times I wasn't sure who my enemies were: the M-19, the Colombian government, or my own people in Washington. Almost every proposal we put forth seemed to die "in committee." I understand now that each group had its own interests to protect — even if those interests were contrary to my own — but at the time I found the reticence of allies to consider seriously our proposals both foolishly counterproductive and frustrating.

Something else I noticed at the time was that the pace of negotiations was becoming considerably more frantic. Whereas nothing would happen for days, even weeks, at a time in the beginning, everything now seemed to happen all at once. Carefully planned schemes went haywire: unexpected and unpredictable turns of events kept us perennially off balance. Ideas — some of them thoughtful and others just desperate — ping-ponged back and forth without order. Trying to stay calm and keep the crisis under control seemed an impossibility.

In the middle of the scrambling around looking for a solution, we heard a radio bulletin announcing that the government had released nine M-19 Prisoners from Picota. From out of nowhere the impossible seemed to have happened: the Colombians had finally taken the initiative to settle the impasse. I quickly called the American Embassy for confirmation since the Colombian press had a notorious reputation for creativity. My staff hadn't heard the news and promised to check it out. I never heard another word about it. (In fact, the Colombians had released nine prisoners who were awaiting trial, but they were released for lack of evidence rather than as a purposeful move to meet the demands of the terrorists. None of the released prisoners was on the M-19's short list, but for the life of me, I still don't understand why President Turbay didn't capitalize on the event. The government acted as though the two events were unrelated.)

The next day, April 19, the terrorists staged a ceremony to commemorate the tenth anniversary of the founding of their movement. The terrorist band lined up in formation and shouted slogans for a few minutes; Commander One then ordered the ambassadors from Haiti and the Dominican Republic to go on the roof and unfurl the black and red M-19 banner from the front facade of the building. Ambassador Mallol wasn't too pleased with his assignment and sheepishly climbed up to the roof, shouting "Don't shoot! It's the Dominican Ambassador!"

A few minutes later the terrorists got an angry call from the Foreign Minister; fuming, he called the flag "an extreme provocation" and took Commander One to task for his inciting tactics. Without so much as a word of protest, the M-19 quickly and silently struck its colors.

To celebrate the anniversary, Commander One ordered the release of the Costa Rican Consul General — he of the misplaced case of champagne. The Commander had two purposes in mind by releasing Blanco Solis: first, he hoped to assuage Diego Uribe, and second, he wanted to reestablish his humanitarian credentials in view of Blanco's advanced age.

We continued to take the terrier's attitude about having the OAS Human Rights Commission and the Colombian government reach a mutual agreement that protected everyone's rights. With the help of Nascimento e Silva's broad experience in inter-American law and with Ricardo Galán's drafting skills, we went through draft after draft working out the sensitive wording. We wouldn't take no for an answer; our insistence was impressive if not awesome. I could feel the terrorists swaying our way, and we grew increasingly encouraged by their reciprocal interest. I believed the prisoner exchange concept was no longer the issue: we were finally over the hump.

As I feared, the M-19 did not stay idle outside the Embassy. On April 17, men kidnapped a well-known journalist, German Castro Caicedo, and spirited him to an interview with the Supreme Commander of the M-19, Jaime Bateman. Bateman wanted Castro to act as an intermediary between his organization and the Colombian government to propose a summit meeting in Panama with a cast of former presidents, ex-presidential candidates, senators, retired army generals, businessmen, former foreign ministers, and even novelist Gabriel García Marquez. The purpose of the summit, in Bateman's words: to discuss "Whether democracy exists in Colombia." Castro dutifully delivered a tape-recorded message to President Turbay. Two days later, on the M-19's anniversary, President Turbay rejected the offer by having Interior Minister German Zea give a radio interview in which he said the government found it "impossible to enter into a dialogue with subversion." I considered Bateman's maneuver political buffoonery, a grandstand play of the worst sort. None of us were surprised when Minister Zea summarily refused Bateman's castle in the air.

On April 22, our fifty-sixth day, Tom Farer, the president of the Human Rights Commission and a professor of law at Rutgers University, came to the Mission with Andrés Aguilar, the Venezuelan delegate and a former president of the Commission, whom I had known in my days in Caracas. Aguilar had also been a member of the United Nations delegation that had visited the hostages in Teheran.

Farer and Aguilar met with Commander One, Norma, and the negotiating group. Farer impressed me. While his Spanish was halting, and he usually spoke through an interpreter when the discussion became too technical, it was obvious he had a good grasp on what was happening. He comported himself well and caught the mood of the hostages and terrorists immediately. He read our draft agreement and pointed out dispassionately that our paper appeared to offer a new and interesting precedent for the Human Rights commission. He said the Human Rights Commission usually stayed in a country for a couple of weeks, left, and wrote its report, which was then sent to the government for comment. Months would go by before a final report was available for publication and compliance often depended on the goodwill of the government being investigated. In this case, however, we were proposing a continuing presence for the Commission to observe the trials themselves in progress, They were also being offered an opportunity to investigate allegations of human rights violations, something that had never happened before. Farer and Aguilar calmly answered the terrorists' questions as to procedures and functions of the Commission. Both men were forthright, and their confidence and depth of conviction impressed us all.

As I escorted Tom Farer upstairs to meet the other hostages, he compared the old battered mansion with some of the places he'd seen in Africa earlier in his career. I told him we were counting on him to be instrumental in gaining us our freedom and expressed my gratitude for his involvement. In return, he made me promise to buy him a corned-beef sandwich after I got out. On rye. This remarkable man lightened our spirits considerably.

Ambassador Galán then offered Farer and Aguilar the nickel tour of our digs. As he led the group toward the kitchen, we joked about our conditions; suddenly, without warning, Ambassador Galán did an about-face and deflected the group away from the kitchen. I could see by the expression on his face that something had upset him, but he was trying hard not to let Farer or Aguilar see it. I was tempted to take a peek myself but thought better of it and followed Galán as he continued his tour in another part of the house.

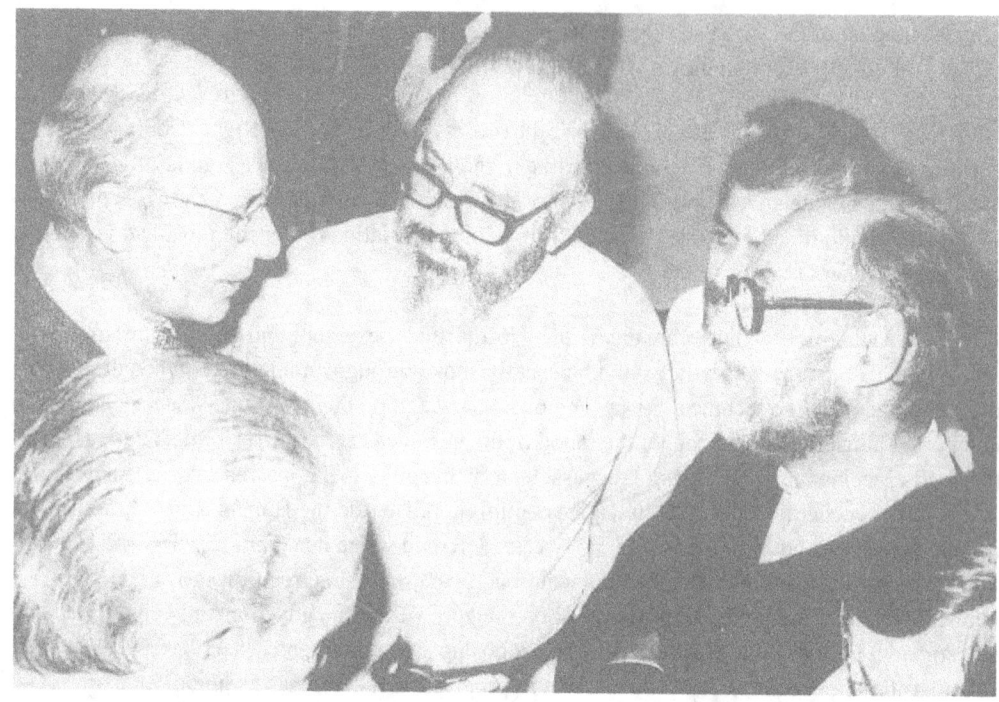

Professor Thomas J. Farer, President of the Inter-American Human Rights Commission, explaining the details of the arrangements for our release. Photo by Luis Guzmán.

What the Ambassador had found in the kitchen was Omar heavily engaged in advanced foreplay with María, Jorge's young "revolutionary wife."

Omar and María had become an item around the house lately, but the Mexican Ambassador no longer found it funny. He returned to the library, seething, and demanded an immediate conference with Commander One. He announced to the terrorist leader testily that it wasn't healthy for those of us in a state of enforced celibacy to have to watch the romantic spectacles of the duo in the kitchen. Further, he didn't know what the ground rules were for "revolutionary spouses" but wondered if we weren't witnessing a good old love triangle made more dangerous by the fact that both men were heavily armed.

By this time I had a hard time keeping a straight face, but the Mexican continued to denounce Omar's overbearing manner, his officiousness, and his constant roiling of the diplomats by his obsessive concern for security. Galán suggested that some discipline was in order with regard to Omar's love life, and that he should be told to get off our collective back. To my surprise, Commander One meekly accepted the Ambassador's criticism and agreed to take care of the matter. From that day Omar put aside his rifle and was all sweetness and light.

184

After our release, a rumor was published in the Bogotá press that Commander One had killed Omar in Havana. I often wondered whether we planted the seeds of homicide that day.

TWENTY-FIVE

Romance knows no restraint and clings tenaciously even in the most inhospitable environment. Adversity encourages it. Amidst all the political turmoil and the impossible living conditions, Pyrarnus and Thisbe continue their age-old tryst. Even though the social and sexual relationships among the terrorists were often confused, there were heartening splashes of sanity from time to time to remind us of the true nature of the world outside. Bishop Acerbi was pleasantly surprised when La Negra approached him privately and asked if he would marry her to Alfredo. Being a "revolutionary wife" was not enough.

Most of us were so starved for entertainment that we thought a wedding sounded like a smashing idea. At the rate negotiations were crawling along, we were bound to become godfathers to their children. But the Nuncio scrupulously avoided getting involved in any such scheme. He tried to dodge La Negra's petition by telling her he couldn't marry her and Alfredo without her parish priest's permission. Someone leaked the news to the press, and the facts got garbled. The next day none of us was surprised by the newsman who reported that the Nuncio had married Norma to Commander One. The Nuncio groaned; we shook our heads knowingly. Love, we hoped, would endure.

That same day we found some bootleg news clippings in one of the Red Cross shipments. Unexpectedly, we found among them what amounted to a treasure trove: a quote from the M-19 Supreme Commander, Jaime Bateman, disavowing that his proposed summit meeting with high officials of the Colombian Government would in any way interfere with the negotiations being held by Commander One:

> The negotiations he is conducting have our complete backing and support. If he reaches an agreement, we are sure that it would be best for the country, for the hostages and for the Commando that is in the Embassy. We are dealing with two facets of the same problem, and they must not be confused.

Here at last was the statement we had been hoping might come from Felipe González, only it was coming from the Supreme Commander himself. Clearly, he was giving Commander One the right to use his own judgment, saying that Commander One's decisions weren't contingent on any other person's. Straightaway we took the clipping to Commander One. "Here, look!" we said. "If you have had any reservations about Gonzalez's ambiguous message, then you can't have any about this one: it rings clarion clear."

It's hard to describe our excitement. With Tom Farer and the arrival of the Commission, with Jaime Bateman's own exhortation for Commander One to decide according to his conscience for the good of the country and the hostages, there was only one way for him to go. We also pointed out that in speaking of the good of the country, the hostages, and the terrorists in the Embassy, Bateman had pointedly excluded the prisoners in La Picota prison, which we interpreted to mean that his declaration superseded any intentions that could have been implied by González. Our argument here was dangerously thin, but the Commander was as anxious as we to find a rationale that would allow him to get out of his rat's nest of intrigue.

Ambassador Galán, a master of timing, launched a spirited allocution which left Commander One nonplussed. Ambassador Galán and I looked at each other, knowing we had just reached the peak of the nearly invincible mountain we had been clawing up for nearly two months. Suddenly, without warning, we were at the top, our heads above the clouds that had muddled our vision. We inhaled the fresh, invigorating air deeply into our lungs, and it felt good. Very good.

Commander One agreed to review the facts with his people and present our case. He seemed convinced that he now had the authority to act on his own. If so, we had just cleared the last major hurdle.

I felt relieved physically as well as mentally. The strain of bad hours and bad food had started to manifest itself as stomach cramps. I worried about ulcers, so I started taking antacids but to no effect. I knew I wasn't eating right: my diet was too haphazard. I lost weight, which I could easily afford. The long sedentary hours behind a desk combined with scores of diplomatic receptions with their rich food and drink had endowed me with about thirty extra pounds in the last two years. I was happy to shed the surplus. I was now able to wear the jeans Nancy had sent me at the beginning of the siege. They had been several sizes too small, but now they fit perfectly (I had lent them to Ambassador Allubah of Egypt, which provoked his wife to ask if he was gaining weight). I talked to a doctor at the U.S. Embassy who felt I might have contracted the curse of the Foreign Service: amoebas. He sent along some medicine for me, but when I read the literature, which warned of bizarre side effects, I demurred at taking any. I wasn't prepared to chance my lucidity at this point in the game. Rather, grin and bear it. I could get proper medical attention after I was released. Until then, I was resolved to stay sharp.

Meanwhile, Victor Sasson kept plugging away. He felt a settlement was close; he was bargaining in the million-dollar range and had offered Commander One a "personal" ransom of an extra $200,000 if he resolved the crisis quickly. There were no hidden snags that he could foresee, and he expected the Commander to accept the $1,200,000 without any further hitches.

President Turbay approved in principle the draft of the Colombian-OAS agreement we'd prepared. A few details needed to be ironed out, but it was only a matter of patience. Foreign Minister Uribe called to confirm the status of the document and grouse about some of the language. We were after substance, not style. As long as the principle of the agreement was acceptable, we didn't care how it read.

For her part, Norma was in the van haggling over details with Zambrano and Jiménez. The Venezuelan government had withdrawn its Consul General, so Norma had the Bolivian chargé, Reinaldo del Carpio, along as company. The government plodded along, insisting that the prisoner issue be dropped altogether, and that Norma sign the agreements. The OAS Commission, they said, could deliver the executed copy of the agreement by first light the next morning.

Commander One blandly materialized late that afternoon and told the negotiating committee that he'd met with the others and proposed they accept our alternative plan. The ideas were sound, honorable, and weighty in short, worthy of serious consideration. The terrorists, to a man, voted to accept our proposal. But they accepted it only *in addition to prisoner release, not in lieu of it.*

After a long moment of stunned disbelief, we nearly went berserk. The Mexican and Brazilian ambassadors foamed with rage. The Israeli Ambassador assumed his inscrutable stance. Euphoria transfigured instantly into morbid scorn. If we had had weapons, we would have attacked the man where he stood for his spinelessness, for his invincible ignorance, for his patent disregard for everything we had slaved over for week after torturous week. Every ounce of my strength was sapped away, while bitter venom filled its place. My anger went beyond words. The rollercoaster of emotions not only plunged but derailed. Except for the shoot-out on the first day, this was the most dangerous point of our captivity. Despair was profound; the tension, unbearable. All I could say to the Commander was that he was crazy. There was nothing else to say.

TWENTY-SIX

As the forlorn and disconsolate negotiating group trooped wearily up the stairs, Norma furtively tugged my sleeve and motioned for me to lag behind. She took me aside where no one could hear us and made me promise not to divulge what she was about to tell me. Norma glanced around to make sure no one was eavesdropping on us and then lowered her voice. Commander One's plan, she whispered, was to continue to insist on a prisoner exchange until Sunday. If the government continued to refuse the demand, then he would give in to the terms and leave without his comrades. That was it: the Commander was bluffing.

Again, Norma made me promise not to tell anyone because she was frightened for her life. I asked her if I could at least tell Ambassadors Galán and Nascimento e Silva to calm them down. We were in a dangerous state; they had to know. Reluctantly, she agreed.

I slogged upstairs, trying to figure out how best to alleviate the despair of my fellow hostages. Personally, I felt as though I had just been granted a reprieve at the eleventh hour, but my colleagues couldn't benefit from the fact without jeopardizing Norma. When I saw that the hostages had retreated into their own shells, I empathized with their dejection and wanted to call out, "It's all right, it's not as bad as it seems." I wanted to betray Norma's trust only to assuage their pain, but I dared not. If I did, and the information ultimately turned out to be wrong, then I would have destroyed my credibility altogether. Worse, Commander One or Omar would deal unsympathetically with Norma if either of them found out she was secretly informing us of their plans.

These risks were unacceptable. But in a moment when I could get Ambassadors Galán and Nascimento e Silva alone, I passed along the privileged news. I suggested that we keep my promise to Norma, but that we make an effort to project such an aura of optimism and self-confidence that the others would at least respond to it unconsciously. We couldn't allow them to become desperate and do something rash. "At last," sighed Ambassador Galán, "we're getting somewhere."

The OAS Commission arrived early on the morning of April 24. The members brought with them the revised agreement in which we had put so much stock. We went over it together in painstaking detail to make sure everyone understood its provisions. We didn't want "technical difficulties" popping up to haunt us later. We also briefed Norma for her session in the van that afternoon. We were the directors giving the actors their last-minute stage instructions. The ideas might have been ours, but success depended entirely on their performance.

Despite the lousy track record, negotiations in the van became more frequent; they were scheduled daily, and the one that afternoon figured to be their twenty-third encounter. Norma was now going into the van without a hostage representative because after Ricardo Galán they served little purpose. The main drawback for us was that we were no longer briefed after each session. I assumed Norma was holding firm to her demand that prisoners be released, just as the government consistently rebuffed her.

To our surprise, Victor Sasson and Rivas Sacconi showed up at the Embassy that morning with the Cuban Ambassador in tow. The plan to leave via Panama, the Cuban told us, had been scrapped for a direct flight to Havana. We would be released after Commander One was safely in the embrace of Fidel Castro. Ambassador Ravelo delighted in giving us a little pep talk, which we endured silently. A Cuban jetliner was expected momentarily at Bogotá International Airport; soon we would be going home! Ambassador Ravelo assured us we would be welcome in Cuba no matter what our particular political persuasion happened to be, and that we would be treated with all due deference to rank. If we wished, we could get in touch with our diplomatic representatives as soon as we disembarked. The Ambassador then made a special point of telling me I would be turned over to the Special Interests Section at the Swiss Embassy. If any of us liked, Ambassador Ravelo generously offered, we could stay as his guests in Cuba for as long as we liked. I still wonder if he really expected any takers to his offer.

I took Ambassador Ravelo, who was all smiles, aside and told him I insisted that the jetliner be under Cuban military control before it took off from Bogotá; otherwise, I threatened, I would refuse to board the plane. Ambassador Ravelo was startled by my threat. I explained to him that from my point of view, Cubans — whether they were red or blue — were Cubans: they represented an established government, even if I didn't much approve of it. The terrorists, on the other hand, were too jumpy and unpredictable. They didn't understand international law and the nature of diplomatic commitment. I had no intention of being under their whimsical control in the air; they were just as likely to change their minds halfway to Havana and strike out for the Middle East. I told Ambassador Ravelo that I preferred any Cuban to a Bedouin.

The Ambassador laughed heartily and told me not to worry: he would make sure Cuban troops were on board and in control. He also promised to see to it that Nancy could meet me in Havana. Barring the unexpected — and I shudder to recall all the times the unexpected disrupted our plans — we would be home within the week.

Cuban Ambassador Fernando Do Revelo Renedo, on the far left, informing the group that the Cuban government was sending a plane to pick up the hostages and terrorists. Photo by Luis Guzmán.

The next day was equally busy with Norma in the van and the Human Rights people coming and going. I had a long talk with Nancy, who read me messages from President Carter and the U.S. Congress. They bolstered my morale wonderfully. More important, the messages were official statements of support.

President Carter wrote:

> The events of the past six weeks in Bogotá have been of grave concern to me and to those men and women throughout the world who work for the common good of all people by peaceful and just means. Your vigorous dedication to the basic principles of diplomacy — presently being tested on so many fronts — personifies the ideals and spirit of the international community. The worthy service you are giving your country and to the countries in which you have served is nowhere better exemplified than in your present post. Thanks to your tireless efforts, the United States and Colombia are full partners in the pursuit of fundamental human rights, including an aggressive battle against the illicit drug traffic, a deadly offender against those rights.

Now, as your own basic rights are violated, your actions are a dignified and courageous reaffirmation of the intrinsic values for which you have worked so long and hard.

You are not forgotten. Your friends and your country are committed to your safe release. The Government of Colombia has my full support in the long and difficult process of negotiations which will bring an honorable solution to this critical situation. Your family is safe, and every effort is being made to provide for their well-being until you return to them.

Congress, never at a loss for words, compounded the premium with a resolution sponsored by Congressman Wydler of New York and Congressman Zablocki of Wisconsin:

Whereas Diego Asencio, the United States Ambassador to Colombia, is a distinguished career diplomat of the United States;

Whereas Ambassador Asencio is an effective and respected representative of his country;

Whereas Ambassador Asencio is held in great personal affection by his Government and his colleagues and by the foreign officials and private citizens with whom he has worked;

Whereas, since February 27, 1980, Ambassador Asencio and a group of his foreign diplomatic colleagues have been held hostage by terrorists;

Whereas, through this ordeal, Ambassador Asencio has served with extraordinary courage and composure;

Whereas his personal qualities have been a continuous source of encouragement and admiration for those who are working to resolve this dangerous incident; and

Whereas Ambassador Asencio's performance under the most trying circumstances has been in the highest tradition of the United States;

Now, therefore, be it Resolved, That the thanks and support of the Congress and of the American people are hereby extended to Ambassador Asencio. The House of Representatives expresses its hope for the immediate and safe release of Ambassador Asencio and the other hostages being held in Colombia.

Among those speaking in support of the Resolution, Congressman Zablocki said, "…House Resolution 641…expresses recognition to a dedicated public servant who is serving his country with uncommon skill and courage, notwithstanding the obvious danger to his life." He added:

> We know that under the most dangerous circumstances Ambassador Asencio has conducted himself with the utmost courage and composure, and has been an inspiration to those who are working to resolve the situation. This Resolution brings recognition and hopefully encouragement to this outstanding diplomat. We hold him in great affection, and it is an inspiration to all to know that this American diplomat is rising to the demands of a trying incident. We thank him for his courage and leadership and pray for his immediate and safe release, along with that of the other hostages held in Colombia.

Congressman Guyer of Ohio charitably characterized me as a "man who has served in many capacities, and his conduct, his stoic absorption of what he must be going through mentally, emotionally, and physically is a Gibraltar of strength to all of us. We wish him Godspeed as he stands symbolizing what Americans believe in and stand for."

Congressman Wolff also of New York, Chairman of the Select Committee on Narcotics and a great supporter of our narcotics campaign in Colombia, also went on record:

> I want to join with my colleagues in objecting to the terrorist captivity of my friend, Diego Asencio. I concur with House Resolution 641, and the statements of support and admiration for Ambassador Asencio made by my colleagues. I know Ambassador Asencio personally, and over the years I have witnessed the dedication he has shown in furthering the amity and understanding between the United States and the countries in which he has served. He has upheld the highest traditions of our Nation in his diplomatic service.

There it was: a hero by resolution of the United States Congress. It felt good. It felt good not so much for the generous acclaim but for the support. I was alone on the inside, and to know people and friends on the outside were worrying, working, and supporting me made a great deal of difference. After Nancy finished reading me the message, I felt the proverbial lump in my throat. After all my years in service, the government rallied around me and said, "Diego, we believe in you; we trust you." The messages were the first solid indications I had that Washington was supporting my somewhat mutinous approach to getting me and my colleagues out of hock. For all I knew, I had wrecked my career by taking matters into my own hands. But I had not; my gamble had paid off.

I told Nancy I thought the solution was only hours away. Soon I would be back home, and soon, back into the grind of politics. But first there would be time for the two of us — time no man or government could interrupt. Nancy told me she was thinking of flying to Miami that evening. Arrangements would be made for me to fly from Havana to Homestead Air Base in Florida, where we would be reunited. I gave her the go-ahead, while Renata, who was monitoring our call, gave me silent encouragement by nodding her head vigorously.

There was an additional reason for Nancy to believe. A few days before, she had been delegated by the other wives to approach the Colombian government and negotiate for something better than the box lunches we had been receiving. She had arrived with menus and figures in hand only to get into a heated exchange with the Director of Protocol over the extra five dollars the new meals would cost. When the Director suddenly agreed to start the meals on the following Monday after consulting his superiors, Mexican Representative Raul Valdéz winked at Nancy, as she nodded in agreement, and remarked "With these cheapskates, I guess that means they will be out by Sunday."

The big event of the day turned out to be the delivery of Armin Kobel's Ping-Pong table, an ironic anticlimax to the efforts of the International Red Cross. The table came from the American Embassy, and it was a real beauty. Its arrival brought the Swiss Ambassador to life; he turned out to be a prodigious player and took on all corners. Norma asked me to contribute the table to the prisoners at La Picota, a request to which I judiciously agreed.

The negotiations continued in the van and between Victor Sasson and Commander One. We no longer had our customary briefings and were unaware of what may have been developing without our knowledge. Again we had to have blind faith, but the signs were all right for our release. We were edgy, afraid to move or breathe the wrong way and upset the delicate balance we had somehow managed to achieve among all these diverse interests. As I look back, the sheer impossibility of what we accomplished seems awesome. It took pluck, it took grit, and it took saintly patience. We learned we couldn't predict the unpredictable (and that everything is unpredictable); we were barely able to manage what we thought was predictable. Only perseverance and brute determination got us through.

Jo Ibáñez, the nurse at the American Embassy, sent me a less radical medication for my stomach cramps, and she sent me a wishbone, which seemed apropos. As I was contemplating the wishbone, Diego Uribe called and spoke to Ricardo Galán about our final arrangements. Ambassador Galán suggested the time had come for the Foreign Minister to talk to Commander One directly in order to massage the Commander's ego and thus provide a little extra push the negotiations needed. The Foreign Minister agreed, although I'm sure he couldn't have cared less about the Commander's ego.

Afterward, a beaming Commander One told us that, except for some minor details, he had finally reached an accord with Mr. Uribe. We would be released within two days, on April 27. There it was: almost sixty days of mind-crushing captivity on a runaway train: the long, torturous inclines and the breakneck drops, the endless tunnels of darkness. Soon we would have arrived, shaken, a bit the worse for wear, and a lot smarter.

Norma also came by to tell us her talks in the van had gone well. The only real hitch was an agreement with the Colombian Association for Human Rights, which was still being drafted. Ransom was finally established at $1,200,000.

Ambassador Lovera went into a huff over the ransom; he was insulted, he said, by such a paltry sum. We were worth a great deal more than that. If the terrorists insisted on going to Europe, the money wouldn't last a month — it was pocket change, he said derisively. If I ever came close to stuffing a gag in Ambassador Lovera's mouth, that was the time. I had no problem considering our ransom transaction as a bargain.

Evening settled in and we settled back, thinking of freedom. The hostages quietly reminisced about their wives, their children, their mistresses in some cases. We went through a round of "The first thing I'm going to do when I get out of here…" and made promises to stay in touch with one another. Everyone was lost in his own private reveries as we began to count the hours.

Victor Sasson showed up early the next morning and stayed through lunch. He brought the terrorists new red berets and material so they could make new bandannas for themselves. Sasson and Rivas Sacconi spent the evening inside the Embassy, making final preparations. Norma had her last meeting with the men in the van, and they produced a document specifically outlining the details for our departure, which was to be managed by the International Red Cross. Like people at the tense countdown before a missile launch, we sat by holding our breaths, hoping we had taken care of all our business. Commander One told us to be ready to leave the Embassy by seven the next morning. We had no complaints; it was one of the few times we didn't argue with him. I offered some of my colleagues a ride home with me on the jet that would be waiting for me in Havana. Ricardo Galán said thank you, but he'd have his own plane waiting; the Ambassador from Brazil accepted the invitation and asked if the Nuncio could tag along.

We finished off our vintage with great ceremony. The backgammon freaks staged their last marathon tourney, and the Ambassador from Egypt, an elegant player, challenged all who dared play him for the championship. Unfortunately for the Egyptian, Ambassador Galán edged him out of the title in the very last game. I had already sewed up the Chinese Checkers title.

There was also a great deal of kidding about Ambassador Barak, whose turn it was to clean the lavatory. He steadfastly performed the chore but promised revenge because I was on the duty roster to clean it the next day: he threatened to wake me up very early to make sure I would have enough time to get the work done before we left for the airport.

That evening Ambassador Barak buttonholed me and said he wanted to show me he hadn't been bluffing about his threat to Commander One to escape if his deadline wasn't met. I followed him to the bathroom, where he showed me a small awninged window over the washbasin that the terrorists had wired shut after Ambassador Gómez had escaped. The Ambassador had carefully cut the wire but left it in place, held with chewing gum. When I climbed up on the washbasin and looked out the window, I could see it led directly to a niche in the facade of the building that was out of view of the sentry posts. Once on the ground, he had only to make a short dash to the parked cars and cover. "Eli, it's perfect," I said. "Why didn't you go?"

Ambassador Barak smiled broadly and extended his arm toward me. "I was waiting for you to lose a little more weight so you could fit through the window and go with me," he said mischievously.

TWENTY-SEVEN

Tactically, some important lessons could be drawn from my experience in the Dominican Embassy in how to conduct barricade negotiations. Some previous experiences were revalidated, some conventional wisdoms put into question. Paul Wilkinson, in his interesting book *Terrorism and the Liberal State* (New York: Halsted Press, 1978), points out that the advantages do not always lie with the terrorist side. He cites the fact that in late 1975, tactics developed by the New York City police in criminal kidnappings were used by a number of governments as a third option to the stark alternatives of absolute capitulation to terrorist demands to save hostage lives or the ultimate shoot-out with the prospect of heavy casualties among the hostages.

Wilkinson speaks of a policy of "standing firm, breaking down the morale and will of the terrorists, and forcing them to surrender peacefully without harm to the hostages." He refers to the calling in of psychologists who advise the police when to bring pressure to bear and when to back off and describes the use of the latest surveillance techniques, cameras, and listening devices to monitor the mood of the kidnappers and the plight of the victims. These are to be followed up by an impressive show of force by army and police units. Such techniques were used by the Irish security authorities during the eighteen-day siege of the kidnappers of Dr. Teide Herrama in October—November 1975. Similar tactics were employed by the British police in the Balcombe Street siege of Provisional IRA members in December 1975 and by the Dutch authorities in the same month in dealing with the South Moluccan terrorists who stormed the Indonesian Consulate in Amsterdam and hijacked a Dutch train near Beilin. "One great advantage of this strategy of pressure by authorities," according to Wilkinson, "is that while they are applying psychological pressure against the terrorists, the hostage has at least a chance of developing a personal relationship with his captors which might make the hostage's execution less likely."

The parallels between these situations and the siege at the Dominican Embassy are self-evident. The New York City police tactics were manifest. There were also some differences. The contrast between the political fragility of the Colombian government and the stability of the United Kingdom and of the Netherlands need not be belabored. The fact that representatives of fifteen governments were being held put unusual pressure on the Colombians as those governments raised their voices to insist on the safeguarding of their envoys, through capitulation if necessary. The unusually large number of terrorists with almost-military training and internal cohesion made the breaking down of their morale problematical. There was also one salient difference between our situation and those described by Wilkinson: the presence of experienced, mature negotiators among the hostages.

This was the element, initially perceived by the terrorists as an exploitable resource and by the governments involved as a potential embarrassment if not an outright obstacle, that made our vigil interesting if not outright historic. Both sides were to be proved wrong. It was here where the outside managers of the crisis, slavishly following the New York police script which provides that hostages should not be used as negotiators and implicitly accepts the validity of the Stockholm Syndrome, first stumbled and then recovered sufficiently to permit our "intrusion" into the negotiation. Our participation, in addition to its substantial and substantive contribution to the eventual resolution of the crisis, provided clear evidence of the way out between the stark alternatives described above. It should engender fruitful discussion between the hard-liners, the no-negotiation, no-concession, gun-on-hip group, anxious to settle matters by shooting it out with the terrorists, and those who, for humanitarian reasons, might be prepared to go further in their intent to defend the life and limb of otherwise innocent civilians. I am convinced that the threat of force as a credible deterrent is essential in barricade situations and has its place as a potential instrument. It must provide the pressure that ensures negotiations on a reasonable basis. However, the time has come, as I stated to my fellow hostages at one point, to think with our heads and not with our balls, not to fight harder or fight dirtier but to fight smarter. In the ultimate analysis, intelligent conversation is always preferable to that atavistic impulse of all males to settle disputes by violence. It is the area of the trained negotiator, the psychologist, the salesman, and it should not be abandoned to violent men wishing to revalidate their manhood by killing each other. Put in blunter terms, bullshit is always cheaper than bullets.

We proved also that each barricade situation is a universe of its own with its own special characteristics and that following the script could have undesirable effects. Flexibility should be the norm, and if an unusual opportunity presents itself to resolve the situation, it should be seized. The Stockholm Syndrome needs more study and research. It has been hyped by the media out of all proportion and context, and it is affecting life-and-death decisions. It may very well exist under special circumstances, but it probably does not mean what the men on the barricades think it means. There are also strong indications that it can be resisted by hostages with a modicum of advice and training.

Interestingly, there are indications from Colombia that the terrorists considered the Dominican Embassy siege a failure. It was, they appear to think, too heavy an investment in time and resources for its accomplishments. They lost control of the eventual outcome once they slammed the door at the Embassy and began to shoot it out with the Colombian security forces. They have since reverted to bank holdups and individual kidnappings where the victims are spirited away to undisclosed locations as much more productive than the Mexican standoff they engineered on February 27. While anything is possible in the inverted world of terrorism, I would be surprised if any such adventure is attempted again in the near future in Latin America by an organized group.

The principal lesson, of course, for the individual diplomat or multinational employee or anyone who works for an international organization, whether private or public, is what to do once you are in the soup.

The first lesson is a truism learned as a child from any cowboy-and-Indian matinée; that is, in any shoot-out stay very close to the floor, preferably behind cover. Religion helps but this is something you take in with you; while Paul on the road to Damascus represents a great example for humanity, it is sufficiently rare to discard as an everyday lesson. Psychologists have informed me that in this type of situation the aggressors have the enormous advantage of increased amounts of adrenaline in their bloodstreams. Victims, on the other hand, are most likely producing acetylcholine, antagonist of adrenaline and the chemical symptom of the terror-driven state typical of captives. This also appears to be the condition most conducive to the Stockholm Syndrome. Passivity is to be consciously guarded against, but by this I do not mean antagonizing your captors, never a particularly healthy approach when the other fellow has the guns. Engage them in discussion, find out what they really think. Attempt to establish a personal relationship, to emphasize your primacy as a human being with feelings, needs, and cares. Work to invoke a climate of cordiality even if you are seething within. Inner rage has its place as a great provider of adrenaline, but its outward manifestation may get you into trouble. Above all, do not confuse cordiality with the Stockholm Syndrome. There is a tactical purpose behind your actions. Essentially, it is to avoid being killed.

It is also a truism that many terrorists, hijackers, criminals, and the like are usually adept at preparing the first act of our type of melodrama but are singularly incapable often of even visualizing the denouement. The Icarian personality is usually compensating for inadequacies and seeking fame, fortune, and the land of Eden through some magic gesture instead of by the ordinary road of preparation and hard work. One analyst wisecracked that terrorists are often foreigners whose medical records are not accessible to us. They are often shocked when, after their spasm of effort, it all does not fall into place. The government does not collapse. Their nonnegotiable demands are rejected out of hand. The land of Eden is nowhere near; rather, they are nose to nose with reality in the form of the guns of opposing security forces. They are, in truth, eternal boys. This is where the mature, well-integrated hostage steps in. I stress that what I am proposing runs contrary to the conventional wisdom embodied in the New York City police tactics. There, it is suggested that a hostage is particularly unsuitable as a negotiator since, being sensibly interested in protecting life and limb, he is likely to be highly desirous of seeing the terrorists accomplish their objective. At worst, if he is appropriately terror-stricken and is particularly susceptible, the Stockholm Syndrome comes into play and he identifies with the terrorists — or even worse, he is considered by those on the outside to be under the influence of the syndrome.

This approach discards an invaluable asset. No one is suggesting that the hostage should be the sole negotiator or intermediary for the official point of view. If, however, the hostage has managed to establish any sort of personal relationship with his captors, he is in a unique position to influence them. Negotiating sessions are relatively formal affairs, brief and intermittent at best. Often they must be conducted at a distance or through electronic means. The interlocutors are, by definition, enemies. The hostage ordinarily is with his captors all day, every day, of his captivity in a barricade situation. His value to the terrorists is symbolic and he typically does not have anything personal against the individual terrorists. I took the tack: "Listen, buddy, I'm anxious to get out of here in one piece. Your demands are unrealistic. Your negotiating tactics will ensure that we are all shot. I am an experienced negotiator. Let me help." When my suggested approaches struck responsive chords with the government negotiators, my judgment automatically zoomed in value with the terrorists. This enabled me, at the appropriate moment, to speak up on behalf of the government's approach, to expand it, to take into account the observations of the terrorists that were consistent with what the government was trying to do, and most important of all, to convince them that they had a good deal. I do not mean to imply that it was easy. It took, after all, sixty-one days. The point is that it was possible, and it probably was the single most important element leading to a satisfactory resolution.

Perhaps Gail Sheehy, of *Passages* fame, was correct when, in an interview after my release, she stated that I had become so accustomed to identifying myself with the United States as its representative abroad that I had a continental-sized ego incapable of being dominated by adversity. I have no delusions of being a titan and I would probably be just as embarrassed as anyone else by the usual flag-waving manifestations of patriotism. There is no question, however, that I was fully conscious of representing the United States of America. I could not betray that trust.

How to stay healthy in a protracted siege situation? What helped most of all was the fact that I was working very hard. I was not just a hostage sitting in a corner but was very deeply involved in the negotiations, not only dealing with the other members of our internal committee but also with the Colombian government, with my own Embassy, with the guerrillas, and in trying to take care of the other hostages. My telephone calls with my wife, and from time to time with my children, were precious moments that revitalized me completely.

Physically, we managed to do some exercise whenever we were removed from our room to speak on the telephones. While other members of our group spoke, we did calisthenics, ran in place, and marched up and down. After the first week, when we were in danger of drowning in our own garbage and conditions had gotten exceedingly gamy, we set up distinct and organized work details with rather high standards. The floor had to be clean, the bathrooms sparkling. We recruited amateur chefs and planned menus. These were not just aesthetic considerations; we also considered that the crowded and unhygienic conditions would lead to catastrophe if we were not careful. I was determined to come out of the siege in better condition physically than when I went in. In addition to the exercise, I was watching my diet, not a particularly difficult task since our food was sometimes barely edible. I was taking vitamins but avoiding tranquilizers and soporifics because I wanted to be both physically and mentally alert: physically in the event it became necessary to make any sudden moves; and mentally because ultimately my wits were my first line of defense and my ticket out of the situation. I rarely had time to brood over my probable fate.

Those who did not require external stimuli in order to entertain themselves or keep themselves busy did remarkably well. Some stared at the television set all day long at some of the most inane programs in existence. The games we played helped. The backgammon, chess, dominoes, Chinese checkers, in addition to helping the time pass, contributed to camaraderie among the players and it helped dispel the feelings of loneliness and abandonment. Those feelings were the most pernicious of all. A person in this situation needs a sense that he is being backed, that people are concerned about him, that someone is working on his behalf that he is loved. The messages Nancy transmitted from the President, the Secretary of State, and the Congress, as well as from my friends, did much to assuage emotions that might have become overwhelming. Little tokens became tremendously important. When I think of the eggs decorated by David Manzur and the collage made by Alejandro Obregón or the column written about me by Daniel Samper, I still choke up. They became immensely important parts of my daily existence. I would look at them often. They were my tenuous link to the outside world.

Being deprived of information was terrible. In addition to government reports, I was accustomed to scanning most of the Colombian newspapers and to reading the *New York Times*, the *Washington Post*, the *Miami Herald*, and various newsmagazines. I could understand why the authorities had prevented the entry of printed news media into the Embassy. I fully agreed with the principle. The terrorists should not be kept up to date on what was going on in the outside world. It could only complicate the situation. It was necessary to increase their sense of isolation. The Embassy attempted to brief me by reading from our wireless file, a compendium of U.S. and world media reports, but this was not enough. I wanted to know what George Will was writing. What did Meg Greenfield think of this situation? What was going on in Teheran? What was the latest from Afghanistan? What was happening in El Salvador? When some copies of *Time* magazine were smuggled in with the Swiss Ambassador's supplies, I devoured them from cover to cover.

Night times were bad. We would prepare our pallets for sleeping in the semidarkness with no light except that from a television receiver. We were fully aware of the surrounding troops as they tried to provoke reactions from our guards. Shots would be fired, bottles smashed, the motors of troops carriers would be revved. When you are asleep at 1:00 A.M. and suddenly automatic weapon-fire goes off a few yards away, it is quite thought-provoking and not particularly restful.

I was asked shortly after my release whether, knowing I would survive, I would be prepared to undergo the same experience again. I replied that having gone through it once, I saw no virtue in doing it again. If that had not been the case, I would probably do it just out of curiosity. It was fascinating, an experience I cherish but do not particularly want to repeat. I believe that I assisted in converting a violent, confrontational situation in which all kinds of juridical norms were being violated, into one where the principles of human rights and the sanctity of human life were upheld. I was given the opportunity of observing men under stress, which broadened my consideration of the human condition. Furthermore, I had not been prepared merely to sit there with my thumb in my mouth, waiting for external forces to come to my rescue. The conventional wisdom, be damned. I had been working, I was in good shape, and I was intent on getting our bottoms out of that particular sling, if necessary, by ourselves.

One aspect of terrorism that needs more careful thought and study is the interaction of the media with it. There are some theorists who believe that without the attention of the media — particularly television — terrorism would diminish considerably, if not disappear completely. One has only to remember the obscene chanting of the mobs in Teheran during that hostage crisis to wonder whether the reaction of the so-called public was staged or if it would have been so violent had television cameras not been omnipresent. Observers noted, for instance, that the crowds played to the cameras: their vociferousness was directly proportionate to camera and microphone range. One also cannot help wondering if the presence of electronic media didn't provide an international stage for the Iranians to perform on, and artificially prolonged the crisis itself. As an old Arkansan adage says: "So long's someone's gonna listen, I'm gonna talk."

The symbology of the events in Teheran and Bogotá is clear. The terrorist, by taking an American official hostage abroad or in taking an American installation, considers the American government — and perhaps American society itself— his captive. From the American point of view, the symbols unquestionably provide an effect: the terrorists are burning *our* flag. An American official, our representative and the personal representative of the President of the United States, is helpless in the clutches of a wild-eyed political zealot who sees himself as the avatar of the Revolution. When a terrorist invades an embassy, he is invading *American* soil. His act, in our eyes, is an aggressive act tantamount to an act of war.

I have often heard people express the rather widespread belief that we must do more to protect these bastions of the United States overseas: we need more marines, more armor, more weapons. We cannot afford to let these "punk" opportunists run roughshod over a nation so great without a fight and without benefit of our sophisticated technologies.

I respond to the criticism by saying that, despite the symbols — the flag, the eagle on the top of the flagpole, the platoon of ready marines — we are talking about an office building. Stripped of its glamour, its mystique, and its symbols, that's all an embassy is. There is no known technology or tactic which will allow you to defend a building against superior forces indefinitely. Our embassy defense plans are predicated on eventual rescue by the security forces of the host government. If these forces should not arrive or if they come late; the result is foredoomed.

The press is one of the major characters in these dramas, for without the means to disseminate the propaganda, the effort is worthless. Terrorists have often claimed that their objective — at least their *prima facie* objective — is to secure the release of prisoners and/or raise moneys for their cause. History has convincingly demonstrated that these professed goals are rarely met and that terrorism for profit or trade is not cost-effective. What does make the exercise cost-effective, at least in the minds of some terrorists, is the international media exposure they are guaranteed. This fact makes terrorism a nonpareil exercise for many foundering factions that need to act convincingly in an oftentimes desperate attempt to recoup lost ground.

What would happen, however, if the media did not focus their attention so forcefully on such events? What if someone gave a demonstration or a riot or an embassy takeover and nobody came? Would the terrorist still consider the effort cost-effective if he could not air his demands or publish his principles or posture in public? I am not advocating a diminishment of the freedoms guaranteed by our Bill of Rights. Nor do I argue with the public's right to know what is happening. The quandary is evident. Aren't we catering to the competitive, commercial urge of newsmen and their desire to out-scoop their colleagues by showing the latest political crisis in painstaking detail? Aren't the newsmen themselves manipulating the same symbols as the terrorists? Their ostensible motive is to inform, but to inform under the aegis of commercialism; in short, to sell jeans and mouthwash. I'm prepared to accept that my job requires me to put my life on the line for my country. But do I have to do it for Calvin Klein?

I remember the indecent urgency of the first days of my captivity when the newsmen refused to get off the telephone so we could call out to make the arrangements for the negotiations that ultimately set us free. I also remember the unnecessary tension and strain caused by the terrorist sentries when they scrambled to take up defensive positions in preparation for a shoot-out, only to find newsmen trying to infiltrate the security perimeter in order to interview someone. At times the terrorists used us as shields while they shot at journalists trying to get close to the Embassy. Many of these journalists, intent only on an exclusive interview, recklessly jeopardized our safety. Whenever I thought of the troop of newsmen gathered in their tent city known as "Scoopsville" near the Embassy, I had the nagging suspicion, that they were waiting, hoping to witness the final denouement: the shoot-out between the government and the terrorists with the hostages in the middle. They were waiting to report my maiming or my execution; in fact, they had already filed false reports of just that. All for a few moments of film that would enliven the television screen and momentarily rival the violence of *Starsky and Hutch*. Is this form of frenetic journalism necessary?

I would be the last person to advocate censorship or governmental control of the media. The media, however, could well do some soul-searching of their own and decide what those limits should properly be. If we are truly at the beginning of a terrorist cycle when such tactics are the preferred instruments of political warfare, is there any reason to think the United States will be spared? If terrorism should occur here more frequently than it already has, it is likely that this will influence our legislators, in which case the media may face restrictions not of their own choosing. A difficult question, of course, but one that merits more attention than it has received.

The question still remains of how best to protect our embassies abroad. The hardening of Embassy sites and the development of missions into veritable bunkers have a place in this crazy world of ours. Such precautions would deter the casual terrorist, the maniac, and the freelancer, but by themselves are not the answer. There is only one method I know of that gives substantial promise of effectively combatting terrorism: a system of enhanced intelligence collection and analysis.

As a political officer for most of my Foreign Service career, I have observed at close hand the operations of the Central Intelligence Agency, particularly those in Latin America. Sometime in the mid-1970s, the Agency gave up most of the resources it had devoted to the internal subversive movements of Latin America. In reassessing its priorities, the Agency eliminated its capability to observe domestic political currents elsewhere in favor of its principal goal of concentrating on Iron Curtain activities. The Agency's mission and tactics were attacked in the U.S. press and in Congress. As a result the Agency cut loose not only many experienced U.S. agents, but more important, its assets abroad that had formerly been used to penetrate, infiltrate, and collect data on the clandestine political world of the Southern Hemisphere. This fact was brought forcefully to my attention while I was working on the case of an American businessman kidnapped in Caracas. After I asked for information on the group that had purportedly organized the kidnapping, our intelligence people sheepishly admitted that the Agency resources once connected with the group were no longer on the job. I ran into the same problem again when a Peace Corps volunteer was kidnapped in Colombia. I asked for information on the organization responsible for the kidnapping, on what it was thinking, and so forth, only to be met with blank stares.

There was a time not too long ago when it was impossible for the proverbial swallow to fall without its being reported by the CIA. Since then, its capabilities have been severely compromised. Some of the slack has been taken up by the overt political sections of our embassies. Any good political officer with normal access to the political groups of a society will, perforce, know a great deal of what's going on in any given country. By their very nature, however, these are open contacts, the normal and legitimate political meetings, parties, literature, political spokesmen, and political currents of a society. The Foreign Service members have little or no access to the subterranean levels of the clandestine world, nor do they seek it because it would compromise the open nature of their activities. An informational gap formed as a result of this compromised capacity for gathering intelligence, and I almost died as a result of it. Intelligence might have warned me of the M-19's plans. Rumors of "something going down" were circulating *abroad* before the actual seizure. A well-developed intelligence community would have picked up on it.

I understand this gap is now being redressed. I hope so. Any democracy that vitiates such a precious political instrument deserves everything that happens to it. The destruction of our intelligence capability in the face of the activities of the KGB and its minions throughout the world strikes me as the height of lunacy. Those who advocate the unilateral dismantling of our intelligence capacity are guilty of incredible naiveté. I'm not in favor of rogue elephants out of control of the appropriate authorities nor do I condone transgressions against the civil rights of Americans or anyone else, for that matter, but I advocate strongly the need for a sensitive and capable intelligence community. Our lives depend on it.

There was another curious condition manifesting itself during my captivity that I believe cries out for greater research by psychologists. Certainly, every crisis manager should be aware of it. For want of a better term, I would call it the "Victim and Victim's Family Syndrome." It goes without saying that, in the case of the victim in any kidnapping or barricade situation, there has to be a considerable amount of unresolved rage and frustration. These emotions cannot be expressed to the captors because it would clearly endanger the victim. Major but often forgotten players in these dramas, are the families of the victims. Although not subjected to the same physical danger as the victims themselves, these families are psychological and emotional casualties of terrorist acts. The family has no way of directing its anger at the terrorists who are simply inaccessible as the focal point of such feelings. There is also no socially acceptable means of expressing grief — no funeral, no ceremony, or other rite — since the victim is simply missing and the state of his well-being unknown. Some psychologists state that, often, the victim is in better mental condition than his family since he, at least, knows how and where he is. Uncertainty affects the family psychologically in ways that are difficult to handle.

The end result often is that the nearest authority figure becomes the target, the lightning rod for the rage that must somehow be expressed. This figure is, of course, the crisis manager and his superiors, whether government official, company executive, Secretary of State, company president, or even the President of the United States. It can also be expressed impersonally in the form of frustration focused on the Embassy, the company, the Department of State, the U.S. government or, simply, "them." I have observed this phenomenon at work in a number of cases where I was directly involved, and I was able to observe its effects on me and my family during my own captivity. I have even experimented in attempting to reach victims' families through applications of large quantities of empathy, information, personal contact, and other means of demonstrating that my staff people were doing everything possible and that we really cared. I have found it impossible, so far, to do "enough" for such a family since — not having resolved the problem — there is a marked tendency on the part of the victim's family unconsciously to discount and even disregard the efforts being made by well-wishers. "How can you be doing the right thing if you haven't obtained Johnny's release?" is not an uncommon attitude.

Nor does the problem end with the release or safety of the victim and the successful resolution of the case. Victims are usually idealized in their absence by their families and take on an almost saint-like aura, often reinforced by feelings of guilt on the part of those who are not suffering directly with them. On their return home, not surprisingly, they are found to possess the same frailties they had before the incident. This departure from the ideal comes as a shock to the family. Since it would be difficult psychically and perhaps not even respectable socially to rail at one who has suffered danger and has, perhaps, even been acclaimed a hero, the resentment on the part of the family must also find its focus elsewhere. Equally potent as a displacer of anger and frustration is the situation in which the victim is, indeed, lionized and then takes the spotlight away from the family members who, up until the moment of deliverance, were the object of universal concern, solicitude and, more important, media attention.

The psychic thickets encompassed in these observations are, I believe, fertile ground for original, interesting, and useful professional research. It should not end there, however. The crisis managers have to know also. Further, I think it interesting for potential victims to be aware of these factors so that they may be prepared to take their own emotional temperature when in captivity and so that victims' families may help themselves in learning to handle rage and frustration.

TWENTY-EIGHT

After a restless night, I woke up early on Sunday morning, April 27. Most of the other hostages — there were eighteen of us left — were already up and about, some complaining of hangovers from celebrating too hard the night before. We collected our things and made ready for our exodus. Bishop Acerbi celebrated Mass downstairs, still using his little chest-of-drawers as a makeshift altar, as hostage and terrorist alike knelt to accept Communion.

We were soon joined by the entire cast of characters: the four members of the OAS Human Rights Commission, negotiators Jiménez and Zambrano, the Cuban Ambassador, and the two ransom negotiators, who had spent the night with us. We stood around waiting for the word to board the two gray and white Red Cross buses, which had their windows painted over. The guerrillas were exceptionally nervous, but the presence of the mediators helped calm them down. We'd come too far to be attacked by the army now; if it had done so, it would have taken a needless, foolhardy risk, but that didn't keep the M-19 from worrying.

Along with the buses, three ambulances were standing by, and they served as an ugly reminder of what could happen. The Munich police had waited until the Arab terrorists holding the Israeli athletes were in the open at the airport before they counterattacked, and it was a bloody and tragic encounter. We didn't believe outwardly that the Colombian army would attack, but inwardly there was the fear it might. Logic does not always prevail, and history has many slaughtered victims to prove it.

The excitement of our pending freedom mixed with the fearful anticipation of the unknown unsettled all of us.

At 6:45 A.M., Commander One gave the go-ahead to start boarding the buses. He carefully interspersed hostages with his own troops as they started to file out of the Embassy and into the buses. Commander One and Norma stayed close to me — determined to use me as a shield until the end — and made me sit in the front of the lead bus. I expected our departure to be highly emotional, but with the bustle and the mechanical way the exercise was carried out, our mood was subdued, almost hesitant. Some of the hostages turned around to take a parting glance at the eerie mansion — an image that will be etched into our memories for a lifetime in our thoughts and in our dreams. It was a silent farewell, a fervent goodbye, good riddance.

Because no one could see out his window, the buses made us slightly claustrophobic and equally paranoid. We didn't know what was out there, and the unknown seemed much more dangerous and unpredictable. Fortunately, I was up front and could see out the driver's window. There was some advantage of being in the open. Once we were aboard and the doors were secured,

Commander One gave the order for the caravan to begin its eight-mile trek to El Dorado Airport outside Bogotá.

The early Sunday morning streets were nearly deserted. The Commander, crouched near the driver, flashed the "V" for victory sign to occasional pedestrians, some of whom were still dressed in evening clothes. A few of the bystanders stared at us blankly; others applauded. I never found out if they were applauding us or the terrorists.

The buses traveled cautiously through the city streets to the airport, where we were met by an army jeep and a stark yellow airport fire truck which escorted us to the end of a remote runway. There a red and white Soviet-made Ilyushin jet was already refueled and waiting for us. From the distance I could see a group of men milling around the gangway. I hoped they weren't army: Commander One was already fidgety enough. As we got closer, I could see the group was made up of photographers and journalists — or at least people dressed up to look like them. The Commander, ever cautious and paranoid, delayed our unloading until Ambassador Ravelo cleared them off the runway. He wasn't about to take any chances, and I couldn't really blame him. It took fifteen anxious minutes for the Cuban Ambassador to shoo them away while we cursed the press under our breaths. The delays, no matter how small, were maddening.

Once Ambassador Ravelo gave the "All Clear" sign to Commander One, we filed off the bus and quickly boarded the plane. The terrorists pulled their bandannas over their faces and stayed close to the hostages so sharpshooters wouldn't have the chance to pick them off. Rosenberg Pabón Pabón — Commander One — overlorded the operation without his bandanna; since he had been identified, he no longer thought it necessary to hide his light under a bushel. The terrorists kept their weapons at hand and off safety as they lugged the heavy suitcase filled with $1,200,000 in cash onto the plane.

The Cubans frisked us as soon as we boarded. They were firm but polite. They also made the terrorists turn over their grenades before they boarded, but they let them keep their firearms. Had Ambassador Ravelo gone back on his word? He'd promised me his people would disarm the terrorists before taking off; now that I was aboard, there was little I could do — the terrorists weren't about to let me disembark in protest. I felt betrayed.

Only twelve hostages boarded; six stayed on the runway. The ambassadors from Egypt and Israel were allowed to return to Bogotá because Commander One had promised not to take them to the Middle East when that was a possibility since their lives would have been endangered. The Ambassador from Venezuela, despite his loud claim to feel like running a mile in the Olympics or going a few rounds with Pambele, the Colombian junior welterweight champion, was also to stay in Bogotá. Commander One also freed the Dominican Ambassador and thanked him for his gracious hospitality during the past two months. Guzmán and Valencia, despite their efforts to get on board with us, were unceremoniously bounced.

Once the cabin doors were closed, I breathed a partial sigh of relief. At least the Colombians weren't about to start any tomfoolery. But I still had the armed terrorists to worry about; something could still go awry. If everything went well and according to schedule, I had only three hours of captivity left. One hundred and eighty minutes. I was, I hoped, a commuter's flight away from freedom. At 8:15 A.M., the control tower at Bogotá International gave us final clearance, and our Air Cubana jet took off into the sparkling morning sun.

Once we were airborne, Ambassador Ravelo lived up to his promise to me: the Cubans confiscated the M-19's rifles. Curiously however, they let the terrorists keep their sidearms sans ammunition — perhaps as token souvenirs or as false security blankets. There wasn't much they could do with unloaded pistols, I reasoned, so I didn't object as I settled into my seat more comfortably.

The cabin attendants worked hard to make us feel at ease. The Ilyushin jet was clean, sleek, and modern — even elegant, except for the roll of toilet tissue I found hanging from a nail driven into the wall of the lavatory. They served us a wonderful lunch: I ordered steak and a bottle of Marqués de Riscal, a Rioja wine to which I am partial. I even indulged in a glass of native Cuban beer, Hatuey, which I had heard exiles mention fondly.

The Cubans brought along their own entourage of journalists so as not to miss the opportunity to exploit the occasion properly. Before long they cranked up their television cameras and set to work on us.

Their questions were surprisingly tame, even gentle. After one interview, I turned to Ambassador Ravelo and with a straight face told him I had just done irreparable damage to his career. "What do you mean?" he asked as the furrows deepened on his forehead.

"I just got finished telling the press what a good fellow you are," I joked. "Coming from the mouth of the American Ambassador, surely that means trouble for you!"

"In that case we're even," he told me slyly. "In Colombia I told the press how you are *my* friend!" International politics would never be the same again.

There was a lot of mutual teasing and jesting. Part of it was nervousness and part of it was genuine warmth. As Ambassador Galan noted: "In sixty days of living together, you learn to admire people as people, if not to admire their ideas." Although he didn't particularly care for the M-19's ideas, "As people," he said for all of us, "some of them were excellent."

Later in the day, Ambassador Nascimento e Silva and María bantered affectionately before the press. "Ideology separated us," she said, "but he was very human."

"I'm a reactionary bourgeois," he teased.

"But he is very human," María repeated.

A little after noon, our jet swung gracefully into the final approach to José Martí Airport outside Havana. The warm Caribbean sun, the startling translucence of the sea and the graceful palms were comforting and endearing. I felt a newfound sense of tranquility. We were beyond the point of no return: Cuba meant freedom. Ironically, I was probably the first American in recent history who was escaping to Cuba for freedom. Cuba meant reunion with my family and my country. I was weary of rhetoric and shadow-talk; I was fed-up with finesse. I looked forward to simpler pleasures: pleasures all of us take for granted too often. Most of all, I anticipated the generous pleasures of freedom and democracy.

I knew I was going to be the man of the moment back home — proof positive that one could deal successfully with terrorist blackmailers without giving in to them — that I was going to be the inspiration and hope for retrieving the American hostages in Iran. But I wasn't ready for the speeches, the interviews, the endless briefings and debriefings: I wanted only some privacy with Nancy so we could take stock of ourselves and what we had, I needed time to reaffirm our love and commitment. I wanted to take a deep, unimpeded breath and give thanks.

When the Air Cubana jet lumbered to a halt, Commander One and his band of freshly primped guerrillas prepared for their heroes' welcome. They marched off the plane in the attitude of returning conquerors resplendent in their new berets and bandannas. They were greeted with applause, admiration, and respect: the Cubans received them as the revolutionaries they claimed to be. Manuel Piñero, the head of Cuba's America Department and a ranking member of the Cuban Communist party's Central Committee, was on hand to accept them and offer his country's sanctuary.

I was pleased to see my own little reception committee waiting for me off to the side. As I disembarked, I spotted Dr. Ferguson Reid of the State Department's Medical Services Division. Standing next to him was another old friend, Sam Eaton, a Deputy Assistant Secretary for Latin American Affairs, and Wayne Smith and Tim Towell of the Special Interests Section in Havana. "Hi, Fergie!" I greeted him as though I were bumping into him on Capitol Hill. "What are you doing here?"

We strode through the terminal where I held a short, impromptu press conference with some of the other hostages. I was happy to see Daniel Samper, the political columnist for *El Tiempo*, whose columns had established my credibility with the M-19; he had turned me from an ogre into someone respectable and human. I also gave Daniel a message to pass along to his brother Ernesto, who was the director of a banking think-tank in Bogotá: we had a long-standing family feud over the legalization of marijuana, and I told Daniel to tell his brother he was taking unfair advantage of my captivity by campaigning for the legalization while I was a hostage.

Diego hugs Deputy Assistant Secretary of State for Inter-American Affairs Samuel Eaton, on the far right Chief of Special Interest Section in Havana Timothy Towell.

The Cubans set up the reception facilities so captor and captive would be segregated, but the terrorists made a point of coming to our lounge to say goodbye. Several of the ambassadors hugged and even kissed the female terrorists. The press reported that I had either hugged or kissed La Doctora, but I don't remember ever having done so. I wasn't so far gone that I wouldn't remember kissing a pretty young girl. I later reviewed a videotape of our arrival at José Martí Airport, but it resolved nothing. All I can think of was that the Ambassador from Brazil bore a superficial resemblance to me at a distance, and he did kiss the girls. Another possibility stems from a later *Washington Post* photo of me embracing Nancy and one of my daughters at

Homestead Air Force Base with the caption, "Asencio Bids Fond Farewell to Guerrillas." I still have that clipping and will treasure it always.

Within the hour of our landing, I started walking over to a beautiful Learjet waiting to take me home. I said goodbye to my colleagues with whom I had shared the ordeal and wished them Godspeed. It would be long before we'd be back behind our desks and bumping shoulders at another diplomatic reception. Many of us grew close in those months, and we'd forged bonds of friendship that would endure. I would miss them: their quirks, their humor, their keen insight, and their warmly human nature.

The flight back to the United States was filled with unrestrained enthusiasm. Despite the constant turmoil, the illusive highs and disconsolate lows, despite the bad food and worse accommodations, despite the hostilities of some of the terrorists and some of our own, and despite the moments when I was certain I was about to die, I had somehow pulled through. I had risked my life, my health, and my career; I was stripped of title, rank — everything but dignity — and I had survived the struggle. In an hour or two I'd be reunited with my family. No more standing in line at five in the morning, no more snorers and sulkers and pedants, and no more scullery and bathroom detail. I was a free man and, for the first time in my life, truly understood what it meant to be free.

During the flight to Homestead Air Force Base, Sam Eaton briefed me on recent developments in the Department of State. Dave Passage, an officer from the Public Affairs Division, who had been sent along to manage the press, remarked with a straight face, "I hate to mention this now, but I've been asked to remind you that you're behind preparing personnel evaluation reports on your staff." Reality was already creeping back in.

I remember thinking, when we touched down at Homestead, how good it felt to be back on American soil. I had taken the privilege for granted in the past, but it meant the world to me now: I will never forget the sensation which millions of others have shared privately: the returning soldier, the immigrant, the exile. I was home at last.

Nancy and my daughter Mary were waiting for me, and we had an emotional reunion. Nancy's sisters and a delegation of officers from the base headed by Wing Commander Colonel E. L. Fischer were also on hand to greet me. Nancy hung a beautiful gold cross around my neck which Louis Flóres, an artisan and the husband of one of my officers in Bogotá, had crafted for me. Nancy also draped a yellow ribbon around me as part of my symbolic welcome home. We were both in a daze, too stunned with emotion to react to our official welcome.

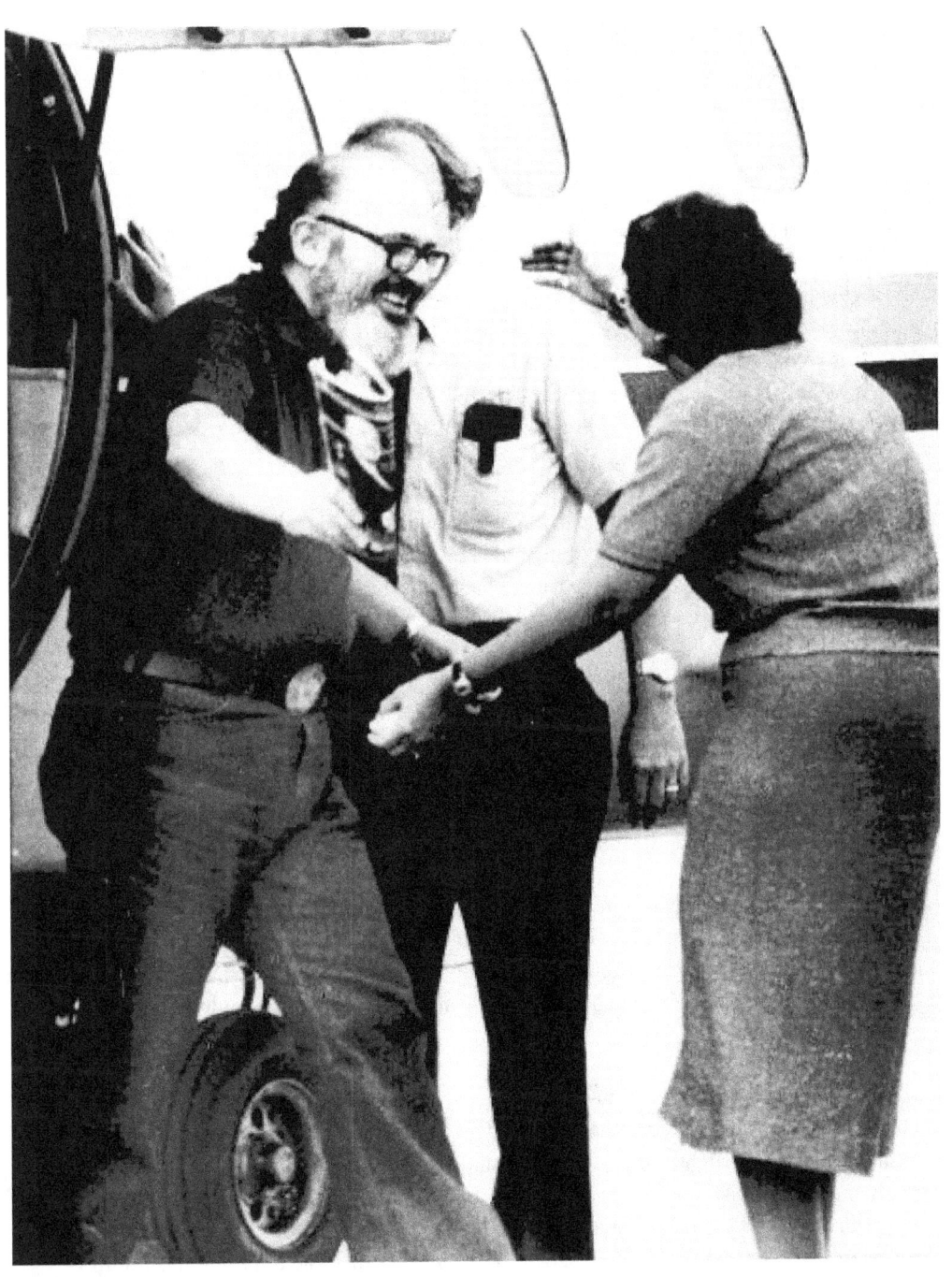

Nancy greeting Diego on arrival from Cuba after the hostages are released.

Sensing our need for privacy, Colonel Fischer had Nancy and me whisked off to a suite in the Bachelor Officers' Quarters where we were put strictly off limits. The base personnel went out of their way to make sure we had everything we wanted, and we began a two-and-a-half-day idyll.

My first luxury was a long, hot bath. Later, after Nancy and I had some time to ourselves, my son Frank, who had been given special leave from West Point to visit me, joined us at a sumptuous meal at the officers' club. I was particularly aware of the fact that I could get up and move around as I liked; I didn't need to ask anyone's permission. There were no more sentries with rifles standing by watching my every move, no more slogans of "Win or Die!" and no more ideological verse being spouted. There were friends unafraid of laughter, there was Nancy and not just her voice, and some of my children in the flesh to welcome me home. I can't describe the feeling I had then and there; I wish I could. I felt the love and support not only of my family and friends, but from people I'd never met before. We had one trait we all shared in common and that's what brought us together: we were Americans.

Before long our dinner turned into a party. We ate and joked and embraced one another. Secretary Vance, amidst the tragedy of the failed rescue attempt in the desert in Iran, made a point of calling me and welcoming me back. I particularly appreciate his gesture because I later understood he had already formulated his resignation.

The State Department people and the Air Force officers gave me a rousing reception. Colonel Fischer told me he almost couldn't get me landing clearance from the FAA because "they didn't want any more refugees coming to the United States from Havana." In the middle of our raucous celebration, Richard Baca, the Director of the Peace Corps in Colombia, picked up the phone and shouted over the din, "It's the President!" There was a dead silence except for one wag in the back of the room who shouted, "Put him on hold!"

President Carter graciously welcomed me back and told me he was glad for some "good news" for a change. Those were hard days for everyone in Washington, indeed for the entire country, and my safe return demonstrated convincingly that patience and diligence pay off. The President asked me to drop by if I ever happened to be in the neighborhood, and I said yes, I thought that could be arranged.

The next morning, after my sister-in-law Sylvia had trimmed my unruly beard, Fergie Reid accompanied me to the Base Hospital, where I was put through the paces of a vigorous physical examination. To my delight, I'd lost twenty pounds. I also had a chat with Pat Haynes, a State Department psychiatrist who'd been among those waiting for me in Havana. I'd figured him out for a shrink before anyone told me he was one: he was the only person who hadn't joined in on the conversation and had sat stone-faced and stared at me in his role of professional observer. Apparently I passed psychiatric muster, but then you never know.

That evening Nancy and I were invited to a dinner hosted by Colonel Fischer. He presented me with a plaque with the Air Wing's motto, "Return with Honor," inscribed on it and was kind enough to say I earned it. The Commander of the Support Staff also gave me a T-shirt that had the motto "We Do It Right" emblazoned across the chest.

The next day we boarded Air Force One for Andrews Air Force Base near Washington. Ambassador Harry Barnes, Director General of the Foreign Service, and Ambassador Abelardo Valdez, Director of Protocol, came along. They warned me about the red-carpet reception awaiting me and tried to prepare me for what was about to happen. If Ambassador Valdez hadn't told me about the fourteen-gun salute, I might have dived for cover.

Son Manuel embracing Diego on arrival to Andrews Air Force Base, Nancy and daughter Maria descend the ramp on the right, Acting Secretary of State Warren Christopher and Vice-President Walter Mondale on the left.

Fourteen gun salute at Andrews Air Force Base.

With Vice-President Walter Mondale at Andrews Air Force Base.

As soon as we landed, Washington, in marked contrast from the other times I'd returned there in complete anonymity, put on its finest ceremonial face: full-dress military band, honor guard, fourteen-gun salute. I didn't realize until I saw the pomp and circumstance that I was being welcomed home as a hero. When Ambassador Valdez had told me about red-carpet treatment, I thought he was talking metaphorically, but as I stepped off Air Force One, there was the red carpet, spread out in front of me leading to a reception line of dignitaries waiting to greet me, including Vice President Mondale, the Secretary General of the OAS, and the ambassadors of the countries represented by the hostages in the Dominican Embassy. My son Manuel was standing at the foot of the ramp, and he lifted me off the ground in a bear-hug. All sorts of people from Washington officialdom were there. Friends traveled from everywhere to share in the reception. The place was packed; normally stoic Washington had turned out for a schismatic son.

Vice President Mondale escorted me to the podium and began his welcoming speech. "We are all very proud of Ambassador Asencio," he said. "His courage, unflagging good spirits and leadership in adversity, as well as the patience and fortitude of his family, are an inspiration to us all. The career of diplomacy has been well served by the example set in the captive embassy these past two months." In the middle of the Vice President's speech, my daughter Anne, who just arrived from New York, came flying up to the podium and threw her arms around me. The Vice President, not used to being upstaged so dramatically, was startled by her sudden appearance but graciously stepped aside as Anne and I embraced. The crowd went wild at the sight of our reunion.

Once we "remembered where we were," Vice President Mondale continued without missing another beat: "Ambassador [from Colombia] Barco, the President has asked that I convey through you to President Turbay and his Government our deep appreciation for the skill, steadfastness of purpose and equanimity they have displayed throughout the lengthy, difficult negotiations leading to the release of the hostages…The taking of hostages and all other forms of terrorism whether in Bogotá, Teheran or anywhere else in the world, are inhumane acts that cannot be condoned. Firmness is needed to combat them. We, together with other like-minded countries, will seek to combat these despicable acts of violence wherever they occur."

As Vice President Mondale read these words, I couldn't help noticing the ocean of difference between the intellectual concept of fighting terrorism and the visceral reality of being a hostage; the Vice President's words were true, but they didn't seem real. Reality of terrorism can be understood only through its victims. We are all victims of terrorism in one sense because it threatens the very fabric of a free society; but emotionally we don't really understand its threat. The image of a child killed by a terrorist bomb or an innocent bystander shot down in the street by an indiscriminate sniper moves us all, but it doesn't teach anyone but the victim a lesson. The Vice President's words were more than rhetoric to me, but as I looked out over the faces in the audience I could see that in most cases those same words were nothing more than a flurry.

From Andrews Air Force Base, Acting Secretary of State Warren Christopher drove Nancy and me to the cavernous diplomatic entrance at the Department of State building where a horde of people were waiting anxiously. I had trouble fighting back the emotion as I hugged my way through the crowd of loyal friends to the podium. Acting Secretary Christopher gave a rousing welcome and proclaimed this day "one of our happiest days in a long time."

Acting Secretary of State Warren Christopher reading Diego's Award for Valor, son Manuel between them, daughter Maria on the right, just in front of the Memorial Plaque of Foreign Service personnel who died in the line of duty.

While hundreds of State Department employees watched from the balcony above the lobby, Mr. Christopher conferred the Award for Valor on me. The honor was so new, in fact, that I had to accept a scroll in lieu of the medal itself, which was still being struck. I thanked the Acting Secretary, my colleagues, and my friends, and then paraphrased Mark Twain by saying that if it weren't for the honor of the thing, I'd just as soon skip it all. I then told everyone about the plaque Colonel Fischer's Air Wing had presented to me with the motto "Return with Honor," and I hoped that I'd done that. On a more solemn note, I added that no Foreign Service officer could consider himself truly free while his friends and fellow workers were still being held prisoner in Teheran. I knew my freedom and honors were a testament for the hope of freedom for our colleagues in Iran: the moment was very emotional for all of us.

Diego speaking to staff at Department of State during award ceremony, daughter Anne in front of flag at far right.

After a press conference, I was ceremoniously checked into a suite of rooms at the Sheraton-Canton. My accommodations were a far cut above what I was usually given when I made my periodic visits to Washington.

President Carter received me at the White House and was kind enough to refer to me as "an authentic American hero" before the White House press corps. I don't really deserve to be called a hero because I didn't do anything I considered heroic. I stood in and fought for what I believed in without resorting to foolish compromise. Surely that isn't heroic. It's part of our ingrained American character.

Diego and Nancy with President Jimmy Carter in the Oval Office at the White House.

THE DAILY DIARY OF PRESIDENT JIMMY CARTER

LOCATION

THE WHITE HOUSE
WASHINGTON, D.C.

DATE (Mo., Day, Yr.)

APRIL 30, 1980

TIME   DAY

11 55 a.m.   WEDNESDAY

TIME		PHONE	ACTIVITY
From	To	P = Placed R = Rec'd	
11:55	12:05		The President met with: Diego C. Asencio, Ambassador of the U.S. to Colombia Mrs. Diego C. (Nancy) Asencio Anne Asencio, daughter Maria Asencio, daughter Manuel Asencio, son. Acting Secretary Christopher Robert Pastor, Staff Member, National Security Council (NSC) The purpose of the meeting was to welcome Ambassador Asencio home after being held as hostage at the Dominican Embassy in Bogota, Colombia for sixty-one days.
12:05	12:20		The President met with: Richard G. Hatcher, Mayor (D-Gary, Indiana) Mr. Watson Bruce Kirschenbaum, Associate for Intergovernmental Affairs Louis E. Martin, Special Assistant for Minority Affairs Members of the press, in/out The purpose of the meeting was to discuss the job situation in central cities and to announce Mayor Hatcher's endorsement of the President's re-election campaign.
12:20	1:00		The President had lunch with Vice President Walter F. Mondale
1:05	1:08	P	The President talked with Charles H. Kirbo, partner with King and Spalding law firm, Atlanta, Georgia.
1:12			The President went Roosevelt Room.
1:12	1:19		The President attended a luncheon hosted by Vice President Mondale for members of the editorial board of the Baltimore Sun Times. For a list of attendees, see APPENDIX "B."
1:19			The President returned to the Oval Office.
1:19	1:40		The President met to discuss legislative priorities with: Representative Harold T. Johnson (D-California) Representative James J. Howard (D-New Jersey) Secretary Goldschmidt Susan J. Williams, Assistant Secretary of Transportation for Government and Public Affairs Mr. Eizenstat

continued

White House Diary noting the Asencio family's meeting with President Carter.

When I left the Oval Office, I found my State Department limousine had left. I was stranded until Jim Wright, the Majority Leader of the House, offered me a ride, which made me realize that something truly noteworthy had come out of my sixty-one days in captivity!

It took me months to readjust to normal life. I found, in walking from the Sheraton-Carlton to the State Department, how wonderful it was to feel the sun and wind on my face, to be able to see the grass and the trees. The movement of people to and fro and the motion of cars on the street fascinated me. I had always enjoyed seeing the rain fall and smelling the fresh, earthy scent of wet dirt, but now it took on a special meaning. It was great to be alive, to feel, to see.

My sense of hearing remained unusually acute for months. I was able to overhear conversation going on several rooms away. The smallest noise would wake me up in the middle of the night — I was always waiting for the other shoe to drop. I had become accustomed to tracking the position of the sentries during my captivity. A part of me had become ever vigilant to the noises around me in anticipation of the ultimate shoot-out. I had rehearsed in my mind where to jump, how to go out the window, if the negotiations should break down or the security forces ringing the Embassy grew impatient and decided to take matters into their own hands. Every time a sentry looked into our room to check on us, I would automatically tense, preparing for action, for flight, to fight, to hide. Some atavistic impulse from our savage, hunting ancestry, blunted by years of civilization, had been reactivated by the danger to my life and limb. My senses became attuned to my environment. Its only effect now was that my hapless receptionist knows I can hear everything that goes on in her office, which is more than a hundred feet away.

I also noticed after a few weeks that I was having difficulty reading. My eyes weren't focusing on the printed page properly. I went to an ophthalmologist on the assumption that the rigors of my confinement or advancing age had caused my eyesight to deteriorate. To my amazement, the doctor told me that my eyes had actually improved. He hypothesized several possible causes: perhaps my eyesight had improved as the result of something new in my diet, or it could have been the result of my weight loss. Then again, he said, it might indeed be the effects of age. I still wonder.

Psychologically, it's been more difficult for me to tell whether my experience has had any lasting effect on me. I seem to be mellower and more tolerant of my fellows. Religion means more to me. Where previously I had been hard-driving and aggressive, I am now content to sit back in the sunshine and enjoy the life that had almost been snuffed out. I am particularly close to my family.

I had gone through an ordeal that gave me, of all things, the time to look at myself. Caught up in the maddening rush of daily life, I hadn't taken stock of myself for too long a time. Being a prisoner denies you many things, but it is generous with time: one cannot help but search oneself painstakingly.

I had time to think about whether I had been a good husband and father, whether my career had been the right thing to do. I had time to think about all the things I had wanted to do, and whether I had really managed my life the way I was supposed to. I reassessed who I was, what I wanted, and whether I had accomplished everything I had set out to do. Under those conditions, one cannot lie to oneself: truth is stark.

I was concerned whether danger had destroyed my appetite for the Foreign Service. Would I be able to return to my post, to any post overseas? Would I be an able diplomat knowing firsthand the realities of terrorism? The Director General of the Foreign Service and the Acting Secretary of State were supportive: they told me I could have just about any major embassy that was coming vacant or any of a number of major posts in the Department of State as part of my hero's welcome. They suggested, however, that I stay home for a while. I'd been overseas since 1967 and had completed assignments in Portugal, Brazil, and Venezuela before going to Colombia. I missed the United States, now more than ever, and I missed my children, who were scattered around the country going to school.

I was worried that my reaction was the result of a delayed-stress syndrome I'd been hearing so much about. Yet I was unsettled, tentative. Part of me wanted to return to Colombia and resume my duties as the Ambassador. I wanted to return to Colombia if only to prove to myself not only that I could, but that I could function effectively despite the threat. I had enjoyed my tour in Colombia, and I had been very well received by the Colombian government. I was not about to be frightened off by terrorists; we cannot afford to be intimidated by them.

Yet again, one of the jobs I'd been offered in Washington was a major responsibility, a decided step up the career ladder and one in which I was sure my particular and peculiar talents might stand me in good stead. I talked it over with Nancy; the decision was not easy, but it came.

A compromise. I would take the post in Washington as Assistant Secretary for Consular Affairs but not before I returned to Colombia to say goodbye and conclude my business in that country. I was not going to leave with my tail between my legs; rather, I would leave with dignity and honor. Many people had extended themselves for me in Colombia, and I wasn't about to abandon them or be thankless.

In the meantime, I walked down Pennsylvania Avenue from my hotel to the Department of State. Everything was brand-new. I could smell and almost taste the city around me. The bustling of the commuters on their way to work entranced me. People in the street recognized me from my appearance in the media and waved and honked their horns. I was particularly touched by one fellow who stuck his head out of his car window as he went by and shouted, "Attaway, Ambassador!" It was good to be alive.

EPILOGUE

And life goes on at its capriciously variable pace.

My wife informs me that there is a strong probability that we will stay married forever. During twenty-nine years we have experienced both happiness and frustration. It is our mutual consensus that no period has been more difficult than that of February 27, 1980, to date. If the subject of this book was our most painful experience, writing the book was a close second. If this collaboration has not caused us to part, only death will. We have also acquired a more profound respect for those who write for a living.

During our farewells in Bogotá, we had a wedding. Our son Charlie and Norma Fehrmann had been planning the event for weeks before the hostage incident. Our new circumstances required a few changes in their plans. The ceremony took place at the Embassy residence and behind the protected walls of the Embassy compound. At the behest of the security authorities, there was a full platoon of silver-helmeted troops surrounding the grounds. Our tuxedo-clad guests had to pass through a magnetometer and ladies' purses were meticulously examined. The gifts were put through an X-ray machine. One guest caused some excitement when he sent a radio as a gift. It was promptly carried to the farthest edge of the garden for examination for fear that it might be a bomb. The happy couple was sped away to the airport in my bulletproof limousine, and flight reservations had been made under assumed names. One guest mentioned that he had heard of shotgun weddings, but this was the first "machine-gun" wedding he had ever attended. I was not about to take a chance with the kids.

It was, in fact, a beautiful wedding and a delightful evening, with our friends around us in a celebration of life made all the more meaningful by what might have been. I still recall vividly sometime during the course of the evening when Clara Maria danced a habanera on one of the tables to the surprise of her banker husband. When Susana began to eat the flowers in the centerpiece, her physician consort gravely assured me that they were a good source of vitamin C.

Finally, on a Sunday morning in June, Frank and Bettie Crigler arrived at the residence to accompany us to the airport. Frank had a newspaper under his arm and a broad grin on his face. He asked if we had seen the article on the front page of *El Tiempo*. It was a fairly faithful account of the conversation at one of our farewell dinners to which I had invited some of my rascally journalist friends. Unfortunately, Nancy had made it clear how upset she had been at the Papal Nuncio's cavalier attitude toward the matter of Easter duties, confession, and Communion, during our captivity. Even more unfortunately, my journalist friend had attributed the marks to me. While waiting to board the plane, we were startled to see coming across the airport terminal the smiling face and outstretched hand of the Nuncio in his guise of dean of the Diplomatic Corps come to bid us farewell. Nancy looked as if she wanted to hide.

Frank whispered, "Do you think he read the morning paper?"

I replied, "No. He's still smiling."

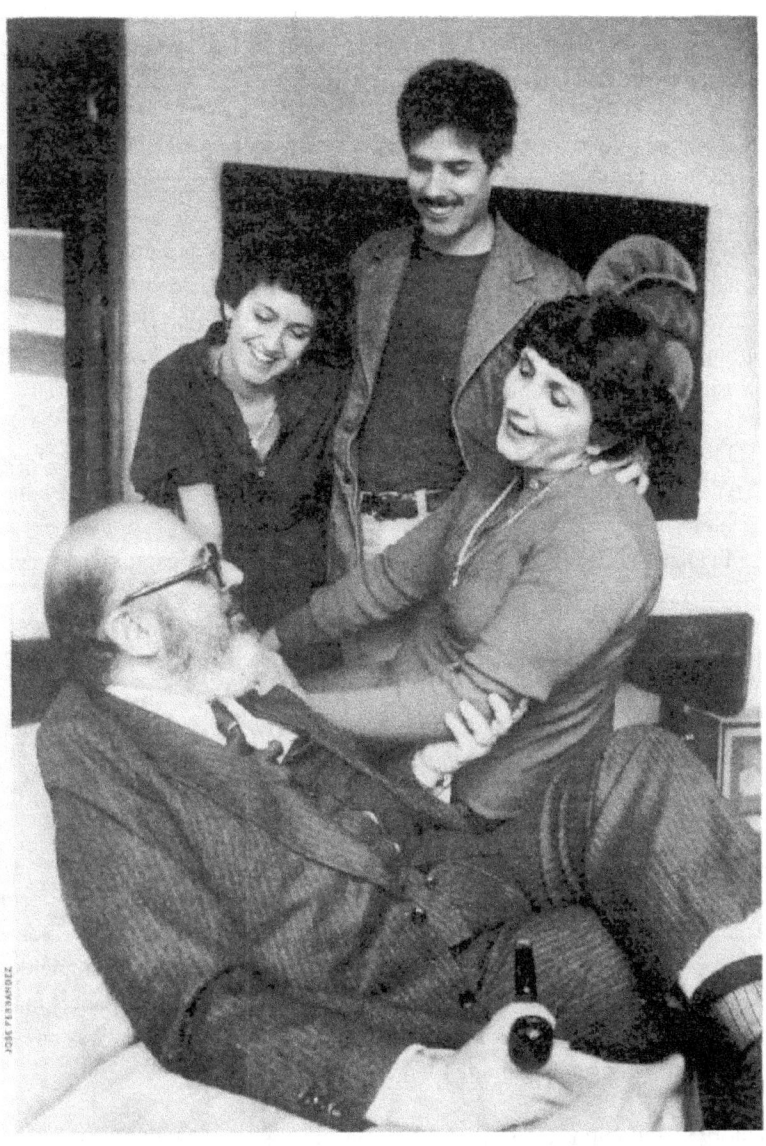

Return to Colombia for wedding of Diego "Charlie" Asencio and Norma Fehrmann.

As I settled into my new duties, Nancy also found employment. Shortly after the first anniversary of my captivity, her duties took her back to Bogotá. As the plane hovered over the tall mountains of Colombia, she reminisced. Closing her eyes, she sought happy thoughts and tried to picture the faces of our daughter-in-law's family, who would be at the airport to meet her. She was trying to maintain her mental equilibrium in the face of news that a heavily armed M-19 group, including a number of my former captors, had invaded Colombia. As the plane touched down, she could not completely escape a touch of fear. Nevertheless, during the counterinsurgency campaign of March and April of 1981, the Colombian military captured at least 130 M-19 guerrillas and ten more were killed.

If one can imagine the folly of an essentially urban terrorist group attempting to take on the Colombian army in the jungle, the result was predictable. Commander One, Rosenberg Pabón Pabón, sought to escape by crossing the border into Ecuador but was returned to the Colombian authorities. Norma, the negotiator, that combination of toughness and femininity who had been so helpful to our negotiating group, was killed in one of the engagements. At least five other members of my little ragtag group were also captured. Norma's death released me from self-imposed restraints on reporting fully the extent of her cooperation with my group. I had feared that any disclosure on my part would put her at risk with her fellow revolutionaries.

Shortly after, I had occasion to lunch with Minister of Defense Camacho Leyva at the table of my friend Virgilio Barco, the Colombian Ambassador in Washington. General Camacho Leyva said in his usual dry, humorous style, "You know, Asencio, you left Colombia with this reputation for being a tough, stand-up guy. Do you know what your captor, Commander One, has been doing since we captured him? Crying! He cries all day long!"

I responded, "For heaven's sake, tell him to buck up. I have a reputation to maintain."

Could this be the Icarian personality come to earth? Actually, I hope someday to interview Commander One. I believe that a sequel to this book, from his point of view, would be most instructive.

Another point of interest is the fact that I met Iranian hostage Don Cooke when we assisted the State Department's Medical Division in a group therapy program for the former hostages from Iran. Destiny and a pushy mother combined for him to meet our daughter Anne. Sometime after, and shying from publicity, they went to Montego Bay and sent us the following telegram: "Got Married. Thought You Would Like to Know. Anne and Don." Many newspapers made much of the fact that the daughter of a hostage was marrying a hostage. My favorite was an item beginning, "My God. They are beginning to inter-breed."

Finally, this story would not be complete without an expression of gratitude on my part to the private Colombian citizen who paid the ransom. Thank you, dear friend.

APPENDIX

The Guerrilla Position Paper and Our Revision

GUERRILLA DOCUMENT

1. We of the Guerrilla Column Jorge Marcos Zambrano, members of the politico-military organization M-19 believe that in these long talks, we have tried to focus on the issues under discussion while you have tried to digress and delay. Consequently, a common interest in achieving a rapid solution does not exist. We have had thirty-five days without any clear solutions being presented by the Government.

2. We believe that there is no need to express doubt because we have none. The Government, during the length of the negotiations has not been telling the truth as the following examples will show:

   A. At the beginning of the negotiations, when we asked for the release of Comrade Cuenca Cortes Montegranario, the response was that we were asking for the release of a delinquent condemned to eighteen years in prison for murder. This was done with the intent of impressing the Ambassadors since Comrade Montegranario has already served most of his sentence and should regain his freedom at the end of the year.

   B. A similar thing happened when we asked for the release of Comrade Coqueco Marco Aurelio.

   C. The Government has issued press bulletins which it has had to retract at the request of the Ambassadors.

3. Since our beginnings as an organization, we have behaved correctly with the people, to power with arms! Our organization has kept its promises. During the operation "Democracy and Liberty," Commander One has kept his promises and this can be verified by His Excellency the Apostolic Nuncio, the Ambassadors, the Consuls, and the rest of the hostages.

4. You have produced frustrations that have demoralized the hostages, because on the telephone you speak of concrete answers and at the negotiations you equivocate.

5. We are aware of the release of Mrs. Fals, of Mrs. Torrado and of the ex-magistrate Tony Lopez Ozuela. This give us great satisfaction because their release would not have been possible without our action and because it serves to show the injustices and arbitrariness of Military Justice, which finds itself obliged to release innocent persons after more than

fourteen months of torture and prison. Meditate upon the words spoken by Mrs. Fals on television concerning Military Justice.

6. With regard to the previous meeting at which our departure with the 311 political prisoners was discussed, we believe that there is "no one blinder than he who will not see." There is nothing on the record about our travelling with persons absolved by the courts-martial.

7. If no one has been detained for belonging to the M-19, how do you explain to the people that your principal objective is to destroy our organization; the eager search for our leaders who are free; that prisoners are obliged by torture to confess that they are members of the M-19; that there are hundreds of our comrades under sentence for having distributed our propaganda. Why do you offer rewards to those who turn over our comrades? As you must know, the law states that a person is innocent until proven guilty; however, in Colombia unfortunately the "law of the jungle" prevails. It is considered preferable to condemn the innocent than to absolve the guilty. Proof of this are the hundreds of thousands of prisoners in our country who have not had their juridical situation defined.

8. If, as you say, our country is democratic and free and military judges are just and honest, lift the state of siege so that the biased courts-martial will be replaced by ordinary justice and so that civilians in Colombia might be judged by civilian judges and not the current situation where the military accuse, torture, defend, prosecute and pass judgment, which is a function reserved to God. In other words, we do not accept the trials in progress against our revolutionary and popular fighting comrades because they should not be judged by murderous torturers. The solution does not lie in shortening the processes in order to end them sooner. It is not a race with the clock. We are not desperate. The problem is that the military cannot judge civilians in courts-martial. The problem is that we have some diplomatic hostages who we are prepared to release for the popular fighters you maliciously call "delinquents" just as, in their time, Bolivar, San Martin and many other heroes were called.

9. Up until this moment we have released twenty-nine hostages without expecting any gift from the Government. We have done this, not because of "pressure," but for humanitarian reasons and to show by example that we wish a dialogue and a peaceful solution.

10. It is very significant that political prisoners in Colombia be acknowledged to be judged unjustly and not be treated in full dignity as human beings.

11. We agree that it is those prisoners who remain behind and those imprisoned in the future that require our greatest attention and it is through our operation "Democracy and Liberty" that we have shown that political prisoners exist in Colombia and that they are savagely tortured and abandoned to their fate because military justice does not offer any guarantees.

12. You say you have no interest in prolonging the present situation indefinitely but, in practice, you are demonstrating the contrary to us and to the hostages. We believe that the Government has within its means the possibility of a decorous and legal solution, and we have demonstrated this in the document presented to the Government delegates for the President of the Republic.

13. With regard to the persons interested in the ransom negotiations, we wish first the freedom of our comrades and then the money. We do not want to "mount the saddle before we have the horse."

14. On invitations to international organizations, we wish to inform that we accept the International Red Cross, the Human Rights Commission of the OAS, and Amnesty International as assistance to get you out of the muddle you find yourselves in and so that they may make clear that the international concept of human right does take precedence over national rights.

15. We propose that your documents and ours be made public, so that public opinion might be the judge of our actions.

HOSTAGE VERSION

We of the Guerrilla Column Jorge Marcos Zambrano, members of the politico-military organization M-19, have made a detailed study of the document that was delivered to us by the Government delegates on April 1st and, before entering into specifics, wish to indicate our desire to avoid the polemic tone evident in your document since we consider that this could obstruct or delay the negotiations. The Command accepts that, since the taking of the Dominican Embassy, it achieved the following gains:

1. Initiation and continuation of the negotiations.

2. Withdrawal of the troops and the Government's promise of not attempting to take the Embassy by force unless there was an attempt against the lives of the hostages.

3. Publication of our communiqué and national and international publicity demonstrating that in Colombia there are tortures and political prisoners.

4. Measures taken by the Government to accelerate the trials by creating a Commission of Jurists for this purpose.

5. From the beginning of the negotiations, the Government has offered to invite international institutions to observe the courts-martial and accelerate investigations concerning abuse of authority, torture and murder of persons linked with revolutionary organizations, syndicates and labor unions; a promise which was complied with only a few days ago as we learned from radio and television. In addition, in our view, the positive points of the Government's document are as follows:

A. The Government's indication that it is those comrades in prison and those that will be imprisoned in the future that require the greatest protection; therefore, we reiterate as one of our accomplishments in operation "Democracy and Liberty" that our comrades will not be abandoned to the military but that their trials will be under the surveillance of international organizations.

B. Similarly, we accept that said organizations will be permitted to investigate charges of abuse of authority and torture committed against political prisoners.

C. We share the Government's desire for maintaining the dialogue, but we make clear that dialogue for the sake of dialoguing is fruitless. The negotiations must be directed toward a decorous and peaceful solution.

D. The expressed hope on the part of the Government that those prisoners in which we are interested could be exonerated by the courts and be able to travel with us.

Finally we wish to be very clear about the following points which are proposals pending from the beginning of the negotiation:

1. From the beginning we have indicated that we have a negotiable list of 311 comrades; what is not negotiable or subject to debate are those on the list who are members of our High Command.

2. Our demand for money is equally negotiable in proportion to the number of released comrades. We accept that progress could be made in this aspect without this signifying any compromise on our part.

3. If, as you say, our country is democratic and free, permit justice to be served and the state of siege to be lifted so as to end the biased courts-martial and that civilians might be judged by civilian judges and not as in the present situation where the military, accuse, torture, defend, prosecute and pass judgment.

4. We propose that your document and ours be made known to the public so that public opinion might judge our actions.

Bogotá

April 1, 1980

By the High Command

Commander One.

BIOGRAPHY

Ambassador Diego Asencio and his wife Nancy are a retired US Foreign Service couple. Most of their thirty year diplomatic career was spent stationed at Embassies throughout Latin America and the Iberian Peninsula. They met in Washington, D.C., while he attended Georgetown University School of Foreign Service, and she a freshman at Dumbarton College of the Holy Cross. Nancy later attended the National University of Brazil and graduated from George Washington University.

Diego was born in Spain but derived his American citizenship from his naturalized father, who had returned to his homeland to marry. He was raised on the hard-scrabble streets of the Ironbound section of Newark, New Jersey, one of the last melting pot enclaves in the United States. Nancy was born in Havana, Cuba, immigrated to the United States with her mother in 1945, and was naturalized at age twenty.

In 1980, while attending a cocktail party at the Dominican Republic Embassy in Bogota, Diego, who was serving as American Ambassador to Colombia, was captured together with a group of other foreign ambassadors. The terrorists belonged to a politically radical paramilitary organization known as M-19. In a departure from the usual turn of events, the hostages directly participated in the negotiations that eventually set them free. Ambassador Asencio was ultimately awarded the State Department's Medal for Valor, and became Assistant Secretary of State for Consular Affairs.

Diego began his diplomatic career as a Vice-Consul in Mexico assisting Americans in jails and shipping dead bodies home, followed by a stint as Political Officer in Panama where he participated in the Panama Canal negotiations and survived the riots of 1964. His subsequent duties included Special Assistant to the Assistant Secretary for Inter-American Affairs/ Coordinator of the Alliance for Progress, Deputy Chief of Mission in Portugal just before the Revolution of the Carnations, Political Counselor in Brazil during a military government, Deputy Chief of Mission in Venezuelan during the nationalization of the petroleum industry, and Ambassador to Colombia, where he became intimately familiar with the ways of terror.

After his tenure as Assistant Secretary of State for Consular Affairs, he was named Ambassador to Brazil at a most poignant moment, when civilian rule returned to that society. The Asencio's upcoming memoirs, ***The Joys and Perils of Serving Abroad***, also recounts Diego's tenure as a member of the US-Moscow Investigating Commission, and as Chairman of the Commission for the Study of International Migration and Cooperative Economic Development.

Having decided that there were too many retired ambassadors looking for interesting things to do in Washington, Diego and Nancy moved to Florida where they have resident children and grandchildren. Governor Lawton Chiles promptly appointed him Executive Director of the Florida International Affairs Commission with a charge to coordinate the State's foreign trade policy.

After a couple of arduous years he returned to private life, concentrating on consulting with American firms, including McDonald's and Coca-Cola, on their Latin American operations. Nancy spends a great deal of her time reading, writing and painting, her passions in life. They live a few steps from the Intercoastal, across from the town of Palm Beach, with their Portuguese Water Dog Filomena, cat Tinkerbell and cockatiel Blanquita, all three refugees abandoned into their care.

Escaping the Floridian heat at Basic Necessities near Wintergreen, Virginia.

www.ingramcontent.com/pod-product-compliance
Lightning Source LLC
Chambersburg PA
CBHW081822280526
45789CB00007B/2304